THEY CAME IN CHAINS

Books by Saunders Redding

TO MAKE A POET BLACK

NO DAY OF TRIUMPH

STRANGER AND ALONE

THEY CAME IN CHAINS

THE LONESOME ROAD

ON BEING NEGRO IN AMERICA

AMERICAN IN INDIA

THE NEGRO

THEY CAME IN CHAINS

Americans from Africa

SAUNDERS REDDING

Edited by Louis Adamic

J. B. LIPPINCOTT COMPANY
Philadelphia   *New York*

For my sons:

Conway and Lewis

CONTENTS

●●

Part One

Part Two

Part Three

THEY CAME IN CHAINS

Part One

1

GREED AND BLOOD

• •

SAILS FURLED, FLAG drooping at her rounded stern, she rode the tide in from the sea. She was a strange ship; indeed, by all accounts, a frightening ship, a ship of mystery. Whether she was trader, privateer, or man-of-war no one knows. Through her bulwarks black-mouthed cannon yawned. The flag she flew was Dutch; her crew a motley. Her master, a Captain Tope. Her true registry? Unknown. Her port of call, an English settlement, Jamestown, in the colony of Virginia. She came, she traded, and shortly afterwards was gone. Probably no ship in modern history has carried a more portentous freight. Her cargo? Twenty slaves.

Not that these twenty were the first black slaves. The ancient world had known them. Parts of medieval Europe, especially those areas bordering Mohammedan lands, had bought and sold their like for two hundred years. Negroes, who were probably slaves, figure in the accounts of Spanish Conquistadors who girdled the new western world with a path of blood and gold. There was one with Columbus. His name was Pedro Alonzo, and he was captain of the *Niña.* Negroes accompanied Balboa when he explored the Pacific. They were with Cortez in Mexico, Ponce de León in Florida, and Coronado in New Mexico. Estevanico, a Negro with De Vaca, discovered the Zuñi Indians. Indeed, near the site where the mystery ship dropped anchor in 1619, Negro slaves had lived almost a hundred years before. But they rebelled, and the Spanish settlement they helped to found was soon abandoned.

Fifty years before the discovery of America black slaves had been imported from Africa to Europe. The Portuguese started it in 1442 as an incident of their country's commercial expansion. Under

11

Prince Henry the Navigator's driving ambition to find a passage to the East, Portuguese mariners established claim to the Canary and Madeira Islands and pushed southward for four thousand miles along the west coast of Africa. In 1440, Antam Gonçalvez captured three Moors who ransomed themselves for ten Negroes. These were brought to Lisbon in 1442. From a second trip Gonçalvez brought back more slaves, and in 1444 a group of merchant-adventurers, known as the Company of Lagos, captured more than a hundred and fifty Negro men, women and children from the island of Nar and Tidar. These slaves, a recompense from God "for all the labor they [the Portuguese] had given in His service," were landed at Lagos. Prince Henry himself was there to receive them in the name of Christ and to claim his share.

This was the beginning of the modern slave trade with Africa, and the beginning, too, of its justification on the grounds of winning souls for Christ.

By the end of the fifteenth century, Portugal controlled Africa and had made an agreement, called the "Asiento," to supply slaves to Spain. The latter country herself joined the trade in 1517. A few years later an Englishman, William Hawkins, sailed to the Guinea Coast and brought back a few slaves, although England did not formally enter the traffic until 1562. France followed, then Holland and Denmark. Within a century slaving had grown into a commercial enterprise of such proportions that no civilized nation could ignore it as a lucrative source of trade. It led to bickering and then to war. Treaties and agreements of all kinds were drawn up to regulate it. In twenty years, down to 1591, Brazil imported fifty-two thousand slaves. More than three hundred ships out of Liverpool, England, were engaged in the trade by 1744; by which time, too, the British West Indies alone had imported two million black slaves. Factories and barracoons dotted the west coast of Africa. A thousand ships were engaged in the plunder, and each voyage averaged a profit of between thirty and fifty thousand dollars.

In 1715 in the American colonies there were approximately sixty thousand slaves. By the period of the Revolution this number had increased to 502,132.

They came in chains, and they came from everywhere along the west coast of Africa—from Cape Verde and the Bights of Benin and Biafra; from Goree, Gambia, and Calabar; Anamaboe and Ambriz;

the Gold, the Ivory and the Grain Coast; and from a thousand nameless villages inland. They were, these slaves, people of at least four great races—the Negritians, the Fellatahs, the Bantus and the Gallas—and many tribes whose names make a kind of poetry: Makalolu, Bassutas, Kaffir, Koromantis; the Senegalese and the Mandingos; Ibos, Iboni, Ibani (like the parsing of a Latin verb), Efik and Fulahs, the Wysyahs and the Zandes. Native villages ran red with their blood. The plains and the valleys of Africa rang with their cries. Chained to each other, neck and foot, under the stroke of the merciless sun and the whine of the slaver's whip, the terrified Negroes were driven to the coast. Two out of five died on these long marches. The barracoons into which the rest were herded stank of excrement and blood. And worse was yet to come.

But slavery was an old, old story even then. It had been in existence since the first man who, by luck or the dim recognition of his superior endowment, discovered that he held an edge over a rival. It was almost a natural consequence of man's pride, of the development of his lust for mastery, and of his compulsion to control his environment. Slavery became entrenched in human customs before man had got well used to walking upright. It was a time-honored institution among the primitive Jews. When Babylonia, Assyria and Phoenicia were young, slavery was old. The cultures of ancient Greece and Rome were founded upon it.

There was slavery in Africa long before the coming of the white man. It owed its origin to local conditions of social structure and to natural conditions of climate and soil. Where land was plentiful and food abundant and a leisure class could develop without hazard to the means of subsistence, slavery could thrive. But these conditions were only relative in parts of West Africa, for nowhere along that torrid coast did nature pamper the inhabitants. Excessive rainfall, averaging sometimes a hundred inches a year, debilitating humidity, steaming heat, tropical diseases, wild beasts and the heartbreaking rapacity of the jungle made it anything but a paradise.

The West African worked hard. Contrary to popular legend, living was not simply a matter of shaking fruit from trees and gathering roots and herbs. Where a living drops into one's lap, there is no need for complex socio-economic institutions, and such institutions in West Africa were quite complex. They had evolved from the family through the clan to the tribe, until by the end of the Middle Ages there were kingdoms like Melle and Songhai where culture was so rich and vigorous that their schools and universities attracted scholars from Asia and Europe. Among the people of these kingdoms the weaving of cloth, the working of metal, the making of pottery and the turning of wood had long been common skills. Indeed, they had clanked into the iron age before Europe climbed from the age of stone. The fall of the great states marked no abrupt end of African culture—merely its dispersion; for everywhere there were lesser kingdoms, and there was always the tribe or the clan.

The general structure of society was socialistic, and specialized to a degree that required the tightest cooperation in the production, distribution and exchange of goods. Class lines were as rigidly fixed as those in medieval Europe. In some tribes the political system was monarchal, in others aristocratic. There were courts and kings, chiefs and headmen, and all degrees of lesser folk. Craft guilds and trade guilds, prescribed markets, the common ownership of land and a monetary system based on the cowrie shell, proved not only that living was complex but that sustaining life meant doing more than stretching open-mouthed under a mango tree.

In sections where hunting (which called for resourcefulness) and cattle raising (which meant roaming) were the sources of wealth, slavery had little chance. The nomadic tribes that prowled the arid and barren regions north of the Equator commonly followed the practice of putting their tribal enemies to death or of selling them as slaves to other tribes. Farther down the coast, from the Gambia River to Benguela, conditions were more favorable to human bondage. This agricultural area, reaching inland for two hundred miles, was comparatively rich and was therefore able to support slaves. But an abundant food supply did not mean that a subsistence was to be had for the mere taking. The prevalence of slavery there argues otherwise. Slavery flourishes where work is arduous, requiring a concentration of laborers. Rich as the land was along the coast, it had to be worked—and under conditions of a grueling kind.

Another circumstance conducive to slaveholding along the west coast of Africa was that the area teemed with barbaric life. In the Niger delta lived millions of people divided into hundreds of small, independent tribes. Proximity led to quarrels on the faintest pretext; quarrels led to war. Strong, victorious tribes, when they did not kill, took captives and made them slaves. Nor was this the only way to servile reduction. Famine sometimes drove men to sell themselves and their families. Within the tribe debtors could be enslaved to satisfy their debts. The destruction of fetishes, and certain other crimes such as adultery and thievery were punishable by bondage.

When the white man went to Africa in the fifteenth century he had only to organize and develop a traffic that was already old. He took with him the commercial skill. He took also a contrariety of inclinations and attitudes that were to make of the overseas slave trade the most cynical, degrading and gruesome enterprise ever undertaken in the modern world.

After Europe had been settled roughly along the lines, national and ethnic, that were to determine its modern structure, and after western man had recovered a little from the domestic eruptions and the internecine strife of the Middle Ages, a great period of exploration set in. European man turned his energies to extending the boundaries of the universe. Out of the intellectual ferment of the Renaissance came the new and breath-taking theory that the earth was round. If this were true, then by sailing west one would eventually arrive at the East. The notion opened up hitherto undreamed-of possibilities: the new mariner's compass made men eager to try them.

Supported by insatiable curiosity, and by proselyting zeal, and by the desire for wealth, the primary ambition of Christendom was to discover a new trade route to India. The Turks, seizing Constantinople in 1453, had blocked the old route overland. Seeking a passage by water, Columbus discovered the new world. In his wake soon followed the adventurer, the soldier, the priest—among whom it was sometimes hard to distinguish: Spanish, Portuguese, British, Dutch, Danish, French. They poured into the Bahamas, then Cuba, Haiti, and all the lesser Antilles—Tortuga, Guadeloupe, Martinique, Barbados, Jamaica, St. Thomas and St. Johns.

At first the new world gave promise of supplying its own slaves. The natives, described by the earliest explorers as mild-mannered and "affectionate" seemed born to the white man's purpose, for they were easily bent to his will. But the trouble was that when bent the Indians tended to break. They were not a strong, nor an ambitious, nor an adaptable people. Diseases which the European imported—diphtheria, tuberculosis and the pox—killed them in droves. Having been used to the placid round of cooperative farming and hunting, their energies could not match the white man's unbridled appetite for the products of the sugar plantation, the rice fields, the tobacco farms and the mines. The excessive demands upon the Indians went largely unfulfilled, and calculated brutality came into play. Murder ran second only to torture, which often resulted in death. Within two generations the Indians proved not only inadequate but almost wholly worthless as a source of labor supply. Within that time, too, they came dangerously close to extinction.

But the masters of the new world were keen for profits. They had come to exploit the natural wealth of the new lands. Commercial expansion was a kind of reflex from the seethe of the Renaissance. Without some show of concrete wealth, without some increase in the physical pleasures of living, the intellectual awakening of Europe meant little to the average European. So the pushing back of the world's geographical boundaries was not the only dream of the adventurers, especially the later ones. Cortez and Coronado, Hawkins and Drake were less explorers than warrior-marauders bent on privilege and property. To the attainment of these and for the greater glory of their monarchs, they blunted, repressed or perverted all sense of social and moral responsibility. Their successors went even further: they cajoled, bribed, tricked and shanghaied men of their own race and nation and placed them, under a system of indentureship, in servile subjection in a foreign and distant land. But such as they got by these means proved unsatisfactory too. They were not craftsmen—neither farmers nor woodsmen, carpenters nor smiths. Being white like their masters, they were inclined to take liberties.

Long before this, however, the way had been opened to another stock pile of forced labor. A peripatetic priest had done this early in the sixteenth century. Bartholomew de Las Casas was wrenched with pity for the Indian helots, against whom "a more cruel judgment had been rendered than against the ancient Hebrews." "Consider," he wrote, "whether this hard usage of the poor creatures be consistent with the precepts which God commands concerning charity to our neighbors." What the good priest's line of reasoning was is idle to speculate upon, but he petitioned the King of Spain to allow the importation of Negro slaves "to work in the gold mines of Hispaniola." Thus, through the intercession of God's holy minister, the African slave trade to the new world was begun.

It was a profitable, a reckless, and a romantic trade, but it was not pretty. The monopoly of it passed from the Portuguese to the Spanish to the Dutch, who lost it finally and definitely in the 1670's, to the French, and at last to the English, who, adapting and combining the methods of their predecessors, brought slave trading to its direst height, first under the Company of Adventurers of London and the East India Company, and then under independent traders, marauders and soldiers of fortune. By any comparison with the English, the slave traders of other countries were small fry. Nearly four times as many African slaves were transported in British bottoms as in the ships of all other nations combined. English sea power proved itself in the cold-blooded traffic in human flesh.

2

Perhaps if African slaves in the Caribbean and in Haiti had not "prospered so much that it was the opinion that unless a Negro should happen to be hung he would never die" they might not have been brought to the mainland of North America at all. It is true that a third of the black men died on the first leg of the journey to the African coast, and another third, in ships seemingly designed as torture chambers, on the infamous middle passage, but these did not count; and those who got to Haiti prospered, though strictly by comparison.

Whereas the native Arawak Indians perished so fast that a million of them in Haiti were reduced to a very few thousand after only twenty years of Spanish occupation, Negro slaves died at only about three-fourths this rate, and not all of them from the natural ravages of overwork and starvation. The Spanish were notorious for maiming slaves for small offenses. Under their Black Code, the French developed refinements of punishment that included hamstringing, branding and merciless flogging. Insurrection, or even the hope of insurrection, if discovered, resulted in death so slow and torturous as to make the most depraved sadist blush. For ordinary punishment the British flogged with "so formidable an instrument in the hands of some of the overseers, that by means of it they could take the skin off a horse's back." An abstract of *Evidence of the Slave Trade* [1] tells how a Captain Cook, in company with two others on a plantation in Barbados, "saw near a house, upon a dunghill, a naked Negro nearly suspended by strings from his elbows backwards, to the bough of a tree, with his feet barely upon the ground, and an iron weight round his neck, at least, to the appearance of fourteen lbs. weight; and thus without one creature near him, or apparently near the house, was the wretch left, exposed to the noonday sun."

If only a relative few were racked by this kind of punishment, many, many more suffered and died from a combination of overwork and a diet of rotten fish. "When the herrings were unfit for the whites, they were bought up by the planters for the slaves." These fish, together with a few handfuls of corn, were the standard slave ration in the Caribbean. No fare for laborers whose hours of toil often ran to eighteen in a day. Not only men, but women went to the fields at daybreak and drudged until dark; or at midnight they went to the boiling house, where cane was rendered, and worked until the following noon. Women, too, shrivelled under the bite of the lash, had their ears cropped off, their bodies weighted with irons. Deaf and blind with weariness, slaves were sometimes wrenched into the gears of the grinding mills and mangled like so many stalks of cane. Many a gallon of syrup was made red with blood and lumpy with gobbets of shredded flesh. Day after searing day, week after week, year after tortured year the slaves toiled and died.

Not only did they die. They either refused to reproduce, or were incapacitated for doing so, or both. On none of the islands of the West Indies was there ever a natural increase in the number of slaves, though on most plantations sexual promiscuity was encouraged. In Jamaica, in 1702, there were 36,000 Negro slaves. Seventy-three years later there was an increase to 194,614. But in that seventy-three years 497,736 slaves were imported, of whom 137,114 were sent to other slave-holding islands. In short, it was necessary to bring in more than 300,000 slaves in order to have an increase of 158,614 in three-quarters of a century. These figures tell a story of disease, debility and desperation—even of race suicide. They are not unusual figures. On the island of St. Vincent there were two and a half deaths for every birth. In British Guiana the number of births was regularly half the number of deaths.

Race suicide was the group's way of protest and escape? The record of importations seems to support it. Brazil imported 45,000 slaves a year during the seventeenth century. In twenty-one years 320,000 slaves were taken to Cuba alone. From 1690 to 1820 Jamaica imported 800,000, yet in the latter year her slave population was only

340,000. Natural increase played almost no part in supplying the Antilles and Latin America with slaves. In the decade before the close of the English trade, the slave population on ten British West Indian islands declined by 60,000; but within ten years after the abolition of slavery the Negro population of these same islands had a natural increase of 54,000. Who can say that race suicide was not a group intent?

For the individual, of course, there was always self-murder, and this was often resorted to. Indeed, there were African tribes, like the Eboe, especially noted for their tendency to commit suicide rather than suffer slavery. More resourceful, life-loving individuals stirred up rebellions or ran away. Laws were passed to throttle such activities, but, excepting the codes of the Spanish and the French, these laws attacked symptoms rather than causes of slave discontent, and gave legal sanction to masters' cruelty. Even the French, whose *Code Noir* has been called liberal and humane, "seem to have treated their slaves at times with a wanton, almost tigerish cruelty which left a deep impression on the Negro mind." But the French paid for it, always in fear and sometimes in blood. The revolutionist Ogé put them in mortal terror, and Toussaint, nicknamed The Opener, finally cancelled out their fiendishness with fire and sword.

But that was later.

In 1685, a hundred years before Toussaint began his bath of blood and flame, a memorandum went to the French Minister of Colonies. It reported tersely, "In the negroes we possess a formidable domestic enemy." The reference was to bands of escaped slaves, called maroons, who waged a constant warfare of depredation and pillage against the planters. It was not uncommon for an army of maroons to number a thousand men and women. According to the record, they had prowled and plagued and plundered since twelve years after the first Negro slaves were dragged to Haiti in 1510. In Jamaica, Barbados, and the British West Indies they were felt and feared. They stirred up revolts in 1649, 1692 and 1702. Without their harsh midwifery in 1804, the Black Republic would have been powerless to be born. "Contemporary accounts are so filled with stories of uprisings and other modes of revolt. . . ." writes Melville Herskovits, "that it is surprising that the conception of the compliant African ever developed." [2]

But not all slaves could revolt or run away, and those who did neither—and did not die—remained to be broken in. Considered tractable then, they were exported to other islands and to the mainland of North America.

By the beginning of the eighteenth century it was becoming grossly apparent that the financial returns from slavery in the West Indies were no longer big enough to support the system and provide the fabulous profits of the early years. Absentee owners continued to pour money into vast plantations with large gangs of slaves, but it was like pouring money down a drain. All they bought was more cruelty from their plantation agents, whose care was for nothing but to show an annual increment. Neither the money of masters nor the labor of slaves could postpone for long the day of social and financial collapse. The worn-out soil demanded more and more workers, who were able to produce less and less. The islands were overpopulated with human chattel—and this at the very time of the dawning realization of wealth to be had on the mainland; this only shortly after the supply of English indentured servants to the new colonies was abruptly cut off.

The history of slavery in the West Indies was the history of greed and blood. But these are as ubiquitous as the winds. The demand for Negro slaves rose on the mainland. The story of human bondage had yet more than two centuries to run.

2

DURANTE VITA

●●●

THE FIRST BLACK slaves on the continent of North America were not
the twenty "negars" brought by the Dutch man-of-war and landed at
Jamestown. In 1526 a Spaniard had brought some. Vásquez de Ayllón
founded a settlement on a coastal river deep in the South, and here
five hundred white men held one hundred Negroes as slaves. The
colony lasted six months, from June to November, and then it was
wiped out in violence. The Spaniards who were left after the massacre fled back to Haiti; the slaves fused with the Indians. A century
passed before black slaves were brought to the continent to stay.

They were brought apparently by accident at first, but the Virginia
Colony had use for them. The labor problem there was acute. Indian
slavery had been tried and found entirely unsatisfactory. The Indians
were treacherous, hostile. They resented the intrusion of the white
men; they definitely did not want to work for them. Nor, it seems,
did the white men want to work for themselves. Neither the gentlemen-adventurers nor the planters, who comprised the Virginia Company of London, considered themselves laborers. As John Rolfe,
that early colonial historian wrote, "They would all be Keisers, none
inferior to the others." Only a handful had any of the skills required
of farmers and mechanics. Many were dissolute, given to "gluttony
and drunkenness." In the heat of the first summer every other man
died, and it was only the coming of autumn with game for the hunting and wild grain for the harvesting that saved the colony from
starvation.

It was necessary for John Smith, the leader, to take stringent
measures. The whole settlement was organized as a working force
in 1610. The colonists, somewhat chastened now, were marched to

their daily work in squads and companies, under officers, "and the severest penalties were prescribed for a breach of discipline or neglect of duty." Threats of labor in the galleys and other forms of penal servitude were held over their heads. Still they could do only just enough to keep themselves alive. The wealth they had dreamed of winning demanded more tribute of toil than they alone could give. Sea and forest and field and the distant frowning mountains were too much for them alone. In 1618 the colonists petitioned James I for vagabonds and condemned men to be sent out from England as indentured servants.

But indentureships, limited to terms of years, had a way of running out. Moreover, contract servants did not come in sufficient numbers to quell the clamor for such services as they could render; and the reason was not far to seek. The Virginia Colony had an evil reputation. The harshness of the controls imposed by successive governors indicates that the reputation was deserved. It was so bad that some condemned men, "rather than be sent there, chose to be hanged, and were." A less squeamish and more dependable labor supply was needed. In due time it was found.

The colonists were blind at first to the potentialities of Negro labor. The first black men brought to Virginia were not true slaves, and, as a matter of fact, slavery had no legal status there for forty years. Each Negro served a period of indentureship, after which he could take up land, as white servants did, "at any other place at his own will and pleasure." But it soon began to be plain that there were exploitable possibilities in Negro labor far greater than those in white and Indian servitude. First of all, the supply was practically inexhaustible, and the nature of the expediency demanded numbers. Secondly, unlike the inflexible Indians who would break before they would bend to a master's will, Negroes were resilient. And finally— most fortunate and persuasive fact of all—they were visibly different from white men. No matter that the difference was sometimes monstrously forgotten and mulatto babies were born into the world, Negroes were unassimilable. The Christian precepts of kindness, charity and humane dealing need not apply to them—was not intended to apply to them, for they were a heathen breed, demonstrably inferior. Thus began in North America the rationalization of race-caste. Before long its knotty, insidious tendrils, seeming to uphold what they would pull down, were clinging to every fissure in the national frame.

In literal terms, what happened was that a twisted body of moral and ethnic assumptions grew up around and fed upon a body of expedient practices. Once this process got fairly started—and it had by mid-century—the Negro was thoroughly enslaved. By 1640 no Negro newly imported into the Virginia Colony could look forward to anything save perpetual slavery.

In New England the frigid, thrifty Puritans pushed the northern wilderness farther and farther back from the sea, unfettering the land which gave gratitude in stones and little else. But woods and water had much to yield, and the Puritans fished and hunted and dried fish and pelts. They cut timber and built ships and sent their furs and fish and leather to foreign markets, thus building up the commerce upon which their prosperity eventually was to rest. They had much to do, including the hammering out of self-government. Men of peace, the Puritans turned soldiers at a war-whoop and fought the Narragansetts and the Pequots; and they kept a constant vigil on their borders to the north, where lived the French, and to the south, where lived the Dutch. But constant watch also did the New Englanders keep over matters of dogma and practice among themselves. They banished Roger Williams for his belief in freedom of the conscience. They persecuted Quakers, hunted heretics, and eventually burned witches. Still they found time to trade.

Later they traded in slaves—Indian slaves captured in "just wars" and sold or exchanged to the sugar islands. "If upon a just warre," Emanuel Downing wrote to the Governor of the Massachusetts Colony, "the Lord should deliver them into our hands, we might easily have men, women, and children enough to exchange for Moores, for I doe not see how wee can thrive untill wee get into a stock of slaves sufficient to doe all our business."

They throve, but not because slaves did all their business. The Puritans were too smart for that. They knew that as a source of labor, slavery could not be successful in New England. There were too many small, independent landholdings; nor could the flinty soil support a plantation culture. New England life came early to crystallize in towns, where industry and commerce were the basis of economy. The slave in the North was important chiefly as an item of trade. The first American slave ship—she was named *Desire*—put out from Salem on the Massachusetts coast. She was owned by a company of Puritans in silent partnership.

The Maryland and Virginia colonists were a more dramatic but less stable lot. While the Puritans were content to pile slow pence on tardy pound, the Southern "cavaliers" wanted sudden showers of gold. Few whose money was at stake came with the thought of settling down. Their hope was to grab quick wealth and return to England, where the lure of London social life was especially strong during the tart and shallow Restoration period. The vicious system of absentee ownership, which had rooted itself in the Caribbean islands, would have been to the gentlemen-adventurers' liking, but it would not work on the mainland. There was no responsible class to trust their holdings to. Vagrants, political offenders and downright criminals were not likely to stink and sweat for the benefit of absent gentlemen.

So, slowly at first, but with increasing momentum, slavery grew in the South. Thirty years after 1619 there were still only three hundred Negroes in Virginia—and not all of these were slaves. Indeed, at least one, Anthony Johnson, was a master. But by 1671, Virginia had 2,000 slaves, and in 1715 almost one third of the total population of 95,500 was in a state of lifelong bondage. Maryland's figures were not far behind.

Some time before the turn of the century both colonies had given legal recognition to slavery and the slave trade. Virginia first went in this direction in an act of 1659 granting "free trade to all peoples in amity with England" and providing especially that the "Dutch or other foreigners" who imported Negroes should pay a tax of two shillings on every hogshead of tobacco actually produced by the imported slaves. Two years later an act was passed which sanctioned the holding of black men in perpetual service to their masters. Again Maryland was not far behind, and this time she was more thorough. "All negroes," her law of 1663 said, "or other slaves within the province, all negroes to be hereafter imported, shall serve *durante vita.*"

But already religious ethics were bothersome. The principles of Christianity just did not jibe with the slaveholding, slave trading practices of its professors. The New Englanders were exercised sufficiently over this as sometimes to make quite proper gestures. In 1646, for instance, when two slaves were brought into the Massachu-

setts Colony by a member of the church, the General Court ordered
them sent back to their native country, Guinea, because they had been
stolen! The Southern colonials were more realistic and far-seeing.
The Catholics of Maryland and the Protestants of Virginia were
satisfied with nothing less than a clear-cut temporal ruling on a spiritual issue. "Baptism," it was officially declared, "doth not alter the
condition of the person as to his bondage or freedom."

From this canonical sprig, once rooted, flowered a tree of sophistry
which bore strange fruit. Only the Quakers were not tempted to eat
of it, and their lithic abstinence must have seemed a futile excess
of pietistic strength when, in 1712, the British Parliament forbade
the enforcement of certain prohibitive laws against the slave trade
in Pennsylvania. For here, in 1688, 1693 and 1696, the Society of
Friends had effectively protested that slavery was opposed to Christianity and the rights of man. They continued to protest, but in time
the Christian teachings of all save the Quakers became a kind of ad-
justable stay in the fast-growing body of slavery.

And there were social questions too. Or were they questions of
economics? It is impossible now to tell which had more bearing with
the Southern colonials. At any rate, the issues had to do with bi-
racial commingling which, under the new dispensation, was found
to have economic consequences. Even after the concept of race-caste
had been coaxed into birth, there were those so shameless and un-
feeling as to ignore its lusty cries. White men cohabited with Negro
women, bond and free. White women married Negro men, bond and
free. Aside from being accounted a moral shame, such marriages
were an economic waste. A stop had to be put to them, and then more
stops, until the severest penalties were imposed against interracial
union.

In Virginia a white woman caught in such a relationship could be
sold into service for five years. If she were already a servant, five
years could be added to her term. Children born of such a tie were
bound out for thirty years. At first white men could be (and were)
publicly whipped and fined a thousand pounds of tobacco for having
sexual intimacies with Negro women. Later they were perpetually
banished from the colony—perhaps to spare them the mean shame
of seeing their mulatto bastards treated in all respects like slaves.

But it was, after all, white women who were the chief offenders
against the carefully building economy of slavery, and Maryland

decreed in 1663 "that whatsoever freeborn women [English] shall intermarry with any slave . . . shall serve the master of such slave during the life of her husband; all the issue of such freeborn women, so married, shall be slave as their fathers were."

If this law—a type of which all the Southern colonies eventually adopted—did not hit the mark it aimed for, it did further validate the Negro's *difference,* hallow the concept of his inherent inferiority, sanctify his social degradation and become in time the compulsive emotional symbol of grave cultural and social conflicts—conflicts that have remained the direst threats to the ideal of American democracy.

As the number of slaves increased, masters jerry-built laws and regulations for the control of their human chattels. Indeed, activity in this line was sometimes frantic, and was almost never discontinued. This unremitting carpentry work on the legal structure of slavery is one of the most distinctive tics of American slave masters. Everything was tried, but nothing was quite good enough, or strong enough, or quick enough. Moreover, the snarl of social problems grew more Gordian-like every year, for social ethics and personal morality had little to do with it. In the Southern colonials' pristine ignorance, the whole object of control at first was fiscal. That was the way "the friends of the slave trade" in the mother country wanted it. They "controlled the government and dictated the policy of England. Her [England's] Kings and Queens, Lords and commons . . . gave to the African slave trade their undeviating support. . . . Her coffers were filled with gold bedewed with tears and stained with blood." [1] Queen Anne herself owned stock in the Royal African Company, and made no bones of wishing the company to have always an adequate supply of saleable Negroes.

The production of wealth, however, could not be the only object of control, and this the colonist had to learn.

Experience was not long in opening a grim school. She taught fear first, last, always. The consciousness of this fear was thick and pervasive, like a black miasmic fog. Laws and proclamations dripped with it. It came early and remained to the end. In 1672, for instance, Virginia offered a bounty for the hunting down and killing of belligerent, runaway slaves. Ten years later her House of Burgesses passed an "Additional Act for the better preventing Insurrections by Negroes," and twelve years later still, the Governor of the colony proclaimed that "slaves in Sundry parts and Countyes in this Colony have mett congregated and gott together" and declared that such meetings were "of dangerous consequences." The Governor ordered a more rigid enforcement of the existing laws. He and succeeding governors promulgated new ones. Yet after two centuries the fear was still there. In 1856 a Scandinavian traveler in the South wrote that planters "never lay down to sleep without a brace of loaded pistols at their side."

3

THE RATIONALE OF FEAR

SLAVEHOLDERS HAD REASON for packing pistols to bed, as any trader might have told them. Alexander Falconbridge, the surgeon on a slaver, could have pointed out that few of the Negroes brooked "the loss of their liberty" and that they were "ever on the watch to take advantage of the least negligence in their oppressors." Insurrections were "frequently the consequences," [1] and they were seldom put down without much bloodshed.

Almost from the beginning there was bloodshed. In Gloucester County, Virginia, in 1663, Negro slaves joined with white indentured servants in a conspiracy to rebel, but the plot was discovered. The alleged ringleaders were drawn and quartered and their bloody heads were impaled on posts in a public place. A slave plot to wipe out the whites galvanized three Virginia counties into panic in 1687, although the ambitious scale of the conspiracy had betrayed it. Again the leaders were caught and horribly done to death; but again the examples made of them did not deter other slaves from desperate bids for freedom. By 1710 there had been a dozen revolts attempted or accomplished in Virginia, Maryland, New Jersey and Massachusetts.

Arson was the facile tool of rebels and avengers. Many a planter leapt to wakefulness in the dead of night to find the sky lurid with flames from his grain pile, his stable, or even his dwelling. In New York, in 1712, a rabble of slaves set fire to some buildings late one night. When the whites rushed forth to put out the flames, the slaves, armed with guns and knives, fell upon them, killing nine. Still unsatisfied, the rebels prowled the fear-shocked streets for several hours threatening death to the whites and putting buildings

to the torch. Nor did they all give up when soldiers converged upon
them. "One shot first his wife and then himself and some who had
hid themselves in town when they went to apprehend them cut their
own throats." But more than twenty were caught and sentenced to
die, one by "slow fire," that he might "continue in torment for
eight or ten hours."

Ships on the brutal Middle Passage from the West Indies to the
mainland were sometimes the rolling stages of rebellion. The American slaver *Kentucky* was one such—but she put it down and forty-
seven slaves, among them a woman, were killed for daring to revolt.
"They were ironed or chained, two together, and when they were
hung, a rope was put around their necks and they were drawn up to
the yardarm clear of the sail. This did not kill them, but only choked
or strangled them. They were then shot in the breast and the bodies
thrown overboard. If only one of two that were ironed together was
to be hung, the rope was put around his neck and he was drawn up
clear of the deck and his leg laid across the rail and chopped off to
save the irons." [2]

How the concept of the patient, docile Negro ever came into being
is a minor marvel of historical delusion. It was created against tremendous odds of fact and circumstance. Perhaps it was a psychological
necessity of the sort that sometimes prompts people to blind themselves to wish-destroying fact, and little boys, frightened of the dark,
to whistle gay, pretentious tunes. Whatever the cause of it, there the
delusion was, bigger than life, and, it might be said, as real—a sort
of sublimation of guilt, or fear, or both. It was there when all actuality
denied it. It was there in complete contradiction to the law, to the
Black Codes which said in effect that the Negro was restive, dangerous, murderous under slavery; that the Negro loved freedom
enough to hazard his life for it on only the dimmest chance of winning; and that in order to quench the leaping fires of his rebellious
nature, the flood of despotism must mount unchecked.

The concept of the Negro as knee-bending, head-bowing slave was
there, but the law courts did not act as if they credited it. The policy
of the law was to avoid the prosecution of masters whose punishment of slaves was "malicious, cruel, and excessive" even to the
point of murder. "The power of the master must be absolute to
render the submission of the slave perfect," declared a justice of the
North Carolina Supreme Court. And the courts of law went ruth-

lessly about the business of developing juridical and social means of carrying out an involved but consummate system of controls.

It took a little time, for the frontiersman was highly volatile, highly individual. Personal precedent and privilege yielded only haltingly to communal law. But eventually a creed emerged, for it was a transfer-in-trust from Caribbean new world history, a necessitous condition of modern slavery, and a resource of sanguine expectation in the heart of new American man. And what a man he was! How clear-mettled and how ambiguous, how irresolute and how obstinate, how self-righteous and how self-condemning, how kind and how callous, how simple, complex and altogether contradictory. And these opposing attributes are shown nowhere better than in the way he handled slavery.

Devices for controlling slaves developed with the slave system or sprang man-size from the womb of expediency. An early device was' the simple but effective one of separating slaves of the same family or tribe. Often the inhabitants of entire African villages, closely knit by ties of memory and blood, were captured and sold individually into slavery. Thus a mother might be traded off into the West Indies, a father in Virginia, and the children scattered among owners in New York, New Jersey and Massachusetts. Later, cries of indignation arose over this dispersion when it affected families that had known nothing but bondage. Indeed, it was called the "darkest crime" of slavery. Curiously enough, while at the same time men argued that slaves had no family-feeling and no finer instincts, those who wished to earn or keep reputations as good masters counted it a mortal sin to drag mother from child, wife from husband, sister from brother. Much of the opprobrium that was heaped upon slave dealers stemmed from a general feeling of revulsion over this practice. Private owners seldom followed it except to save themselves from great financial embarrassment, or except as punishment for the most unruly slaves. From the beginning however, no horror attached to disrupting the family ties of slaves just brought from Africa, and yet it must have been most cruel for these bewildered strangers in a strange land. All they had—if not family love—was tribal memory and the sense of community they shared with each other. Sundering these bonds of consanguinity, of group experience and identity, was the ultimate ravishment.

Nor did it always produce the desired end. Some slaves of course, cut off from all the things and people they had known, committed suicide. But such cases were exceptional, for even under slavery and given to spells of deep melancholy, the Africans had a robust love of life. Forced because of the separation from their own kind, to learn a strange language, take on an alien mode of life, acquire a foreign culture-pattern, the early slaves knit up ties with white indentured servants. The mixing of these two elements in the population compounded discontent. Indentured servants had grievances too. The legal and customary distinctions between them and slaves were so slight as hardly to be observed. They were, most of these servants, "unruly" and "spirited," and the Oliverians among them had a green knowledge of what group rebellion meant. They made common cause with the slaves.

Indeed, as already mentioned, the first serious servile conspiracy to rebel found servants and slaves allied in 1663. Nine years later the colonial Assembly of Virginia deemed it wise to point up an enactment permitting runaway slaves to be killed with impunity with the following words:

Forasmuch as it hath beene manifested to this grand assembly that many negroes have lately beene, and are now out in rebellion in sundry parts of this country, and that noe means have yet beene found for the apprehension and suppression of them from whom many mischiefes of very dangerous consequences may arise to the country if either other negroes, Indians or *servants* should happen to fly forth and joyne with them.

The threat to slave control that these alliances held was very real in some of the other colonies too. New Jersey was aware of it and took steps to put it down. New York was startled in 1741 by the sworn testimony of Mary Barton and Peggy Kerry, white indentured servants and the confessed love-partners of slaves, who revealed a servile plot in which at least twenty-five white redemptioners were allied with four times that number of Negro slaves. The testimony of these two women brought to punishment more than a hundred persons—among them Peggy Kerry's lover and the father of her child—some of whom were burned at the stake, some hanged, and some banished.

All during the late years of the seventeenth and the early years of the eighteenth centuries servant-slave rebellion flared with frightening persistence. A rumor was enough to throw whole countries into panic and to pull the colonial legislative trigger in alarm. Laws for the control of slaves grew steadily more rigorous, until, in general, the master's right of property in his slave involved absolute control over the slave's person and conduct. Thus a master could whip his slaves at will, cut their rations, crop their ears, brand them, pillory them, or inflict upon them any other punishment that seemed, in his judgment, "right." Slaves could not leave their masters' premises without a pass. They had no right of assembly. They could not own property and therefore could not buy or sell or trade. Arms were forbidden them. Dogs were taboo. Slaves could not sue or be sued, prosecute for a battery, nor enter a civil suit. They could not give evidence against a white person. Not even in self-defense could they lift their hands against a "Christian" white, and in Virginia until 1788 it was legally impossible for a white man to murder a slave. The death of a slave under punishment was either accidental homicide or manslaughter, neither of which made white men liable to prosecution.

For the execution of the distinctive body of "Negro laws" most colonies, and later the states, had distinctive courts and procedures. Virginia early instituted a special court for the "speedy prosecution" of slaves. In most states slaves had no right to trial by jury and got none. They could be, and most often were, tried, usually on the warrant of a commission of oyer and terminer, in "Negro courts." The justices might, and frequently did have only the most casual acquaintance with the technicalities of the law. The slave himself, of course, had no acquaintance whatever. He did not really need any; nor, had he had, would it have done him any good. Putting into words the original and long-prevailing fact, the Constitutional Court of South Carolina ruled:

A slave can invoke neither Magna Charta not common law. . . . In the very nature of things he is subject to despotism. Law to him is only a compact between his rulers, and the questions which concern him are matters agitated between them. The various acts concerning slaves contemplate throughout the subordination of the servile class to every free white person and enforce the stern policy which the relation of master and slave necessarily requires. Any conduct of a slave inconsistent with due subordination contravenes the purpose of these acts.

This was in 1847, when by some accounts the ironhanded repressiveness of customary attitudes and of law had somewhat relaxed and, by these same accounts, slavery in the South was a benevolent paternalism.

But when the Black Codes started generating their blacker progeny, the middle of the nineteenth century was a long way off. Meantime the spirit of their increasing purpose seeped into factors of psychological conditioning so various, so subtle and pervasive as to defy complete analysis. There was propaganda; and yet it was not wholly this, for these prolocutors—politicians, preachers, and professors—believed it. Doctrine and the sincerity with which it was uttered were a hard combination to withstand. That belief came after the substance of the law only proves the influence of matter over mind. The law had said that the Negro was inferior; now pointing to the slave's mudsill status as empirical proof, anthropologists and sociologists declared so too. "The political responsibility for bringing slavery to this continent," said the politicians, "can be wiped from our escutcheon." The professors at first were more restrained and cautious. "We think we are prepared to say that when all the evils of slavery [in the South] are put together . . . the fair conclusion will be that the whole sum is but a small fraction of the same classes of evils that from time immemorial have belonged and still belong to the barbarism of the fatherland of this race. . . . We see, then, that the *evils* of American slavery are blessings as compared with the general fate of the African race in their native continent." But professorial restraint went by the board in the 1830's, when Professor Thomas R. Dew, of the College of William and Mary, advanced a philosophical defense of slavery. It was a defense fashioned after the Positivist social order of Auguste Comte, and it boldly cast aside the principles of brotherhood and equality. Liberty and equality? Mere romantic nonsense. Brotherhood? A snare and a delusion. "And what is the meaning [of equality] in the Charter of our rights? Simply, that royal blood, and noble blood, is no better than any other blood; and therefore, that we will have no king, and no aristocracy. . . . It goes no further than to cut off the hereditary claims of kings and nobles."

Nor was this all by any means.

In the beginning slaveholders generally opposed religious instruction and baptism for slaves. They believed that an understanding of Christianity would create grave disturbances among the black people. It was better that the African priests continue to practice the heathen rights of Obi and perpetuate their outlandish gods of sticks and straw among the slaves. The law of 1667, which declared that baptism did not alter "the condition of a person as to his bondage or his freedom," aroused no proselyting zeal among the master class. "Talk to a planter of the soul of a negro," an English observer said in 1705, "and he'll be apt to tell you (or at least his actions speak loudly) that the body of one of them may be worth twenty Pounds; but the souls of an hundred of them would not yield him one Farthing." An English lady of the West Indies wrote the Reverend Morgan God-wyn, a rector in Virginia, that one "might as well baptize puppies as Negroes." Still later, in 1765, a Quaker missionary was moved to complain that "it is too manifest to be denied, that the life of religion is almost lost where slaves are very numerous."

But the English Society for the Propagation of the Bible in Foreign Parts did not campaign for the religious instruction of slaves entirely to no avail. Before the close of the eighteenth century, many churches had slave galleries and many masters hired carefully chosen ministers to preach to their congregated blacks. There were even some Negro preachers, but they were harried bootleggers of the Gospel, like the Reverend William Moses, of Williamsburg, Virginia. Frequently arrested and whipped for holding meetings, Preacher Moses nevertheless carried on between 1770 and 1790, secretly preparing other Negroes for his high calling. Black congregations presided over by black ministers aroused the quick fear and suspicion of the slaveholders, and for a time after 1800, the year of the slave revolt led by Gabriel Prosser, Negro preachers were rated dangerous criminals, for some of them were suspected of being involved with Gabriel.

Still, in spite of the hindrances to participation in the religious life, about one in twenty-five slaves was a member of a church in 1800. To preach to these, ministers were chosen for their skill at squaring the fact of slavery with the word of God. Apparently it was not a hard skill to acquire, and though the established churches—Episcopal and Catholic—did not actually require it, their bishops and arch-bishops, some of whom owned slaves themselves, looked upon it with smug approval. The right kind of preaching was a method of slave-control. And, indeed, compelling slaves to go to church, as masters did increasingly, might help save both souls and slavery.

"Cursed be Canaan, a servant of servants shall he be unto his brethren!" The eternal righteousness of God had reduced the blacks to their low estate. That was Gospel. It was expounded nicely, emphasized persistently, promoted fervently. "Masters are taught in the Bible, how they must rule their servants, and servants how they must obey their masters," preached the Reverend Alexander Glennie to the slaves in his South Carolina parish. To make sure of its being heard, he read the biblical passage twice over, and continued with kindly persuasiveness, with gentle exhortation: "Our Heavenly Father commands that you, who are servants, should 'be obedient to your masters according to the flesh'; that is, to your earthly master, the master that you serve here while in the body. Here is a very plain command: 'servants be obedient': be obedient to your masters. . . . As you ought to understand well what is the will of God respecting you, I will read to you again this part of the Bible. 'Servants, be obedient. . . .' " [3]

It is no wonder that Frederick Douglass was to say later that he "learned that 'God, up in the sky,' made everybody: and that he made *white* people to be masters and mistresses, and *black* people to be slaves. This did not satisfy me. . . ."

Nor did it satisfy thousands of others before him and after, for slaves were not always fooled by casuistry and sophistry. Their starved emotions did not leap to the lure. They needed a stronger stimulus, and many of them were regular attendants at secret "brush-arbor" meetings and at clandestine gatherings in some slaves' quarters where in the pitch-black of freighted midnight they could evoke some red-eyed god out of the time of their beginnings. They practiced strange medicine then, brought out perhaps the fetishistic survivals of Obi or of Oxala, and chanted in low voices what they could remember of the white folks' hymns set to the pulsing, melancholy minors of African rhythm.

Yet, somehow they evolved a notion of the Christian God. He was a less temperate, but a kinder, more loving God than their masters'. He understood their troubles and would make things right in the sweet by'n by. Sometimes they grew impatient with the white preachers' notions about God. Sometimes they asked questions. Old Uncle Silas who rose in the middle of a sermon to ask whether "us slaves gonna be free in Heaven" got a sophistic brush-off, but the question was the measure of his misery in bondage on earth.

More immediately effective than propaganda in controlling slaves were the personal punishments and rewards that were practically standard on every large slaveholding plantation. For an offense that violated the rules of propriety, a slave might be severely flogged or branded on one or both cheeks. Acts of impropriety ranged from a certain look in the eye of a slave to open impudence; and impudence itself might mean anything, or, as Frederick Douglass put it, "nothing at all, just according to the caprice of the master overseer, at the moment." It was an offense that could be committed in various ways, "in the tone of an answer; in answering at all; in not answering; in the expression of the countenance; in the motion of the head; in the gait, manner and bearing of the slave." No doubt many a slave was marked for life because of a gesture made in a moment when his customary vigilance was relaxed. No doubt, also, many a master had practical cause to regret his ready recourse to brand and whip. Micajah Ricks, a slaveholder of North Carolina, advertised for a runaway: "A few days ago before she went off, I burnt her with a hot iron on the left side of her face; I tried to make the letter M, and she kept a cloth over her head and face, and a fly bonnet on her head so as to cover the burn."

In the final analysis, though few masters seemed to realize it, rewards paid larger and more certain dividends. The loyalty of the body servant and house slave, of old Black Mammy and Uncle Tom and Zeke, over which the Southern romanticists go into their purplest paeans, would have been much less but for the remainders from festive boards, the cast-off clothes, and the occasional coins that were thrown their way. As for the field hands, gay headcloths and chewing tobacco accomplished what lashing could not. Thomas Ruffin, a chief justice of the North Carolina Supreme Court, said that "trivial matters have exceedingly great effect in improving the slave and uniting him to his owner." He knew one successful planter who had produced this effect simply by putting a cheap looking-glass in his slaves' quarters, and another who had done it by having a fence built around the slaves' burial plot.

For good work and for being tractable, slaves were occasionally rewarded with small amounts of cash. Christmas, a holiday that lasted a week on liberal plantations, was usually the time of this happy dispensation. A woman might get as much as a dollar; a man twice as much. This was great plenty for those who had so little. The slaves could do what they wished with their money. Some got drunk. Indeed, for a slave "not to be drunk during the holidays was disgraceful" and aroused masters' suspicions. But to be drunk at any other time also aroused suspicions. An inebriated and foot-loose Negro was a dangerous thing.

But some slaves had other uses for their money. The North Carolina *Standard*, a paper published at Raleigh, lamented satirically that Negroes too often spent money for "expensive costume, whereby very respectable white dandies are scandalized, being insulted by the successful imitation of the style and manner of exquisite and exclusive gentility." Some of those who were vain and improvident enough to buy expensive clothes were also ungrateful enough to run away in them. A Pennsylvania slave master, for instance, advertised a runaway slave as having "a beaver hat, a green worsted coat, a closebodied coat with a green narrow frieze cape," other clothes and a violin. In 1793, one John Dulin, of Maryland, after describing the absconder's rich haberdashery, declared that his runaway slave also had an ample supply of funds.

From giving slaves Christmas money to do with as they wished, to giving them time which they could hire out was a hesitant step in an uncertain direction. Some masters, liberal beyond common and uncommonly affected by pangs of conscience, took it as a means of lightening the slaves' bondage and went on from there to give slaves their freedom or to allow them a share of the earnings, and trusted slaves who had wangled liberal terms could lay by considerable sums. One Milly Lea, of North Carolina, an expert seamstress, saved more than a thousand dollars in a dozen years. Her case was unusual, not because of the comforting size of the sum but because the court gave her a legal right to it. Generally the courts frowned upon slaves having more than enough coin to jingle in their pockets.

Slaves were hired out to industry. Hezekiah Coffin, a manufacturer of Rhode Island, wrote to Moses Brown in 1763 wishing to know "by the first opportunity what the negroes wages was" that he might settle with the masters. The tobacco factories of Richmond, the warehouses and bustling waterfronts of Norfolk, Charleston and New Orleans, and the labor-hungry lumber plants of the mid-South hired the time of slaves. Slaves were used in foundries as forgemen and blacksmiths. In the process of building America and making it go, these slaves learned many skills. They mined coal and tended the engines that burned it; they felled timber and planed the boards for building; they quarried stone, and wrought iron, and tempered steel, and created tools. They were more free than the "free" Negroes and more secure than the free poor whites.

But the unequal competition between bond labor and free was one of the grosser evils of slavery. Interclass and intra-sectional at first, it came to have an impact on the economic competition between North and South in direct proportion to the dependence of one section upon the other. But this was somewhat later. The interclass impact aroused resentment against the hired-out slave and led to demands for his restraint.

Advertisements such as the following appeared frequently in the latter half of the eighteenth century:

Five hundred laborers wanted. We will employ the above number of laborers to work on the Muscle Shoals Canal, etc., at the rate of fifteen dollars per month, for twenty-six working days, or we will employ negroes by the year, or for a less time, as may suit the convenience of the planters. We will also be responsible to slave holders who hire their negroes to us, for any injury or damage that may hereafter happen in progress of blasting rock or of caving in of banks.

Wanted to hire, a negro wheelwright. Master's interest protected.

The free white mechanics and laborers realized their disadvantage, but there was not much they could do about it. Politics was one weapon, and violence was another, but the first was ineffective, as the second was dangerous. Slaveholders were not going to stand for trifling with the incomes which their hired-out hands brought them; they were not going to have valuable slave artisans and craftsmen molested. Men of the master class had most of the power in the South. The great tobacco plantations and the tobacco factories belonged to them. Later, the land on which the cotton grew, the gins that cleaned it, and the mills that spun it into cloth were theirs. The political interests were nearly all gathered in their hands, and in South Carolina at least they manipulated them to their exclusive advantage by setting up qualifications for office that slammed the door on all but members of their own class. On the expanding

Southern frontier, the planters exercised the raw frontier right of the strong to dominate and even utterly destroy the weak. By their connivance and their naked contempt for the poorer whites, they built solid the tradition of class enmity and they cultivated the resultant hatred between laboring white and laboring black, slave and free.

The residue of power reposed in a sturdy, middle class of whites —Scotch Presbyterians, German Lutherans, and Irish Protestants— who were non-slaveholding, independent farmers, business men and professionals. White labor made its appeal to these and gained some indefatigable friends who abhorred slavery and all its works. These were the men who wrote letters and signed petitions. In Athens, Georgia, they complained that hired-out slaves had so much cheapened white labor that all but a few white masons and carpenters were forced to leave the city. In other places in Georgia they protested against "negro mechanics whose masters reside in other places, and who pay nothing toward the support of the government." Registering their own dissatisfaction, white craftsmen in South Carolina, North Carolina and Tennessee inveighed against the training of slaves in skilled trades and against masters who used their slave mechanics to underbid free workers in contracts, to the great injury of said free workers. Middle class Virginians considered it a "public evil" that the increase of white seamen was discouraged by the use of slaves as pilots, navigators, and sailors, and they did something about it. In 1784 a law was passed which limited the number of Negroes used in river and bay navigation to one third the total of persons so employed. Within ten years restrictive legislation on hiring out slaves was pretty general, and North Carolina had made it a serious offense for a master to allow a slave to hire his time "under any pretense whatever."

2

By the middle of the eighteenth century strange ideas called "humanitarian" were being bruited about. They dealt with such concepts as the dignity of the human personality, the inalienable rights of man, the responsibility of government, and the place of man in a world from which magic and witchcraft and mystical metaphysics had been forever banished by the bright-eyed philosophers who followed after Descartes. Humanitarianism, which was eventually to abolish slavery, bring new spirit to penal codes and institutions, and build refuges for the weak and unfortunate, was disturbing. The notions to which it gave rise had an unsettling effect upon slavery, an institution which, anyway, was not calculated to ease the conscience.

Indeed, the psychology of the average slaveholder was already warped and intorted; his acts were often contrary to his beliefs, his head often in mortal conflict with his heart. His was a split personality, baffled and hypersensitized and infected with an insidious illness. Humanitarianism feezed him. The rationale of slavery was in direct contradiction to the doctrines which, after the 1740's, were getting clearer and clearer statement. It was contrary to the flux of the romantic tide that was beginning to swell and beat against the shores of the western world. The effort to engraft slavery on the whole way of American life and to have its acceptance unquestioned lacked moral conviction. The best minds and the leading minds commenced to probe for more tenable positions, less shaky ground. Thomas Jefferson made known his opposition to slavery. Later his first draft of the Declaration of Independence indicted the King of England for violating the "most sacred rights of life and liberty of a distant people, who never offended him, captivating them into slavery in another hemisphere or to incur miserable death in their transportation thither." Less vocal, Henry Laurens, George Mason and St. George Tucker stood at Jefferson's shoulder.

It is a curious fact that the stirring slogans of the western worldwide revolution, which trumpeted the principles of philanthropy—"Liberty or death!" "Liberty, fraternity, equality!"—seemed to abate the tensions of American slavery. Men took the word for the purging deeds and welcomed it with fervor. But riding furiously on the winds of these slogans came the early abolitionists. They, too, were welcomed—but dubiously and with reservations. They pleaded, coaxed—especially the Quakers, Baptists and Methodists—formed societies, and set examples. Their earnest preachments converted some who, already half convinced of human brotherhood, freed their slaves.

When the war itself came, Negroes fought. Some in New England were freed to fight. Some fought as substitutes for their masters. The first man to die under the guns of the Redcoats was Crispus Attucks, an escaped slave. Peter Salem distinguished himself at Bunker Hill by killing the British Major Pitcairn, and Salem Poor was cited for heroic action in the Battle of Charleston. In that first year of war, there was scarcely a skirmish or a battle that black men did not fight in. But it did not make sense that slaves should fight to win for others a freedom they could not enjoy. It travestied the principles of the Revolution, as James Otis was quick to declare.

If Otis thought that something was wrong in abstract principle only, he was soon disillusioned. Negroes were going over to the British, who promised them freedom. Lord Dunmore, the Royal Governor of Virginia, had issued a proclamation to that effect. He armed slaves to fight against their masters. This disaffection of the Negroes made a bad situation worse. At first opposed to the en-listment of Negroes in the Continental Army, General George Washington was forced to relent enough to admit free Negroes. But escaping from slavery to go over to the British—or just escaping— continued to cause grave concern. If Thomas Jefferson was right, thirty thousand slaves escaped from Virginia masters in one revolu-tionary year alone. As the situation grew more desperate, following the gloomy winter of 'Seventy-eight, the colonies themselves relaxed General Washington's policy still further. New Hampshire, Massa-chusetts and Rhode Island enlisted battalions of blacks. Maryland mustered a troop of seven hundred and fifty, promising them free-dom and paying bounty to their masters. New York did the same; Virginia and North Carolina took similar steps. By the Constitu-tion of 1780, Massachusetts practically abolished slavery. Pennsyl-vania, New York, Connecticut and New Jersey passed acts for gradual emancipation. Maryland prohibited the importation of slaves and made manumission easier.

So Negroes fought all through the war. They were at Ticonderoga, Bemis Heights and Stony Point. With Lafayette was one James Armistead, so astute a spy that he completely fooled the British Lord Cornwallis and saved Lafayette's army from defeat. In desperate battle against Hessian mercenaries at Point Bridge, New York, Rhode Island blacks "sacrificed themselves to the last man" in defense of an important position. The only woman to bear arms in the Con-tinental Army was a Negro, Deborah Gannett, who enlisted as Robert Shurtliff and discharged "the duties of a faithful, gallant soldier, and at the same time," read the citation of the state of Massachusetts, "preserved the virtue and chastity of her sex. . . ." A Negro, Captain

Mark Starlin, commanded the Virginia naval vessel *Patriot,* and Negroes served on the *Royal Louis,* the *Tempest* and the *Diligence.* They were at Red Bank, Princeton and Eutaw Springs. Black Samson of Brandywine, whom the Negro poet Dunbar eulogizes, was not a myth: he did "do great deeds of valor." Negroes crossed the Delaware with Washington, died at Valley Forge, and quartered arms with their white comrades at Yorktown, where, legend has it, one black fellow, forgetting military protocol, yelled out, "Mr. British General, you am Cornwallis, but I'se going now to change your name to Cobwallis, for General Washington, with us colored pussons, has shelled all the corn offen you!" [4] When the war was done at last, many Negro soldiers were reenslaved, but by 1790 there were fifty-nine thousand free blacks, forming, as many came to feel, an ominous cloud on the social horizon.

The convulsive struggle of the Revolution brought to furious boil many simmering problems. There was the war itself to recover from. The Articles of Confederation, strong enough to hold the states together in time of mutual danger, were now pendulous and weak under the unlooked-for burden of victory. That the thin membrane of confederate government threatened to rupture was well recognized by 1787. There was a great deal of jealous ambition on the part of each state, and the "diplomats" in the Congress were each concerned with the particular rights and privileges of his own state. In short, the Confederation could scarcely be called a government; "it was an assemblage of governments."

In the opaqueness of their inexperience, men tried to separate political issues from social and social from economic, but there was no way of separating them. The common people had little left them save political liberty, which was still something of an abstraction, and land, which was largely devastated. Commerce was gone, and money had all but disappeared. The public debt was $170,000,000. In Massachusetts, two thousand men, led by Daniel Shays, rose up with demands that the collection of debts be suspended. It was a spontaneous rebellion that lasted several weeks. The concept of aristocratic rule was challenged. The common people demanded land reforms and guarantees of human rights. Adding their strident voices to the clamor, anti-slavery men called for an end to human bondage.

Though slavery was only one of the issues that faced the Constitutional Convention of 1787, its influence was so pervasive and its resilient fibers had become so entwined about the structure of colonial life that it could not be ignored. Indeed, two questions—the taxation of imports, and proportional representation—dragged the slavery issue out in stark and ominous nakedness. It was an ironic and a mixed-up business. For one thing, the Virginia and Maryland delegates stood with the North, where opposition to slavery had grown steadily through the Revolution.

The North argued largely on moral grounds. As a matter of fact, the Pennsylvania Society for Promoting the Abolition of Slavery, founded in 1775, had prepared a resolution to be presented to the Convention by Benjamin Franklin, president of the Pennsylvania group and a delegate to the Convention. George Mason of Virginia declared that "slavery discourages arts and manufactures. The poor despise labor when performed by slaves. . . . [Slaves] produce the most pernicious effect on manners. Every master of slaves is born a petty tyrant. They bring the judgment of heaven on a Country. As nations can not be rewarded or punished in the next world they must in this. By an inevitable chain of causes and effects providence punishes national sins, by national calamities." The North, where steps had already been taken to end slavery importation, wanted an end put to "the infernal traffic." Counting slaves in the population, Luther Martin, of Maryland, thought, would encourage the traffic, and that it was "inconsistent with the principles of the revolution and dishonorable to the American character to have such a feature [as slavery] in the Constitution."

The South argued largely on economic and political grounds, though Charles Pinckney, a delegate from South Carolina, begged leave to point out that "slavery was justified by the example of the world." John Rutledge, also from South Carolina, declared that "religion and humanity had nothing to do with the slavery question. Interest alone is the governing principle with Nations. . . . If the Northern States consult their interest, they will not oppose the increase of slaves which will increase the commodities of which they will become the carriers." Pinckney echoed this same thinking: the traffic in slaves is "for the interest of the whole Union. The more slaves, the more produce to employ the carrying trade; the more consumption also, and the more of this, the more of revenue for the common treasury." The South thought slavery consistent with the interest of the country, and did not want the traffic stopped by any means. As to the question of proportional representation in Congress, the North which professed to look upon slaves as human beings did not want them counted as part of the population. The South, whose laws had the practical effect of making slaves *things,* wanted slaves counted on an equality with whites.

The great debate dragged on for four months. It ended less in compromise than in the North's capitulation and in a sweeping victory for the South.

"We The People of the United States, in Order to form a more perfect Union, establish Justice, insure domestic Tranquility . . . do ordain and establish . . ." that:

"Representatives and direct Taxes shall be apportioned among the several States which may be included within this Union, according to their respective Numbers, which shall be determined by adding to the whole Number of free Persons, including those bound to Service for a Term of Years, and excluding Indians not taxed, three fifths of all other Persons."

And that:

"The migration or Importation of such Persons as any of the States now existing shall think proper to admit, shall not be prohibited by Congress prior to the Year one thousand eight hundred and eight, but a Tax or duty may be imposed on such Importation, not exceeding ten dollars for each person."

And that:

"No Person held to Service or Labour in one State, under the Laws thereof, escaping into another, shall, in Consequence of any Law or Regulation therein, be discharged from such Service or Labour, but shall be delivered up on Claim of the Party to whom such Service or Labour may be due."

The humanitarian light of the Revolution, blown out in the breath of fearful compromise, was not to come on again for almost three-quarters of a century.

Indeed, what had been a happy if partial and fortuitous exercise of equalitarian principle during the Revolution was become a curse by 1790. The presence of so many escaped slaves was embarrassing to the North, now that the Constitution provided that they should be delivered up on demand. In the South the presence of free Negroes was embarrassing, for such Negroes were a constant threat to the slaveholders' control. Disaffected Negroes, ran common opinion in the slavery section, were usually free Negroes. Laws to restrict the increase of this class were passed. Most Southern states, following a pattern set by Virginia in 1793, prohibited the immigration of free blacks. In North Carolina the free Negro could not go beyond the county adjoining his home county. Arriving at Southern ports, free colored sailors were not allowed to leave ship, or were beaten and thrown into jail. Restriction, prohibition, proscription. The free Negro could not vote, could not own or carry arms, could not sell certain commodities, could not be employed as a clerk or typesetter, could not obtain credit without the permission of a guardian, could not be without a guardian, could not testify against a white man in court, could not entertain slaves nor be entertained by them. Smothered under the limitations imposed upon him by law, the free Negro might almost as well have been enslaved.

What had happened was that several factors and events had made the South more sensitive about slavery after the Revolutionary War. First of all, the period was one of economic uncertainty. The war had brought heavy losses in personal wealth. The British had carried off "thousands of slaves, helped themselves to costly silver plate . . . and left many plantation homes in flames." Rice and indigo, with fewer slaves to produce them, were in a state of acute depression. Transportation was badly disorganized; markets scattered and uncertain. The price of slaves was way down. A good female slave advertised as "ripe for child-bearing and strong in wind and limb" could bring no more than two hundred dollars. A good male slave, offered for five hundred dollars, was thought to be overpriced. Tobacco, the great cash crop of Maryland, Virginia and North Carolina, was a glut on the market. The institution of slavery seemed to be in a precarious state of health.

Moreover, the abolitionist, a grim, persistent breed, had never given up. Anti-slavery men like Benjamin Rush and Jeremy Belknap, John Jay and John Filson, David Rice and Robert Pleasants spoke, wrote and made schemes against slavery. "A thousand laws," shouted David Rice, "can never make that innocent which the Divine Law has made criminal; or give them [slaveholders] a right to that which the Divine Law forbids them to claim." [5] In 1794 various local abolitionist groups—and there were a dozen such from Massachusetts down to Delaware—formed a cooperate body, and the direction

and combined force of anti-slavery thought put the South on the
moral defensive. It could no longer blame the continuance of American slavery on England. Indeed, aroused by Wilberforce, Sharp
and Clarkson, the Mother Country was having anti-slavery troubles
of her own.

But also in England something more was happening, and its
impact upon the slave economy of the South was to be terrific.
Industrialization was happening; coal was happening; steam was
happening. The invention of the power loom made the manu-
facture of great quantities of cloth a matter of throwing an engine
switch. All at once the demand for cheap textile fibers rose to a
strident pitch. Cotton was the answer, but the preparation of cotton
for milling was slow and laborious, by hand. If only a quick way
could be found to separate the fiber from seed and stalky trash, cotton
would be cheaper than silk or linen and more comfortable and
versatile than wool. Just at the right time, wandering down from
New England, Eli Whitney built the first cotton gin. Moribund
slavery, having a powerful restorative now, took a new lease on life.
Cotton meant workers, and workers meant slaves—more and more
slaves as new lands were opened up and more people bowed down
to cotton as king.

Just as this development was getting under way however, a hundred thousand slaves rose up in revolt on the French island of Haiti.
Within a few weeks they destroyed "200 sugar plantations, 600 coffee
plantations" and a like number of cotton and indigo plantations.
More than two thousand whites were killed without mercy. The
island became a fire-drenched waste. Bryan Edwards, visiting Haiti
almost a month after the start of the nightmare, wrote: "We arrived
in the harbor of Le Cap at evening . . . and the first sight which
arrested our attention as we approached was a dreadful scene of
devastation by fire. The noble plain adjoining Le Cap was covered
with ashes, and the surrounding hills, as far as the eye could reach,
everywhere presented to us ruins still smoking and houses and
plantations at that moment in flames." But after a month, six months,
sixteen months, the terrible destruction was not done. It looked as
if the Haitian revolutionaries had set in motion a stupendous chain
reaction that would blast slavery from the earth. For two years,
under their great leader Toussaint L'Ouverture, they struggled un-
quelled, defeating the British, the Spaniards and the soldiers of

Napoleon. At last the First Republic granted freedom to all slaves loyal to France.

The bloody vengeance done in Haiti revitalized the South's old fears and gave deep concern to the whole country. Nor did these lessen with the restoration of order in the Caribbean, for that order was of the Negroes' making, and St. Domingo was practically a Black Republic. The potentials in the American situation were plain. Would American slaveholders be driven to the same expediency of granting freedom to the slaves—and that at a time when the economic promise of slavery was just risen like a golden sun? Thomas Jefferson at least thought this, or worse. "I become daily more and more convinced," he wrote in 1793, "that all the West India Islands will remain in the hands of the people of colour, and a total expulsion of these whites sooner or later will take place. It is high time we should foresee the bloody scenes which our children certainly, and possibly ourselves (south of Potomac), have to wade through, and try to avert them."

Rumors flew. Aided by the French, who were intent upon world conquest, the revolt-freed Haitians were going to invade the United States and set American blacks at liberty. Failing this, picked agents, even then filtering through the South from the ports of New Orleans, Charleston and Baltimore, were to spread sedition among the slaves. Thomas Jefferson, more sagacious than most, and then Secretary of State, had some part in giving these wild reports currency. He wrote the Governor of South Carolina:

A French gentleman, one of the refugees from St. Domingo, informs me that two Frenchmen, from St. Domingo also, of the names Castaing and La Chaise, are about setting out from this place for Charleston, with a design to excite an insurrection among the negroes. He says that this is in execution of a general plan, formed by the Brissotine party at Paris, the first branch of which has been carried into execution at St. Domingo. My informant is a person with whom I am well acquainted, of good sense, discretion and truth, and certainly believes this himself. I inquired of him the channel of his information. He told me it was one which had never been found to be mistaken. . . . Castaing is described as a small dark mulatto, and La Chaise as a Quatron of a tall fine figure.

Whether these rumors were true or not, credulity was grandsired by fear and given substance by events. Slave revolts and conspiracies to revolt broke out like an epidemic in the States. Undoubtedly the news of the Haitian insurrection was partly to blame, but it is also likely that the remembered "spirit and philosophy of the American Revolution were important in arousing . . . discontent amongst the Negroes." Louisiana, then owned by Spain—which country was at war with France—was disturbed by slave uprisings in 1791 and 1792, but not much is known about them. Better known are the slave plots devised in South Carolina. Indeed, the Charleston trouble of 1793, during which fires apparently of incendiary origin blackened part of the city, bears out the warning of Jefferson's letter. A correspondent wrote: "It is said that St. Domingo negroes have sown these seeds of revolt, and that a magazine has been attempted to be broken open." When fires again broke out with fiendish regularity three years later, the seditious connivance of St. Domingo Negroes was further suspected. North Carolina and Maryland were kept constantly alarmed throughout the 1790's.

These outbreaks were hardly quieting to the slaveholders. They were already laboring with problems that seemed insoluble. Their economic hopes were not being realized. In the upper South, the soil was impoverished by the cultivation of tobacco, which crop was itself a drug on the market. Bankrupt planters were a dime a dozen. Plantation fields lay idle; fine old colonial mansions stood deserted. Slaves, grown surly from hunger, loafed in their mouldy cabins, or, tired of this, ran away. Poverty clutched the land. Nor were things better in the lower South, where rice rotted in the swamps and indigo was not worth the cost of cultivation. Still, planters looked upon the times as merely an interlude between promise and fulfillment, and, though some of them gave up, selling or abandoning their holdings and selling or freeing their slaves, most held on.

But if there was a bond in poverty, there was a greater bond in terror, and in 1800, when only the intercession of nature saved Richmond and the surrounding country from the fate of St. Domingo, the South fully realized it. No other slave conspiracy was so well planned as that of Gabriel Prosser's; none, either, came nearer to success.

Gabriel Prosser was no ordinary slave, nor, for that matter, was he an ordinary man. Of giant stature, he possessed the kind of magnetic energy that inspires fanatic confidence in the followers of a leader or a prophet. Gabriel himself had no doubt that he was both.

His face was a scarred black rock. Like many a revolutionary before and after him, he believed that he was God-intended to bring "a great deliverance" to his people. If this was mystical nonsense, there was none in the planning that went on for months. Aided by his wife, his brothers, and Jack Bowler, another giant Negro, Gabriel recruited from his own district and from Carolina County, Goochland, and Petersburg upwards of a thousand slaves. Some of these, having been in the Revolutionary War, had an elementary knowledge of military tactics, for which reason they were made group leaders. Gabriel supplied them with crude arms—pikes and bludgeons made of wood, swords made of scythe blades, and a few antiquated guns. Gabriel cautiously sounded out the Catawba Indians, but decided against their help. He planned to steal horses for greater mobility. Finally, satisfied with his planning, he set a time when the fields would be ready for harvest, the cattle fat for slaughter. The insurrectionists would live off the land.

The operation was to begin on the night of August 20. All the whites (save the French and the Quakers) in the neighborhood of the Prosser plantation were to be killed. Picking up hundreds of pledged recruits from the surrounding country and augmented by hundreds—even thousands—from the city, the slaves were to descend on Richmond. Gabriel knew the city as well as he knew his master's barn, for he had made it the object of special study every Sunday for months. Once in Richmond, where it was expected that all bondmen would rally to the cause, the slaves were to set fires as a diversionary tactic, seize the arsenal and the State House, put all whites to the sword, and establish a black monarchy with Gabriel as king. Failing in this, they were to take to the mountains and defend themselves to the end. Their flag was to bear the legend "Liberty or Death."

Everything went well—for a while. No fewer than a thousand slaves kept the rendezvous at Old Brook Swamp, six miles from Richmond. Even the rain that began to fall at dusk was good for the plans of the insurrectionists, for it would keep unsuspecting folk indoors. But the rains came harder, blew a storm, a gale weirdly lit by lightning. Roads turned to goo, bridges were swept away, houses blown down, crops destroyed. Progress toward the city was utterly impossible. Pledged to a later rendezvous, the rebellious slaves scattered.

It was only later that they knew that they had been betrayed by other than the gods. Two of their own kind had betrayed them. Governor Monroe learned of the plot in the late afternoon of the twentieth. When the slaves kept their rendezvous, the city was already mobilized, the arsenal and State House were guarded. Cavalry troops clattered through the streets trying to cover all points at once. But nothing had happened when the storm broke, and after that nothing could happen.

The next day evidence of the epic scope of the conspiracy poured in and threw city and state into panic. Martial law was declared. The militia went to work, and Negroes were arrested indiscriminately. Some, according to Thomas W. Higginson, were hanged the same way, and almost as soon as caught. Gabriel himself had escaped, and for a time it looked as if the $300 offered for his capture was not enough. But within a month, once again betrayed by his own, Gabriel was discovered hiding in the hold of the schooner *Mary* which had sailed from Richmond to Norfolk. The outcome of his trial was a foregone conclusion. With fifteen others, Gabriel Prosser was hanged on October 7, 1800, before a wildly cheering mob.

3

But by 1800 the interlude of mere anxious hope was over and the promise of the industrial revolution was being fulfilled. Cotton was truly golden fleece. The area of its production spread to Georgia and Arkansas, and the purchase of Louisiana in 1803 extended it still further. Despite unlimited cultivation, the price of cotton soared, and with it the price of land and slaves. For slaves were as necessary to cotton—so at least thought the South—as the very earth that produced it. And there were not enough slaves.

The upheaval in St. Domingo had thoroughly frightened the South. To import slaves, particularly "seasoned" slaves from the Caribbean islands, was to run the risk of servile revolt. North Carolina, South Carolina, Virginia and Maryland had already passed laws prohibiting slave import. Presumably to help offset this voluntary cutting off and to round up some of the estimated forty-five thousand Negroes who had run away during the war, Congress enacted a fugitive slave law in 1793. But also in the very next year Congress moved to stop the slave trade to foreign ports and to prevent the fitting out of foreign slave ships in American yards.

But these measures were largely ineffective after 1800. Cotton was a powerful club. Returns promised to outweigh risks, and the slave trade to the United States continued to flourish. Trafficking under foreign flags, New England traders flouted the law. Southern planters and buyers connived with them. Anti-slavery interests undoubtedly would try to push through prohibitive measures the first moment the Constitution allowed, and slavers raced against the deadline. In the year 1802 alone, it was estimated that twenty thousand Negroes were imported into Georgia and South Carolina. "So little respect seems to have been paid to the existing prohibitory statute," said one member of Congress, "that it may almost be considered as disregarded by common consent."

But the sickening dread of slave revolt, of suddenly waking to find his life at the mercy of a vengeful black mob, still held validity for the average slaveholder. This dread was sometimes magnified by conscience and by the green awareness of what a precious thing was freedom. The Quakers kept conscience alive. They memorialized Congress; they tramped from door to door; and now and then they went to the length of helping slaves escape.

That there were men who needed no such goads is proved by the facts. In 1803, a Virginia planter, William Ludwell Green, set up an estate for the education of his slaves and willed them freedom. A fellow Virginian, Samuel Gist, purchased lands in free Ohio and settled his manumitted slaves upon it. Other slaveholders bought areas in Indiana, Illinois and Michigan and transported their ex-slaves thither. "I tremble for my country," Thomas Jefferson said, "when I think that God is just," and freed some of his slaves. Then, in 1806, President Jefferson reminded the Congress that the slave trade could be outlawed. In March of the next year a law was passed to prohibit the African slave trade. But the law was practically useless without the cooperation of those very states in which the pro-slavery forces were most powerful and cotton most precious. The wonder crop incited greed. It promised the abundant life; it promised the ease of wealth. The more slaves the more cotton, the more cotton the more land. It was, it seemed, an immutable round upon which even the landless poor aspired to set their weary feet.

So the law got scant observance. Perhaps, as some have held, it "begot a sort of dare-devil spirit on the part of Southern blood . . .

to overcome any doubts arising in their minds." But certainly this much is true: it had the effect of increasing the profits of the slave traffic two and threefold. And if by 1820 there were two hundred thousand free Negroes, they were vastly outnumbered by more than a million and a half slaves.

A million five hundred thousand slaves, the property of, roughly, three hundred thousand people, more than three-quarters of whom owned less than five slaves each! The great gray, faceless mass of Southerners owned no slaves. Indeed, though most of them did not realize it, the slave institution was their greatest enemy. It intensified their economic struggle. It deprived them of opportunity and atrophied ambition. Its class-structure pattern was as rigid as that of medieval Europe, and it left the masses powerless to resist. In the final analysis, it robbed them even of resisting will and made them party to their own degradation. Yet one pride was allowed them—played up, encouraged: they were white after all, and therefore better than the Negroes free or slave. This blinded the majority to the total domination by the slaveholders who determined the South's political and cultural structure, who wrote her laws, who established her mores, who molded the group mind into that sectional oddity known as the mind of the South. It was the slaveholding element that erected an oligarchical superstructure upon the foundation of democracy, and created the fortress of myths within which, it was hoped, the mind of the South could grind out its dream of life in peace.

The threat to the myths reposed in the slaves themselves. It lay in their day to day and hour to hour disaffection—in their silent, passive, mocking resistance: the dawdling, the pretending to be dumb, the pretending not to see and hear and understand, the pretending to be sick. And in the sudden, explosive leap of violence— a slave alone, or many together daring to be bold, defiant, murderous, daring to die. This was the threat, the South knew, to its entire economy, its way of life. To contain that threat and to maintain that way of life, it was necessary, as has been said, to hammer out the Black Codes and to enforce them with such persistent stringency that even the freedom of the master class was curtailed. Almost no act of the slave's, either of nature or of will, but was watched, guarded, spied upon. "Go to de woods to relieve yo'se'f, oberseer heel you der. Go to de cabin when work all done an' you try to res', pattyrollers li'ble to bust in. Go to meetin' on Sunday, white mens. Cain't even down worshup yo' Gawd. White mens. White mens a-watchin' an' a-lis'nin' all de time."

Declared the highest court of South Carolina in 1818: "The peace of society and the safety of individuals require that slaves should be subjected to the authority and control of all freemen when not under the immediate authority of their masters."

And the slave was subject—to the guilt-swelled abuse of master and overseer, to the tender mercy of patrollers, to the tricky whim of any white man who chanced to meet him away from home. He had no more social status than a mule. One white witness could convict him in a court of law. For sedition, and often on suspicion of sedition he could be hanged or burned alive. For reading or distributing incendiary literature he could also be put to death. Running away was an offense for which, if he did not yield when caught, his captor could shoot him down.

If a slave were lucky—and there were degrees of luck—he might live on a small plantation or farm; or he might be a personal servant in a large household; or he might have a kind master. Sometimes he might have the luck to be in two of these circumstances. If he lived on a small plantation, the chances are that there was no overseer and that he worked side by side with the master and the master's children. Personal contact with his owner was to the slave's advantage. He could prove his value; he could ingratiate himself. Sharing experiences tended to humanize the relationship. The slave worked hard, but so did the master, for on the four- and five-slave places life was an elemental struggle against ruin. On such a place the slave's rations might be short, but "sho't rations wont nothin' to de long cat-o-nine" in the hands of an overseer or a "mean, hard" master.

A body servant had even more intimate contacts with his master, and sometimes these led to deep affection and respect on both sides. The house or body slave had many advantages over the field slave. He was a privileged character, the aristocrat of the slave class, and, more frequently than not, a source of envy to other slaves. Cooking the master's food, serving his table, running his personal errands, laying out his clothes and dressing him, standing always within earshot, the body servant learned many things and met many kinds of people. He grew sophisticated, knowing, arrogant and place-conscious. He generally married on his occupation level, for he despised field hands and "common niggers." He dressed much better, ate better, talked better. Coin clinked in his pockets. Sensing that his personal advantage and, indeed, his fate were tied to that of his master, his loyalty was likely to be profound. Moreover, in the unbalanced equation of the Southern culture, master might equal cousin, half-brother, father. Through house slaves many a servile plot came to light, for masters used even the place-jealousies of slaves as instruments of control.

Luckiest of all was the slave who had a kind master. That there were such masters is clearly a part of the record, though many of the contemporary accounts, written by runaway slaves or biased travelers, or ghosted by abolitionists, tended to slight or overlook them. There were masters who were wisely kind, who kept slave families together, who fed and clothed them decently, who forbade cruel punishment. Thomas Jefferson's remaining slaves were "struck dumb" with misery at their master's death, although he had willed them freedom. Thaddeus Herndon, addressing his slaves for the last time, was reported to have said: "Servants, hear me, we have been brothers and sisters, we have grown up together. We have done the best for you. Besides your freedom, we have spent $2,000 in procuring everything we could think of to make you comfortable—clothing, bedding, implements of husbandry, mechanics' tools, tools for the children, Bibles. . . . And now, may God bless you. I can never forget you."

There were those masters who were kindly wise—for profit. But no matter what the souce, *kindness* was goodness to the slave. If he could escape being sold down the river and ward off the bite of the abasing lash; if he could jump the broomstick with a woman of his choosing, worship God in the way that appealed to him, and be made to feel secure in his old age, he was not likely to examine into reasons. For, anyway, much less than these usually made up the paltry sum of his happiness—a runt shoat at Christmas, a cracked mirror, a broken watch, a dance.

"Ole Marsa stan' off in de corner wid his arms folded jus' a-puffin' on his corn-cob pipe as ef he was a-sayin' 'Look at my niggers! Ain' my niggers havin' a good time!' . . . Den ole Missus say to Marsa, 'I b'lieve you lak dem niggers better'n you do me.' Den Marsa say, "Sho', I lak my niggers. Dey works hard and makes money fo' me. . . . I'se gwine stay an' see dat my niggers has a good time.'

"An' we sho' use to have a good time. Yes, sir. We was walkin' an' talkin' wid de devil both day an' night. Settin' all 'round was dem big demi-jonahs of wiskey what Marsa done give us. An' de smell of roast pig an' chicken comin' fum de quarters made ev'ybody feel good." [6]

Yet the slave system was against even such small indulgences as these. When all is said and done, the system could not afford them, for charitableness was its enemy as surely as hate is the enemy of love. The South was in the position of the police state, creating oppression and terror in order to function at all. Truly it was a police state, and all its citizens were policemen. Fanny Kemble, the English actress who married a slaveholder and lived for a time (1838–1839) on a plantation in Georgia, remarked on the extent and nature of the South's militarism. A governor of South Carolina declared that "a state of military preparation must always be with us a state of perfect domestic security." And Frederick Law Olmsted, as objective an observer as ever took a journey, wrote in *A Journey in the Back Country* that one sees in the South

> Police machinery such as you never find in towns under free government: citadels, sentries, passports, grapeshotted cannon, and daily public whippings of the subjects for accidental infractions of police ceremonies. I happened myself to see more direct expression of tyranny in a single day and night in Charleston, than at Naples for a week. . . . There is . . . an armed force, with a military organization, which is invested with more arbitrary and cruel power than any police state in Europe.

So for all the laws, the final control of the subject black population was by arbitrary men. There were the men of the federal military, and men of the states' militias; police and private guards. In emergencies, there were the headlong, skylarking youths and men of the volunteer vigilantes. But most tyrannous of all these public agencies were the men of the local patrols, the dreaded "pattyrollers." Every community in every slave state had its patrol. In some places its members were drawn from the state militia; in others they were drafted from the body of citizenry and any adult white male was liable to service.

Finally, in private capacity were the overseers, bred of the diseases of slavery. As a class they earned the reputation they got. "Passionate, careless, inhuman, generally intemperate, and totally unfit for the duties of the position," not even the masters, whose creatures they were, spoke a good word for them. Yet they were considered indispensable, and the laws of some states made them mandatory. The overseer had over the slave all the rights of control of the master, but none of the master's ultimate responsibility. He ordered, made food and clothing allowances, assigned work and saw to its carrying out, issued passes, punished. He was the gross reflection of the master from whom his authority was derived. The aim of that authority was profit; its means cruelty. "If they [the overseers] made plenty o' cotton, the owners never asked how many niggers they'd killed." [7]

For, of course, sometimes a nigger had to be killed, or maimed, or tortured, or at the very least lashed. The slaves were not inclined to extend themselves for the profit of others. They were lazy and irresponsible, to say which is to point up the way the slave system worked. Every moment of the slaves' day was locked into a routine of almost sidereal precision. The rising horn or bell before day, breakfast in the hushed gloom of morning twilight, the fields at dawn. Plowing, planting, hoeing, chopping, picking. Land to clear, ditches to dig, fences to mend. Noon—sidemeat, blackstrap molasses, hoecake. The fields again. Supper—hoecake, blackstrap molasses, cowpeas. And then at night wood to gather, water to draw. In Mississippi slaves could be legally worked eighteen hours in twenty-four; in Georgia and Alabama nineteen. There was no law that said they could not be worked to death.

The slaves had no initiative, no sense of duty; they were dishonest, thriftless, immoral, the planters said. They were "more brute than human . . . they accepted the white man's civilization only through fear and force of habit; they were mean, restless, and dissatisfied. . . . This class of human brute was subdued only through fear, just as the lion is made to perform in the show through fear." [8] They were also stupid and insensate beyond belief.

But the threat to these concepts, too, reposed in the Negroes themselves, slave and free. Benjamin Banneker, for instance, was free, but his remarkable talents, once they came to light, mocked the accepted beliefs. For the first forty years of his life he was just another farmer, with a little more book learning than he actually seemed to need and not enough money and leisure to follow his interests. One thing he had done however: he had made an excellent clock that attracted attention in his local Maryland community.

Then, in the 1780's a Quaker miller, George Ellicott, took an interest in Banneker, lent him books on mathematics and astronomy, and gave him the use of surveyor's tools. By 1789 Banneker had proved himself so skilled in the engineering sciences that President Washington appointed him to the Commission to survey the District of Columbia and lay out the city of Washington. For two years Banneker engaged in this work. When he returned to Maryland, his interest in astronomy asserted itself, and, beginning in 1791, he issued an annual almanac which for the eleven years that he published it was a household reference in America and won praise abroad.

But if Banneker's accomplishments proved something, they were not enough entirely to eradicate, as he had hoped, the "false ideas and opinions" generally held about Negroes.

Nor were Paul Cuffe's. Born free, like Banneker, but a New Englander, Cuffe went to sea on a whaler at the age of sixteen. Four years later he bought his first vessel, and by 1780 Paul Cuffe's ships were sailing to Europe and Africa. Increasing wealth made him liable to taxes, but these he refused to pay so long as he could not vote. The philosophy of the Revolution was on his side of the argument, and he presented it convincingly. Largely through his efforts, Massachusetts extended the right to vote to free Negroes who paid taxes.

Cuffe was a Quaker. In common with his sect, he had a concern for the plight of Negroes unbounded by selfish interests. Realizing the importance of education, he built a school in New Bedford. Knowing the self-respect that regular employment promotes, he operated a shipyard and employed Negro mechanics when he could find them. Negro seamen shipped on his vessels. But even these things were not enough to narrow the immeasurable distance to Negro self-sufficiency. Too many social and psychological barriers stood in the middle ground. To be free of these, the Negro must go back to Africa. He must have his own land and his own government and himself be subject to himself. In 1811, sailing his own vessel, Paul Cuffe went to Africa, where at Sierra Leone he made arrangements looking to the establishment of a colony of free Negroes. The prospects must have pleased him, for after the War of 1812, he sailed again to Africa, taking with him at his own expense a shipload of Negroes.

But America was home for the vast majority of Negroes. Here many of them were born, though in slavery. Their sweat was going into its building, their blood was spilling in its defense. Here—

since to labor and to die were not enough—they must prove themselves. Here they must confound the concept.

At about the time that Banneker was catching the interest of George Ellicott, a fragilely molded, delicately constituted slave girl in Boston was writing:

> Should you, my lord, while you peruse my song,
> Wonder from whence my love of Freedom sprung,
> Whence flow these wishes for the common good,
> By feeling hearts alone best understood,
> I, young in life, by seeming cruel fate
> Was snatched from Afric's fancied happy seat:
> What pangs excrutiating must molest,
> What sorrows labor in my parent's breast!
> Steeled was that soul, and by no misery moved,
> That from a father seized his babe beloved:
> Such, such my case. And can I then but pray
> Others may never feel tyrannic sway?

This was not Phillis Wheatley's first poem. In 1770, when she was seventeen, she had written one "On the Death of the Reverend George Whitefield," and in 1775, during the British siege of Boston, she had addressed General Washington in heroic couplets:

> Proceed, great chief, with virtue on thy side,
> Thy every action let the goddess guide.
> A crown, a mansion, and a throne that shine,
> With gold unfading, *Washington,* be thine.

And later the General had received her at his headquarters in Cambridge. For Phillis was an oddity, especially to a slaveholder from Virginia. She was a slave who could read and write poetry. She was an artist!

Bought in Boston directly off a slave ship from Senegal, Phillis was reared in the pious and cultured home of the John Wheatleys. She was treated more like a member of the family—which at one time numbered seven—than a slave. She was taught to read from the Bible and given lessons in Latin, history, and geography. Voluminous reading helped to make her at eighteen undoubtedly one of the most cultured women of her day. Manumitted and sent to London for her health at twenty, she was entertained by the Countess of Huntington, and Brook Watson, the Lord Mayor, made her a gift of a handsome edition of *Paradise Lost,* now the property of Harvard College. It was in London also that *Poems on Various Subjects, Religious and Moral,* Phillis' first volume, was published. Later the book had many reprintings in America. It was used as a strong argument against the Negro's inherent inferiority in the anti-slavery campaign of the next century.

Returned to America, Phillis found life much less pleasant than it had been. Freedom was precious, but freedom was hard. Mrs. Wheatley was dead, and Mary, the surviving daughter, married. Mr. Wheatley himself died in 1778. Phillis knew little of the real world. The promises of the facile rascal whom she married proved empty, and bit by bit she was reduced to drudgery for the sake of her three children, two of whom soon died. Her own end is told by the anonymous writer of the *Memoirs of Phillis Wheatley.*

In a filthy apartment, in an obscure part of the metropolis, lay the dying mother and child. The woman who had stood honored and respected by the wise and good in that country which was hers by adoption, or rather compulsion, who had graced the ancient halls of old England, and had rolled about in the splendid equipages of the proud nobles of Britain, was now numbering the last hours of her life in a state of the most abject misery, surrounded by all the elements of squalid poverty.

The Boston *Independent Chronicle* noted simply:

Last Lord's Day, died Mrs. Phillis Peters (formerly Phillis Wheatley), aged thirty-one, known to the world by her celebrated miscellaneous poems. Her funeral is to be held this afternoon, at four o'clock, from the house lately improved by Mr. Todd, nearly opposite Dr. Bulfinch's at West Boston, where her friends and acquaintances are desired to attend.

The date was Thursday, December 9, 1784.

This was the very year in which Richard Allen, who had bought his freedom in 1777 and become an inspiring preacher, began attracting the attention of white Methodism. Moving from Delaware to Philadelphia a decade later, he joined the St. George Church, where he was sometimes called upon to preach. But St. George's was a white congregation and there were those among it who objected to worshipping with Negroes. Once at a service Allen's prayers were interrupted by church officials who were determined to enforce the new policy of segregation. Allen resolved to establish his own church.

In 1794 he opened the doors of Bethel Church—now known as Mother Bethel—in Philadelphia, and within ten years branches of this church were running in North Carolina, Virginia, Maryland, New Jersey and Delaware. By 1816, when they incorporated as the African Methodist Episcopal Church, they had a combined membership of forty-five thousand Negroes.

Negro Protestants in other places, stymied by segregation, also established separate churches during the late 1700's. In New York James Varick, Peter Williams and Christopher Rush were instrumental in setting up the African Methodist Episcopal Zion Church. In the South where, after the Revolutionary War, there was determined opposition to Negro congregations under Negro leaders, who might be refractory, black Baptists set up a church in Savannah, Georgia, and kept it alive even though they were persecuted and Andrew Bryan, their preacher, was jailed. The African Baptist Church of Williamsburg, Virginia, was driven underground, but William Moses and Gowan Pamphlet, free Negroes, continued to serve it until the "black laws," following Nat Turner's bloody rebellion in 1830, stopped the mouths of all Negro preachers in Virginia.

The education of colored people was even harder to accomplish in the South, though, strangely enough perhaps, the first American-born Negro to be thoroughly educated lived most of his life in that section. Born in North Carolina, John Chavis was sent to Princeton (then the college of New Jersey) where he seems to have been taught by the president of the college, Dr. Witherspoon. Returning to North Carolina, Chavis taught for thirty years a school which white boys attended by day and Negro boys at night. He was forced to relinquish his service to Negro boys in 1831, when the education of colored people was generally interdicted in the South.

There was also more than a little opposition to it in the North. It was expensive. It did not seem necessary to a people who were doomed to the lowliest occupations: it could only make them unhappy. Yet, with the aid of some philanthropic whites, Negroes did get a yeasty taste of formal learning. As early as 1777 the Philadelphia Quaker, Anthony Benezet, provided funds for a colored school.

There were off-and-on schools in New Jersey. The African Free School in New York taught hundreds of Negroes between 1787 and 1815. One of its students, Ira Aldridge, won European acclaim by his playing of Othello to Edmund Kean's Iago. Whites in Wilmington, Delaware, New Haven, Connecticut, and Boston, Massachusetts, lent support to Negro schools. By 1826, the year of Thomas Jefferson's death, the race had its first bona-fide graduate of an American college in John Russworm, who finished at Bowdoin, and there were ex-slaves who were practicing medicine, teaching school, and preaching sermons to attentive white audiences.

If these lives and works were no clinching proof of anything, they at least were an earnest, and they at least gave some people pause. Jefferson, whose humanitarian interest in the Negro's welfare did not stop him from holding the usual notions about the race's imperviousness to civilizing influences, was impressed by Banneker's accomplishments. He praised the black man's almanac. Indeed, since he sent it to the Academy of Science in Paris, it is not too much to say that he valued it as the product of an American mind. Washington, who had believed black men unworthy to fight in the country's cause, must have been struck by Phillis Wheatley, by the shaping influence of Anglo-Saxon culture upon her. In the deep South too—in Charleston, Savannah and New Orleans—many must have seen beyond the blinders of the concept. Many must have wondered how a people "so stupid, so bereft of mental endowment" could build with axe and adz and simple facing tools fine mansions for their masters, shape stone to monuments of arresting beauty, and forge and anvil iron with subtle artistry.

And ever and again, "insensible as they were of the high dreams of honor and liberty that inspire white men to grandeur," slaves made bold efforts to assert their human dignity. They ran away to freedom. Between them and it stood all the machinery of control, all the pathological watchfulness of frightened masters. Between them and it sucked the ooze of primordial swamps, prowled the shadows of unknown forests, roared rivers, reared mountains. Between slaves and freedom screamed torture, crept starvation, lurked death—yet they ran away. Many thousands ran away.

4

TO CONTAIN CONTAGION

●●●

IN 1776 there were half a million slaves. Federal law prohibited the African slave trade in 1808, but by 1810 there were a million and a half slaves, and the number doubled statistically every twenty years. The increase is symptomatic not only of expansion but of amorphous change. Many forces were at work. The first two decades of the nineteenth century seethed with ideas and activities, were strident with clashing attitudes.

The industrial revolution proceeded apace. The steam engine was being studied for possible application to land and water travel. As the country expanded there was talk of digging a canal through the Mohawk Valley to the West. Eli Whitney, having perfected the cotton gin, now turned his restless mind to firearms, which were soon to be needed. The tensions of the Revolutionary struggle between England and America had not relaxed. Rather, like nearly everything else, they were growing. The British took an arrogant attitude toward the Non-Intercourse Acts and toward the United States declaration of neutrality in European affairs. Britain continued to impress American seamen into service under the Crown. She continued to egg on the Indians against American emigrants to the West. Finally, her failure to give up the western forts, as provided in the Treaty of Paris, and the unfriendly act of supplying the Indians at Tippecanoe with arms proved to be the big sticks that drummed up a war.

Had England not been locked in a debilitating struggle with Napoleon in Europe, the War of 1812 conceivably might have undone the victory of the Revolution. As a matter of fact, even as things were the British were no shoddy opponents. Because her shipping stood to suffer, the manufacturing heart of New England beat no enthusiasm for the war. Moreover in some of the sections inhabitants frowned on the prospect that the country's westward expansion, which was the ultimate aim of the war, would foster the extension of slavery southwestward. Connecticut, Rhode Island and Massachusetts flung their disaffection into the face of the Southern-dominated Congress by refusing to order out their state militias, and New Jersey and Delaware were almost equally disinclined. This sectional schism did not increase the country's strength in the field. America lost all of the first land battles, and, in spite of a few stirring American victories at sea, the British Navy had completely blockaded our coast by the end of 1813.

In this unpromising state of affairs, Negroes were once again allowed to serve their country. Pennsylvania enlisted Negro troops. New York, having passed an enabling act granting freedom to all slaves who got their masters' permission to join, raised two regiments of colored soldiers. The British, not to be outdone, offered freedom to all slaves who served with the Crown and, as in the Revolutionary War, an unestimated number went over. The Negroes who bore arms for the United States acquitted themselves with valor. No name among them is bathed in the glory of Peter Salem's or Black Samson's, but when the Soldiers of 1812 met in New York long after, they cited the heroism of their dusky comrades. After the Battle of Lake Erie, even Captain Perry, who had objected to Negroes on his ship, praised the colored sailors.

But it was for the part they played in Louisiana and in the wholly unnecessary Battle of New Orleans that the Negro fighters got their best-remembered citation. Jackson had recruited them in desperation to help offset the advantage in disciplined numbers held by the British under General Cochran and General Sir Edward Pakenham. Beginning on Christmas Eve, 1814, the final battle in the Louisiana campaign raged for sixteen days. During that time Negro troops held down a flank of the main body and repelled attack after attack. It was in the hope of this kind of facing-up to challenge that the hollow-cheeked, hot-eyed General Jackson had addressed them earlier.

To the Men of Color. Soldiers! From the shores of Mobile I collected you to arms,—I invited you to share in the perils and to divide the glory of your white countrymen. I expected much from you; for I was not uninformed of those qualities which must render you so formidable to an invading foe. I knew that you could endure hunger and thirst, and all the hardships of war. I knew that you loved the land of your nativity, and that, like ourselves, you had to defend all that is most dear to man. But you surpass my hopes. I have found in you, united to these qualities, that noble enthusiasm which impels to great deeds.

Soldiers! The President of the United States shall be informed of your conduct on the present occasion; and the voice of the Representatives of the American nation shall applaud valor, as your General now praises your ardor. The enemy is near. His sails cover the lakes. But the brave are united; and, if he finds us contending among ourselves, it will be for the prize of valor, and fame, its noblest reward.

With the end of the war it seemed that the expansion which had started at the turn of the century could go on unchecked. Ohio had been made a state in 1802, and westward lay the great plains. The English were no longer a menace. Mile upon mile of territory had been taken from the Indians by broken treaty after broken treaty. "In the dozen years preceding 1809, the savages had 'sold' 48,000,000 acres, not seldom when made drunk for the purpose, and without any apparent satisfaction of the whites' insatiable demand for land." [1] The great Shawnee Indian, Tecumseh, had been put down. The West lay like an unsurfeited woman waiting to be taken.

Southwestward were the rich lands suited to cotton culture. The embargo and the blockade of the coast during the late war had sent manufacturing zooming in New England, and this in turn had increased the demand for cotton. But the never-rich cotton lands of the upper South were wearing out. The center of gravity of agrarian economy was shifting. Profits from tobacco culture no longer concentrated in Virginia and North Carolina, but were fanning out into Kentucky. South by west was the direction for ambitious men to take. A single good crop of cotton might raise a poor redneck— around whom society tended to set with inexorable fixity—into the class of the aristocratic planter; or it might, and often did, increase a planter's wealth by a thousand acres and a hundred slaves. Southwest was indisputably the direction! Louisiana was already a state. Mississippi and Alabama came in before 1820. Planters from the old South began migrating, taking, of course, their movable wealth with them. Far and away the greater portion of such wealth was in slaves. Virginia lost population alarmingly. Land and real estate values declined. Jefferson's Monticello, which had been made constantly more beautiful and imposing down to his death in 1826, sold for about three thousand dollars. Madison was forced to sell his slaves one by one, and John Randolph, as pathetic as a wounded game cock, cast about for ways to stave off bankruptcy. The new South was sucking the life blood of the old. In ten years forty thousand people in the Alabama-Mississippi area grew to two hundred thousand, and in ten years more a half a million slaves were only three-fifths of the population.

Though the southwestward expansion proceeded like an avalanche, there was opposition to it. The Indians, also victims of the white man's greed and the objects of a heartless policy of extermination, gave trouble in Alabama, Florida, Louisiana and Arkansas. Of course they were "hostile," but only presumptive arrogance could term them "interlopers." They had to be fought on their own terms and their terms were costly.

There was opposition, too, to the expansion and the rapid growth of slavery from many in the North and upper South—among them the piedmont and mountain-dwelling Scotch-Irish. The Quakers had a long and ripe tradition of moral opposition to slavery. At considerable pains first to liberate their own slaves (which, because of the legal proscriptions set up in the 1790's, took some doing), the Quakers of North Carolina formed the General Association of the Manumission Society of North Carolina in 1816. They invited all professed Christians to join with them, and the Society numbered Baptists, Methodists, Moravians and Presbyterians among its members. It interceded in cases of slave-kidnapping; it helped manumitted slaves to reach free soil; it circulated anti-slavery tracts; it petitioned the state legislature and Congress. By 1825 the Society had twenty-eight branches and more than a thousand members. There were similar organizations in Maryland, Virginia, Tennessee and Kentucky.

That the slaveholders could tightly suppress such activity in the upper South after 1830 bespeaks their power; that they did suppress it bespeaks their fear. But they could do nothing with the anti-slavery sentiment which continued to glow in the winds of reform bearing down from the North. The Reverend T. F. Clarke, writing of the Kentucky in which he had lived during the 1830's, asserted that "the sentiment in Kentucky in those days, among all the better class of people, was that slavery was a wrong and an evil, and that it ought to be abolished. It was also believed that Kentucky would, when the time came for altering the Constitution, insert a clause in the new Constitution that would allow slavery to be abolished." He was referring to the days when David Rice and David Barrow were preaching emancipation across the state. Those were the days, too, of Daniel Reaves Goodloe who gave up a successful law practice in his native South to become editor of the *National Era,* a leading anti-slavery newspaper, and of B. S. Hedrick, a professor at the university in his state of North Carolina, who was burned in effigy by his students, dismissed by the trustees, and barely escaped being tarred and feathered for expressing views that the slaveholders did not like.

But it was in the North that anti-slavery sentiment crystallized— less readily perhaps around the moral than around the political and economic issues. It is true that humanitarian reform was in the air, and that later, indeed, "reform was a touchstone which differentiated people more incisively than did party allegiance," but Dorothea Dix and prison reform, Elizabeth Cady Stanton and women's rights, and Samuel Howe and education reform were not heard of in the 1820's. On the other hand, the rapidly growing new South was feeling her oats, flexing her political muscles, and casting covetous eyes toward still other realms.

When Missouri petitioned for statehood in 1819, the political issue involved in the old constitutional compromise on proportional representation appeared in a new light. To the eyes of the North, it had all the look of an enemy, dangerous and hydra-headed, and the North fought it on the floor of Congress. James Talmadge, Jr., of New York, started it when he proposed forbidding the further introduction of slaves into the territory and then moved an amendment stipulating that all slave children born after Missouri's admission would be free at the age of twenty-five. The debate raged on for months, growing in bitterness and acrimony and swelling alike on the tongues of sages and fools. John Randolph, of Virginia, was in favor of his Southern colleagues withdrawing from Congress en masse. Jefferson, in retirement now, thought that slavery should be extended into the territories, "so that the evil might be lessened by diffusion," but he repeated that it would be his "last and fondest prayer that emancipation be effected." In the end, when a compromise was struck, when it was finally decided to permit slavery in Missouri but to prohibit it in all the territory north of thirty-six thirty, it was Jefferson who foresaw that the establishment of a geographical line by which men stood divided "would kindle such mutual and mortal hatred as to render separation preferable to eternal discord."

And Jefferson was right. States' rights, sectionalism, even secession had already reared their troublesome heads. The South felt that it could get along without the North, but could the North . . . Well, John Q. Adams had discussed it with John C. Calhoun, and Adams had said that rather than be thrown back upon its stony soil to starve, the North would be forced to move southward. To which Calhoun had replied that in that event "the South would find it necessary to make her communities all military." And was it not this same Calhoun who, incensed by the Tariff Act of 1832 (as was the whole South), led South Carolina to provide for the purchase of arms and the raising of a military force as the first step in secession? The South felt that it could not lose. "Thousands of square miles of rich lands within easy distance of navigable rivers gave the people of the region a sense of new opportunity, a feeling that the world belongs to him who can exploit it, and a restless craving for a new life and wide acres—all of which influenced profoundly not only the lower South but the whole course of American history." [2] In the three decades up to mid-century everything seemed possible to the voracious men of the cotton country. Mississippi, Alabama, Florida and Missouri were already theirs, and Texas was a ripening fruit.

2

The vast area of land which the South already claimed required labor to clear and cultivate, and a labor supply was right at hand. As pointed out earlier, the panic of 1819 and the subsequent depression had hit the planters of the upper South very hard. Prevented by the exhausted soil and the tide of economic destiny from producing enough to pay for their keep, the million slaves of the region had little more than prestige value. Only the very rich—and there were few such—could afford to retain them. John Randolph talked with bitter humor about deserting his slaves in order to avoid bankruptcy, but there were those who did more than talk. Nor did they do what

Randolph, the Quakers of Virginia and North Carolina, and a few others did in the years from 1816. They did not emancipate their slaves and settle them on free soil, nor send them with God's blessings to the new free colony of Liberia in Africa. What most did was to migrate with their slaves to the rich lands southwestward where in 1830 the government was selling good cotton ground at a dollar and a quarter an acre, where cotton grew no more readily than corn, and where crops of vegetables could be raised two or three times a year.

Many of the planters who remained in the old South had no choice but to sell off their slaves. For some, reared in the patrician concept of the moral and social responsibility of slaveholding, this was a rending choice, doubtless. When Bushrod Washington, nephew of the first President, sold ninety slaves to Louisiana planters in 1821, the Leesburg (Va.) *Genius of Liberty* carried a comment:

On Saturday last a drove of negroes, consisting of about 100 men, women, and children, passed through this town for a southern destination. Fifty-four of the above unhappy wretches were sold by Judge Washington, of Mount Vernon, President of the Mother Colonization Society.

The Honorable Justice had been more considerate than many who sell their slaves. He had exacted from the purchaser the promise not to separate individual families, for which agreement he had accepted $2,500 less than the price [he] had at first fixed upon.

Slave dealers, who as a class had reputations as black as overseers, were not likely to be too scrupulous about such agreements. Wills disposing of slaves often stipulated that slave families were not to be separated, but wills were not binding beyond the sale on the open market. Besides, by 1825 the domestic slave trade had grown to great proportions. The law of 1808 abolishing the African slave trade and the law of 1820 making the first law's violation a crime punishable by death, though flouted by the reckless, stimulated business. Exporting slaves from the upper to the lower South became a great economic enterprise, and slave breeding was its chief prop. Thomas Dew of the College of William and Mary, a pro-slavery economist-philosopher of wide influence, pointed out that the sale of Virginia slaves brought a return greater than the return from tobacco. Virginia bred six thousand slaves annually, Kentucky only a thousand less. It is estimated that in peak years these states, together with

Maryland, Tennessee and North Carolina, supplied the lower South with upwards of eighty thousand slaves a year.

Though nearly everyone had hard things to say about slave dealing, it was like the profession of overseeing—no one did anything effective about it. It was a sort of metaphysical evil, like dying in war, which given the conditions, could not be helped. But there was an even greater sub rosa evil. In 1839 a committee of the Yearly Meeting of Friends reported that:

The sphere of action of the kidnapper is much more extensive than that of the legitimate dealer; they are found in every part of the country, preying alike upon the freeman and the slave, and are employed in their vocation both night and day! In the day, they often single out their victims, and in the night they secure them, and bear them off. In other cases, having first ascertained the practicality of his plan, he obtains a warrant by virtue of the well-known fugitive law; drags the individual he had marked out before a Justice of the Peace, and by the aid of an accomplice, and a forged advertisement prepared beforehand, succeeds in identifying the man with the pretended slave thus advertised, and of whom he is in search.[3]

Scarcely a town but had its slave market (some of which stand today as historical monuments); scarcely a community south of Maryland where human chattels could not be bought and sold. Auction blocks and noisome pens "strongly built and well supplied with thumbscrews and gags, and ornamented with cowskins and other whips oftentimes bloody," were reported by a newspaper editor in 1823. Women and men and boys and girls were sold without regard for anything save profit. Some slave dealers, like Robert Lumpkin of Richmond, specialized in young female slaves, some specialized in "studs," some handled every kind.

Southward the human freight went from Baltimore, Washington, Norfolk, Wilmington by boat on voyages remindful of the Middle Passage from Africa. Fractious slaves were bolted to the deck, or kept chained up short under battened-down hatches. The rest were herded together like cattle. William Wells Brown, the first novelist and one of the first historians of the Negro race, tells of a meeting with his mother. Brown was owned at the time by a slave dealer who traded between St. Louis and New Orleans and for whom he acted in a personal capacity. Brown's mother, escaped from slavery in Kentucky, had been recaptured, and, says Brown:

At about ten o'clock in the morning I went on board the boat and found her there in company with fifty or sixty other slaves. She was chained to another woman. On seeing me, she immediately dropped her head on her heaving bosom. She moved not, neither did she weep. Her emotions were too deep for tears. I approached, threw my arms around her neck, kissed her, and fell upon my knees. . . .[4]

Winter and summer for the roving trader who gathered his merchandise as he went along, the route to the deep South lay overland. It was a long march from the old South to Alabama, Florida, Mississippi and Louisiana. The slave gangs of men, women and children slunk along in a double line. The manacles that fastened the left wrist of one to the right wrist of another chafed the flesh. Running through a link in the gyves and binding the whole gang together was the coffle chain with links of iron as thick as a man's finger. The sun was hot, or the wind was raw and piercing; the roads were rutted. At night the gang rested; at dawn the march began. G. W. Featherstonhaugh, an English traveler to America, tells of meeting a coffle somewhere in North Carolina.

Just as we reached New River, in the early grey of the morning, we came up with a singular spectacle, the most striking one of the kind I have ever witnessed. It was a camp of Negro slave-drivers, just packing up to start; they had about three hundred slaves with them, who had bivouacked the preceding night in chains in the woods; these they were conducting to Natchez, upon the Mississippi river, to work upon the sugar plantations in Louisiana. . . . They had a caravan of nine waggons and single horse carriages, for the purpose of conducting the white people. . . . A great many little black children were warming themselves at the fires of the bivouac.[5]

The new South was a-building, fast. In 1800 Georgia had 59,404 slaves and 101,678 whites; Alabama 41,879 slaves and 85,451 whites; Mississippi 3,489 slaves and 5,179 whites; Louisiana 34,660 slaves and 34,311 whites. By 1850 Georgia had 381,682 slaves and 521,572 whites; Alabama 342,844 slaves and 4,261,514 whites; Mississippi 309,878 slaves and 295,718 whites; Louisiana 244,809 slaves and 355,411 whites. By mid-century these states were producing 1,726,349 bales of cotton, 48,000,000 pounds of rice, and 226,087,000 pounds of sugar. The new South had outstripped the old in everything but free population.

If the old upper South was losing her economic dominance, and if the results of the election of General Andrew Jackson to the Presidency in 1828 effectively diluted her political prestige, she was to reassert herself in another sphere. Dangerous sectional schisms had already been uncovered in the squabbles over Missouri and the tariff bill. The political hazards, compounded by the fundamental differences between the socio-economic structure of the North and South, were to be epitomized by the most visible element, slavery, and were to grow more and more naked and determinative as the philosophy of government came into dispute.

In this many-sided controversy—though John C. Calhoun of South Carolina was the South's great political champion—the upper South took the lead. She produced the first widely heralded philosophers and apologists for the Southern way of life. Heretofore, at the same time that she was thoroughly grounding the institution of slavery in law and in custom and making it "an inseparable constituent of her whole way of life," she had shrugged off the criticism of Quaker societies and bothersome individuals by pointing to the accomplished facts. Slavery *was;* the Constitution recognized it. Who would dare do something about it?

(But the atmosphere of "reform" acquired density in the North in the 1830's. People gathered themselves into communities and cohorts pledged to the better life, or to awaiting the Second Coming, or to some principle of political or moral government. Such organizations multiplied like rabbits, and all the forces for "good" that had been discrete and aimless now found focus and burst upon the country with incredible fanaticism. Universal manhood suffrage was now an acknowledged principle. Temperance speakers were everywhere. The rights of women, children and laborers came under discussion. Abolition was a cry to which thousands rallied. In 1831 William Lloyd Garrison founded the *Liberator,* a paper that was quickly to become the bane of Southern slaveholders and a needle sufficiently pointed to force cries of indignation from conservatives in the North.)

I shall strenuously contend for the immediate enfranchisement of our slave population. [Garrison wrote in the salutatory.] . . . I will be as harsh as truth, and as uncompromising as justice. On this subject I do not wish to think, or speak, or write with moderation. No! No! Tell a man whose house is on fire to give a moderate alarm; tell the mother to gradually extricate her babe from the fire into which it has fallen—but urge me not to use moderation in a cause like the present. I am in earnest—I will not equivocate—I will not excuse—I will not retreat a single inch—*and I will be heard.*

And he was heard. The next year, 1832, the New England Anti-Slavery Society was formed, and in 1833 the American Anti-Slavery Society. These interests were greatly encouraged in this latter year too, for the English abolitionists won a great victory when slavery was done away with in the British colonies. Nor did the English crusaders content themselves with this. They made common cause against American slavery. Though William Wilberforce died in the year of victory, his name was still to be reckoned with in the United States, and Thomas Clarkson's letter to the "Planters, Slave-Holders of the Southern Part of the United States," in which he attempted a point-by-point moral, economic and political condemnation of slavery, was widely read. Zachary Macaulay and Sir Thomas Buxton carried on until their deaths in 1838 and 1845 respectively.

This fresh boiling-up of abolitionist sentiment forced the South to prepare a more careful shield for slavery, a more elaborate defense than hitherto. The chief engineer of this defense was Thomas Roderick Dew. Like Alexander Hamilton, but more like Thomas Carlyle (who was to lend his iron-hard notions to the social concept of slavery), Dew had come too much under the influence of the Prussian class theory of society. So long as his point of view remained historical rather than socio-cultural, there was no harm in showing that slavery was a condition of ancient society and that the Bible gave it sanction. But for Dew these were merely the introduction to an argument which, to say nothing of its complete repudiation of Jeffersonian democracy, was not only specious but dangerous. It denied the equality of man. It averred that "the great object of government is the protection of property," and it went on from there to the conclusion that "the relation which the different classes of society bear towards each other, the distinction into high and low, noble and plebeian, depend almost exclusively upon property.

It may be with truth affirmed, that the exclusive owners of property ever have been, ever will, and perhaps ever ought to be, the virtual rulers of mankind." [6]

Dew met the extremes of Garrisonian abolition with extremes of his own. Garrison wanted immediate emancipation; Dew fought even gradual emancipation as a horror making for chaos in economic and social life. Garrison believed that men were born with inherent rights; Dew conceded this, but declared that rights were differentiated and limited by the class into which one was born. As William A. Smith, another Southern educator, President of Randolph-Macon College, and one of the highly articulate followers of Dew, was to say later:

The only difference between free and slave labor is, that the one is rendered in consequence of a contract, and the other in consequence of a command. . . . Hirelings *assent* to it, in most cases, as a necessity of their condition . . . they do not *consent* to it. In the general, hired service is in point of fact, as involuntary as slave labor. . . . That the abstract principle of the institution of slavery, and the principle of natural rights, coincide, and that both have the unqualified approbation of Holy Scripture, cannot be successfully controverted. Natural rights and the principles of slavery do not conflict.[7]

Both the abolitionists and the slaveholders were often inconsistent, reflecting no doubt the boggling, unsettled temper of the times. The arguments of both groups were more dependent upon the prejudices of their audiences than upon the support of logic. The abolitionists did not believe in the use of force, and yet they mocked the fugitive slave laws by promoting the Underground Railroad. The pro-slavery group was an ardent advocate of states' rights, and yet it declared that the obligation of federal government was to safeguard the institutions of each state whether or not those institutions conformed to the will of the federal body. For the slaveholders there was common sense in their rejecting the belief of the abolitionists that the tight knot of slavery could be cut by the axe of emancipation. There was ineffable wisdom in their denying the theory that slavery was a sort of evolutionary economic passage which they could promise to transcend in the course of time. The fabulously productive cotton fields were as yet giving no sign of petering out. Defending and promoting slavery as necessary to the existence of their economy was natural to the slaveholders. If the defense did not accord with a theory of government that emphasized the freedom of the individual, then the theory was wrong. For slavery was right. "I hold slavery to be a good," said John C. Calhoun in 1837. In order to have a progressive flowering of civilization, there must be inequality of men. As ancient history, the doctrine was valid. But the abolitionists refused to see slavery except as an evil institution weakly supported by an evil precedent. The South resorted to an exegesis so subtle and of such recondite reference as to constitute an exercise in historical metaphysics.

There was no lack of brilliant men to expound it. There was Henry Foote and the young Jefferson Davis; John Slidell, the New Yorker turned Louisianian; William Harper, of the highest court of South Carolina; George Fitzhugh and William A. Smith. There were of course Thomas Dew and John Calhoun. There was the whole, small, powerful planter class, who interpreted doctrine in terms that the poor whites could understand and appreciate.

For these latter must not be encouraged to understand that slavery's doctrines were a thwart to their ambitions and their sublimest hopes. The ignorant poor whites were in the case of those to whom salesmen fail to read the small print in a contract. If slavery consigned them to a despised caste in a solidifying culture, they did not know it, for now and then and here and there one of their number was allowed to claw and kick and wrestle his way upward. The doctrines sounded all right, since by them only blacks were committed to perpetual bondage. And that was what, according to Scripture, blacks were created for. It was *their* bondage that made freedom possible for the superior whites:

Slavery "makes [white men] not the bottom of society, as at the North—

not the menials, the hired day laborers, the work scavengers and scullions—but privileged citizens, like Greek and Roman citizens, with a numerous class far below them. In slave society, one white man does not Lord it over another; for all are equal in privilege. . . . Free society is a failure. Do not the past history and present condition of Free Society in Western Europe . . . prove that it is attended with greater evils, moral and physical, than Slave Society? Do not the late writers on society in Western Europe, and in our own free States, generally admit that those evils are intolerable, and that Free Society requires total subversion and re-organization? [8]

Moreover, in the slave society even the poor whites had the honor of a holy obligation, of receiving a holy injunction: "God has committed to you these ignorant, these suffering poor [blacks]. He requires you to care for their souls as well as their bodies," and to make them happy.

If the slaves were made happy, the abolitionists did not believe it. What they heard about and read about and knew about was the degraded misery of the slaves' lot. Garrison gave publicity to this side of slavery in the pages of the *Liberator*. Escaped slaves told their stories from the platforms of anti-slavery meetings. Published slave-narratives appeared in numbers, and their tales of suffering and inhumanity found corroboration in the accounts of such reputable travelers as Harriet Martineau, J. S. Buckingham, Philo Tower. Indeed, in the cold afterlight of history, cruelty seems to have been the rule rather than the exception in slavery.

Yet the charge of cruelty brought against the slaveholders was insufficiently weighty in a time that liked to argue in abstractions. More effective was the charge of pervasive sexual immorality, which the Grimké sisters, Sarah and Angelina, themselves the daughters of slaveholders, hammered home in addresses "to companies of women in private houses" in the North; the charge that slavery was contrary to the precepts of Christianity, which prominent ministers made the subject of sermons and of books; the charge that slavery prostituted democracy, which was the theme of many an editorial and speech; and the charge that slavery was an incubus implacably destroying the resources of the South's land and people.

Between the slaveholders and the abolitionists there seemed to be but one potential meeting ground—colonization. In both groups, especially at first—during and right after the Revolution—there were enough strong men who supported the idea of colonizing Negroes to give it the appearance of an effective compromise. Thomas Jefferson had expressed interest in it as early as the 1770's, and a few years later he had come to think it feasible for the United States "to undertake to make such an establishment [of a Negro colony] on the coast of Africa." Granville Sharp in England and the Reverend Ezra Stiles and Thomas Branagan had been for such a scheme.

But, generally speaking, until the nineteenth century there was no clear-cut difference between the colonization movement and the movement for emancipation. In Thomas Jefferson's mind, the one was the corollary of the other. He was for "emancipation and deportation" by slow degrees. Quakers looked upon colonization as a benevolence properly suited to the ends of justice. By 1880 the idea had withered.

When it was revived in 1815, Negro colonization was given an entirely different slant. Apparently well-meaning people like Dr. Lyman Beecher, Samuel Mills and the Reverend Joshua Danforth found themselves supported by a questionable phalanx of Southerners who had formed the American Colonization Society. The new society, with such slave-holding notables as John C. Calhoun, Joseph Gales, Henry Clay, and Bushrod Washington in its ranks, had surprising growth. Chapters sprung up in Maryland, Virginia, North and South Carolina, Georgia and Mississippi. Many Northerners who supported colonization did not know that its Southern adherents were interested chiefly in drawing off the free Negro population, which was a dangerous anomaly in the slave area. While Southerners threatened free Negroes who refused to be sent to Liberia, Northerners, unmindful of the nasty coercion, went blithely about the business of giving the Society their backing.

Then in 1832, William Lloyd Garrison, who had supported the colonization mildly, turned savagely against it with a ten-point indictment. Among other things, *Thoughts on African Colonization* charged that the American Colonization Society was an apologist for slavery, was pledged not to oppose it, recognized slaves as property, and was therefore the enemy of abolition. A more moderate and circumstantial attack was Judge William Jay's *Inquiry* which appeared in 1834. Judge Jay thought that the Society was made up of three classes, each with a different end in view:

"First, such as desire sincerely to afford the free blacks an asylum from the oppression they suffer here, and by this means to extend the blessings of Christianity and civilization to Africa, and who at the same time flatter themselves that colonization will have a salutary influence in accelerating the abolition of slavery. Secondly, such as expect to enhance the value and security of slave property, by removing the free blacks; and thirdly, such as seek relief from a bad population without the trouble or expense of improving it." [9]

But Jay's dispassion could not disguise the fact that (colonization was another wedge between slaveholder and abolitionist, between North and South.) The invidious Negro question had crept into the structure of American thought like a hardy, many-rooted clinging vine into every crevice of a wall. (Any word uttered about slavery and the Negro—synonymous terms—brought South and North nearer to absolute sectionalism. Almost every national question found its ultimate reference in slavery.) Never has a politically passive minority people had so decisive an influence for so long a time upon the thinking, the customs, the history and the very destiny of a sovereign majority. This influence is still, in this century, the outstanding characteristic of American life.

5

AWAKE AND REHEARSE

●●

For slaves, slavery was not politics and theories of government and philosophical controversy. It is true that they somehow sensed and were made restive by the storms that broke out over them, but after all life had to be lived, and slavery was a way of living. It could even be, under the rarest circumstances, a not unpleasant way of living. Thomas Jefferson's slaves were happy. They lived in comfortable quarters, had fare that would have been feast-food for most slaves, and "were the envy of all Albemarle County." It is said that when Jefferson, then ex-President of the United States, returned to Monticello in 1809, his slaves "rushed to meet him, unharnessing the horses and dragging the carriage to the entrance—bearing their master bodily in their arms into the Monticello house." Many years after his death, Jefferson's ex-slaves used to "climb from Charlottesville to stand in silence at [his] grave on the side of his little mountain."

There were other slaves, too, who were contented in slavery and loved their masters. There were a few who, being freed, voluntarily returned to their former state. But, the simple historical record shows, there were many, many more—the vast majority—who hated it. These were the ones who had the ordinary run of masters, who lived the ordinary day, following the required round.

Their shelters were windowless one-room cabins, "miserable hovels" on slave row. A cabin might be no more commodious than a chicken coop and yet house a family of seven or eight. Such furnishings as it had were invariably crude and homemade. There would be pallets, sometimes attached one above the other to the walls, sometimes made up on the dirt floor; benches made of rough logs; and an iron pot or spider suspended over the fire for cooking. Here the slaves ate and slept, bore children, moaned through their numerous illnesses, and finally died.

Old Uncle Zack, of whom Roscoe Lewis reports, in *The Negro in Virginia,* as constantly muttering "slave young, slave long," was very mistaken. Most slaves died at a comparatively early age. The picture of the cotton-topped retired slave resting in blissful security outside the cabin door is largely romantic fiction. A few faithful house servants might enjoy comfort and leisure in their old age, but even in Virginia, in the times of the classic paternalistic system before the Revolution, the slave condition took such a toll of human vitality that an old slave was something of a rarity. Later, on the plantations of the deep South ancient slaves were scarcely tolerated. Most planters believed that there was greater profit in working a slave to death in eight or ten years and buying a fresh, strong replacement than in working him moderately for twenty. If a slave happened to outlive his usefulness, or to become broken, or crippled, or incurably ill before his time, the master, to be rid of the responsibility, would likely free him to become a public charge. This practice, indeed, created such a nuisance that most slave states took steps to end it. The laws that prohibited the immigration of free Negroes represented as much an effort to keep down pauperism as to avoid the slave disaffection that free Negroes were accused of spreading.

Profit was the slaveholders' motive. On the smaller plantations, where the work was owner-supervised, slaves were less brutally punished perhaps than those handled by overseers, but they worked just as hard. Children were commonly sent to the fields at the age of seven or eight. Some went earlier.

"Had to go roun' stickin' slabs and branches in de fences where de hogs done pushed dey heads through, tell I was 'bout six years ole. After dat dey put me in de fiel' 'cause I was big an' strong for my age. Used to plow fo' I could reach up to de handles. Would stick my head under de cross bar an' wrap my arms roun' de sides whilst another boy led de mule." [1]

Not all of them were as strong at six as West Turner was. Some could not do anything but root out stones from the plow-path and tote water, but between six and eight was considered a good age to get slave children used to the field. Earlier, as toddlers, they might have the run of the quarters. It was generally agreed that colored babies were "as cute as puppies" and sometimes master or mistress made pets of them until they were old enough to do light door-yard chores. Once field age, there was little let up. At ten they set plants, wormed tobacco, hoed corn and cotton, picked cotton, followed the plow. By the time they reached twelve they were veteran laborers, a quarter of the way to death, doing all the jobs that any adult might be assigned. Working in supervised gangs, as most slaves did, meant bowed hams and bent backs. If there were a lead man or a "driver," it meant keeping a rhythmic pace at any tempo the boss desired. A moment to lean on the hoe, or to rest between the plow handles when the overseer's back was turned; permission to go to the water bucket or to "trot to the woods" to satisfy the demands of nature, were respite.

Even on wealthy plantations masters sometimes tried to beat the percentage of one slave for every three to five acres under cultivation. Small slaveholders were forced to beat it, and commonly worked a hundred acres with half a dozen Negroes. Such planters, of course, supervised the work themselves. They could not afford an overseer either on wage terms or share terms. But where there were twenty-five or more slaves—a number that could not be profitably worked by the master alone—an overseer was the rule and brutality the order.

The overseer had no human interest in the slave even to match the minimum interest of a callous master. Generally entrusted with the sole management, the overseer had a free hand so long as he produced—and production was exacted at the end of the lash, the mouth of a pistol. On many large plantations the only contact that slaves had with whites was contact with overseers. Food, clothing, punishment, the assignment of jobs, the granting of passes—these were the duties of the overseer.

The plantation work day started before dawn and went on into the night, when such tasks as husking corn, spinning cotton, cleaning pens and coops, currying horses and mules, and repairing farm gear had to be done by lamplight. At harvest season all hands worked nineteen and twenty hours. They did this on a diet of cornmeal and salt pork or salt fish. It was sometimes less, but it was also sometimes more. If the Polish traveler-poet, Niemcewicz, can be believed, in

1798 George Washington's slaves were receiving less, and he treated "his negroes far more humanely than the greater part of his Virginia countrymen, who generally [gave] to their Negroes nothing but bread and water and lashes."

But the practice of giving "nothing but bread" must have persisted down through the 1830's, for at that time the President of the Agricultural Society of Virginia wrote that "bread alone ought never to be considered a sufficient diet for slaves except as punishment." Fortunate slaves got in addition dried beans, black-eyed peas and molasses. Here and there in the upper South slaves were allowed to keep gardens, but this was unusual in the deep South, where every arable foot of ground was planted in precious cotton.

Grueling toil on such fare as was common scarcely left the slaves the energy which they are usually supposed to have put into frolics during their free times. Some of them did muster energy from somewhere, but they were either the house slaves, whose lot was easier, or the very young. One of the revealing things in slave narratives is how young the frolickers were and how invariably the narrators in relating occasions of jubilee recall that "I wus a girl," or "we wus jes' chillen," or "I wusn' nothin' but a boy." To be a *boy* was generally to be under sixteen. To be a *girl* was to be below marriageable age. A likely slave girl would be married at sixteen, or she would certainly be a mother—sometimes against her will.

For there was little stability in family relationships. Indeed, as B. A. Botkin's collection of narratives shows time and again, most slaveholders made a mockery of the marriages of their slaves.

"Mother was named Becky Moore, and Dad was Thomas Henderson, an' dey both had de same Marsa, ole Charles Sherman. Dey say dey made up dey minds one Sunday an' went up to de kitchen and sent word by de cook, Ant Mollie, dat say dey would like to see Marsa. Well he come out an' Dad he say, 'Marsa, pleasin' yo' goodness, Becky here an' me is aimin' to git married.'

" 'How ole is you, Becky?' asked Marsa. 'Sixteen, Marsa,' she tole him. 'How ole is you, Charlie?' 'I'm sixteen too, Marsa.' 'Dat's all right den. Cain't have no chillun marryin' on my place. Tell Ant Lucky to go 'haid marry you.'

"So my mother an' dad went down to de quarters an' tole Ant Lucky dat Marsa say it was all right fo' 'em to git married. So she went outside— was Sunday, mind you, an' all de slaves was lyin' roun' sleepin' an' restin'.

She called 'em together an' right den an' dere married 'em. Dey all form a ring 'rounst my mother an' dad, an' Ant Lucky read somepin from de Bible, an' den she put de broomstick down an' dey locked dey arms together an' jumped over it. Den dey was married." [2]

Slave marriages had neither legal status nor spiritual meaning. They were generally performed without benefit of clergy, and they could be broken up at the master's, or even the overseer's will. The love relationship of Negroes was degraded by other considerations. In Virginia and Maryland strong and potent slave men were hired out as studs to increase the stock of slaves for the deep South markets. It was common everywhere for comely slave girls to be used as the concubines of white men. William Wells Brown, in his autobiography, describes the lively bidding among some wealthy young white men for such a girl at an auction in Richmond. But if the beautiful quadroon girl Brown describes was reluctant to accept the fate in store for her, there were others who embraced it. This is not to be wondered at. To be the concubine of a wealthy white man meant escape from drudgery; meant advantages in physical comfort; meant, frequently, security and respect. To the slave, any position to alleviate the wretchedness of the common slave lot was respectable.

And the slave paramour was usually more fortunate than the wife of a slave. Her children stood a better chance in the world. They were often manumitted; often they were educated. Indeed, in the Gulf area of the South, where concubinage was little frowned upon, it was usual for wealthy fathers to have their illegitimate colored offspring educated abroad. It was usual for them to provide substantially for the mothers of such children. Many slave girls willingly gave up "honor" for this, or for lesser considerations, so that three-fourths of the freedmen and half a million slaves by the time of the Civil War were mulattoes. Some of the mulattoes and quadroons who held high places in Louisiana, Mississippi and South Carolina during Reconstruction were the cherished sons of white fathers.

On the other hand, if the child of slave parents had a chance it was a long, long one. If he was freed, it was generally through his own efforts. If he learned to read and write it was because someone broke the law against teaching slaves. (The law was broken, of course—by naïve mistresses like one that Frederick Douglass had; by Quakers; and by some masters who believed that teaching slaves to read the Bible could do no harm. There were schools in the border states of Delaware, Kentucky and Missouri which slaves, properly permitted by their masters, could attend. But these were glaring exceptions.) If the child of slave parents could remain under maternal control to the age of six he was lucky. Frederick Douglass, to cite him again, saw his mother not more than a dozen times. He never saw some of his half-brothers. Henry Highland Garnet, another Negro anti-slavery leader, did not know who his father was. Harriet Tubman, who conducted hundreds of slaves along the Underground route to freedom, lost some of her own brothers "down the river." But the record is full. Slavery did not encourage family love among slaves. It gave strange, tragic twists to many family relationships. Roscoe Lewis, who set out in 1938 to interview hundreds of ex-slaves before they should all die, heard the following story from one of them:

"De mother was sold to one trader, her son to another, and de baby daughter to a third. After de war Bess walked all de way from Georgia to Richmond lookin' fo' her mother an' her older brother. But she couldn't fin' 'em. Den dere was a man who ast her to marry him an' she did. Pretty soon dey had two chillun, both of 'em boys.

"One day de husband come home happy an' excited 'cause he don foun' his own mother. De nex' day when she come to live wid him an' Bess, de mother knowed Bess right away, but she didn't say nothin', 'ceptin' she was mighty glad to know her. But de mother couldn't keep it to herself, an' she tole 'em dat she was de mother to dem both, an' dey was brother an' sister. Dey was sick over it, but dey was really in love so dey 'cided to stay married. Pretty soon arter dat de mother died, 'cause she couldn't stan' seein' her son and daughter livin' wid each other."

The half million slaves who lived in the cities were in somewhat better case than those on the farms and plantations. Their contacts encouraged acculturation. They were not the "dull, idiotic, and brute-like" field slaves Frederick Law Olmsted noted. Under the system of hiring their time, many followed the trades of carpentry, brick masonry, blacksmithing, tailoring, shoemaking, and the like. Others worked in industry—in the textile mills of South Carolina and Georgia, in the mines of Alabama and Kentucky, in the iron works and the tobacco factories of Virginia. Joseph Anderson, who ran the

Tredegar Iron Works outside Richmond, hired more than a hundred Negro slaves. It was a common practice in industry to pay overtime beyond the eleven-hour work day, and it was perhaps with the extra money thus earned that the Negroes could dress with the "foppish extravagance, and a great many in clothing of the most expensive materials, and in the latest style of fashion."

The white man who complained that his hired-out slaves "earned money by overwork and spent it for whiskey, and got a habit of roaming about and taking care of themselves; because, when they were not at work, nobody looked out for them" was both right and wrong. The urban slave artisans' regular intervals of free time were subject to control by the police. In Charleston, South Carolina, and cities deeper south, this control was ludicrously restrictive, extending to such things as forbidding the carrying of a cane, watching military parades, visiting dram shops, smoking, and "making any joyful demonstrations." In Richmond, Virginia, there were numerous complaints that masters accorded too many privileges to urban-dwelling slaves and that the police were too lax. Everywhere there were grumblings that slave artisans made unfair competition for the whites.

But slaves in the cities were learning a degree of independence, and it was this which Olmsted said caused "great trouble and anxiety [to] Southern gentlemen." In New Orleans, in Mobile, in Norfolk they had their own burial and fraternal organizations; they attended their own churches—under white surveillance; and in some places they were suspected of having forbidden schools. Many of them followed the example set by the white middle and upper classes, putting a premium upon stable family relations and respectability. They learned many things.

Yet they were subject to the disruptive whims of the white man's law and the master's passion. They had to be armed with the proper passes. They had to observe the curfew. They could not marry without the master's consent. On "hiring-out day," which fell on New Year's, they did not know where they were. They might be hired to a mean employer, or kept with a mean employer they had served for a year; or they might be sent far from home, from wife, children and friends. Like their brothers and sisters back on the plantations, they were slaves, and they were not happy.

2

The South's claim that Negro slaves were "the happiest of mortals" is refuted by the South's own official records. The stories of the slaves' resistance to slavery stand in direct contrast to the memoirs and histories written by Southerners and their sympathizers. Court records [3] covering the span from the 1700's to the Civil War are burdened with such items as the following:

Josephine (a slave) is indicted for murder of [her master], by poison.
Munford (a slave) indicted for murder of [his master].
Alred (a slave) indicted for murder of Coleman, a white man.
The Grand Jury found a true bill against Lingo, a slave, for arson.
Simon (a slave) was apprehended for setting fire to a dwelling house. [When he confessed,] there was great excitement among the people. . . . The people would have taken him into their hands. . . . He was convicted and sentenced to be hung.
Martha (a slave) indicted for arson . . . and the sentence of death must be carried into execution.

Court items sometimes throw probing lights deep into the dark recesses of slavery, revealing strange details.

Examination of Sansoucy, runaway Indian slave, aged about twenty. "Marooned," because he was afraid to return after failing to find an ox that had gone astray. Took refuge in a village . . . where there were fifteen other fugitive slaves. These runaways had eleven guns and some ammunition, and meant to defend themselves if molested for capture.
Kitty (a slave) indicted for administering poison to her master Smelzer. . . . She was afraid she was going to be carried to Texas.
Mary Glass . . . a free quadroon from "the North of the Carolinas" . . . had tortured and slowly done to death . . . Emelia, a fifteen year old white girl. . . . Witnesses testify that they saw Marie Glase [sic] cruelly whip the young white girl . . . that they told her . . . that a white woman was not whipped, that it was done only to slaves, that . . . she answered that this young girl was her slave.

Female slaves murdered masters, mistresses and children. They wiped out whole families, as did Cicely, a slave woman in Mississippi, who killed her master, his wife and two children with a broad axe;

or Sallie, who knocked her master unconscious and roasted his head in the fireplace. Usually the women slaves were more subtle and more averse to the sight of blood. They were poisoners, using ratsbane, strychnine, arsenic and the seed of the jimson weed, which, skillfully administered, brought a lingering, mysterious death.

On the whole, male slaves seemed to be less vindictive and calculating. They usually killed in sudden passion, with brutal forthrightness. Axes, knives, scythes, hoes, stones, sticks were their weapons. Guns were rarely used, for they were hard to come by. Even had not the law forbade slaves to own or carry them, guns were expensive.

Lacking the proper object of their passionate resistance to slavery, slaves might take it out on the mule they worked with, on the harmless hound, or in acts of sabotage of the kind they had every opportunity to commit. They destroyed tools so arrantly and persistently that special "Negro tools," particularly durable and heavy, were manufactured for them. They disabled work animals, drove off valuable stock, wrecked machinery, damaged crops. In the perpetual warfare between masters and slaves, fire was the Negro's most devastating weapon. States made arson a capital crime; towns and cities kept mobilized in fear of it, but incendiarism persisted. Unestimated millions of dollars went up in flames, and the setting of fires was so common that the American Fire Insurance Company of Philadelphia, in 1820, had to "decline making insurances in any of the slave states."

The frequency with which slaves committed suicide made another problem for the slaveholders. Although the files of court cases, insurance claims, and the like seldom mention slavery as the cause of self-destruction, the circumstances surrounding such acts are generally stark accusers. Slaves did themselves to death for a variety of immediate causes. They were threatened with punishment; they were under accusation of crime; they were to be sold from their families; they were sick, or just "morbidly inclined"; and as sometimes must have been the case, they could not endure even the thought of bondage. C. W. Elliott cites the case of two cargoes of slaves newly brought from Africa, who starved themselves to death in 1807. Time and again slave narratives mention suicide (and infanticide, which frequently went together). Slaveholders were not disposed to mention the subject "because of the possibility of imitation." But Charles Ball, an escaped slave, who had reason to know, asserted:

Self-destruction is much more frequent among slaves in the cotton region than is generally supposed. When a negro kills himself, the master is unwilling to let it be known. . . . Suicide amongst the slaves is regarded as a matter of dangerous example, and one which it is the business and the interest of all proprietors to discountenance, and prevent. All the arguments which can be devised against it, are used to deter the negroes from the perpetration of it; and such as take this dreadful means of freeing themselves from their miseries, are always branded in reputation after death, as the worst of criminals; and their bodies are not allowed the small portion of Christian rites, which are awarded to the corpses of other slaves.[4]

What planters did not keep quiet about was the slaves' trick of feigning illness. The master class saw in this the black man's "natural laziness" and his proclivity for lying. The master class also mistook the dawdling mein, the loose-lipped speech, and the laggard bearing for stupidity. Only a knowing master could discover the deception when a slave pretended to be sick. Slaves knew herbs that would pepper them with rash, induce vomiting and fever. A whole body of amusing if caustic folklore grew up around the cunning slave who could gull the white man. This is the essence of the Uncle Remus' tales; it persists, like the Negro's alleged shiftlessness and improvidence, and immorality, in the race-concept images of whites today. Yet the story of Dirtin Ferry who "played off" sick for seven years and grew fat in the interval is something other than an amusing tale. The slave's power of mimicry and his lively imagination made such a feat entirely possible. It is another matter to find a master indulgent to the required degree.

But there was another level of behavior in resistance to bondage. There were wicked slaves as well as wicked masters. In the terrifying vis-à-vis of oppression and resistance, in the confused uncertainty of all human relationships, all classes were victims—master, poor white and slave. Suspicion, hatred, fear and far simpler things demoralized them all: all harbored tendencies that no philosophy could curb or warrant and that none but an abnormal psychology can explain. The slave who killed one of his fellows because he did not like his looks; the slave nurse who dragged the mistress' baby from her black breast and dashed its brains out against a stone—the deep psychic trauma which such crimes reveal makes one shudder.

Almost equally incomprehensible is the leniency shown the slave criminal by the courts—and this quite contrary to the harshness of the laws. In that time of grave ideological and moral conflict the very ruthlessness of the law seemed to call forth the courts' forbearance. In some cases, of course, leniency operated from the less worthy motive of preserving to masters the value of the property represented in slaves. Nevertheless slaves were often vigorously defended by the courts, even when they stood accused of crimes against white people. The legal loopholes were all explored—change of venue, appeals on writs of error, bills of exception—and frequently the accused slipped through. In cases in which a slave committed an offense against a free Negro, the latter had little chance of satisfactory redress.

In 1845 Chancellor Harper of the Supreme Court of South Carolina made plain the reason for this discrimination against the free person of color. "A free African population," he said, "is a curse to any country . . . and the evil is exactly proportional to the number of such population. This race, however conducive they may be in a state of slavery . . . in a state of freedom and in the midst of a civilized community, are a dead weight to the progress of improvement. With few exceptions they become drones . . . governed mainly by the instincts of animal nature, they make no provisions for the morrow. . . . They become pilferers and marauders, and corrupters of the slaves." [5]

Corrupters of the slaves? It may have been that the Chancellor knew history as well as law. He may have recalled how back in the previous century free Negroes (and whites) from the Spanish colony of St. Augustine cultivated the seeds of rebellion in the fertile soil of South Carolina and helped the slaves reap the bloody harvest at Stono in 1739. No doubt he remembered how in 1822 the free Negro, Denmark Vesey, "corrupted" several hundred slaves. In a state where by 1810 slaves outnumbered whites three to one, slave plots flared and hissed like the fires of perdition.

But no one of the slave states escaped this group resistance to slavery. For the slaves, insurrection was a deliberate plunge into a holocaust. Even to conspire toward this end was to take a step that led to the rack, the gallows—for, no matter how hopeful the prospects, how bold and sagacious the leader, nor how resolute the followers, slave rebellions were invariably lost causes. The reasons were not far to seek.

Scattered as slaves were, opportunities to get together for effective planning were few. Communication by word of mouth through second, third and fourth parties was a weak and dangerous thing. When surprise was the great element and timing its primary condition, instructions could not be delayed, or miscarried, or misinterpreted, or whispered into the ear of the wrong person. To guard against the danger of the "contagion of insurrectionary excitement," there was (to quote Olmsted again) "nearly everywhere, always prepared to act, if not always in service, an armed force invested" with omnipotent powers. But also masters planted informers and spies, and these betrayers, bribed by promises of rewards or corrupted by selfish hope, were great hazards to success. Gabriel Prosser was confounded by such as these. Denmark Vesey was distrustful of "waiting men, who receive presents of old coats." Indeed, it was some of these same who did betray him.

The revolutionaries were not insensible of the dangers. Fanatics many of them were, but scarcely fools. Moreover quite aside from the immediate experience of being enslaved, there were powerful stimulants to fanaticism. As already pointed out, the Haitian revolution was one. Gabriel Prosser's attempt was another. Every tongue that thickly whispered "Slaves done riz"—in Georgia, Alabama, Florida, Louisiana, South Carolina, anywhere—were others.

While many of these stimulants had no intellectual recognition from slaves, a sort of emotional distillation must have filtered down to them from their masters. Most slaves of course knew nothing of Greece and her struggle for independence, but their masters, in common with Christendom at large, pretended to be outraged by the pagan Turkish threat to the "Cradle of Civilization." And if the pretensions of the Southern master class were a mockery, the North was quick to challenge them as such. How, asked the northern Democracy, could Southerners be aroused over Greek freedom when they themselves held Negroes in bondage? The Southerners responded to this by wanting to know how Yankees could be stirred by the cause of freedom in the Levant when they themselves made virtual slavery of white labor? [6] Thus a struggle across the seas had repercussions upon America's growing sectionalism.

And sectionalism itself was but the manifestation of forces—

more economic and political than cultural or truly moral—which played like lightning, and with lightning's potential danger, over the American scene. New England and the West—the one to safeguard her manufacturies, the other her grain—were for a new protective tariff. A heavy importer of European goods, the South was convinced that a new tariff would be a vicious blow to her. When the struggle over this question came up in the Congress the lesion on the body of America was revealed in all its angry ugliness. The fight for the tariff became a fight against the slave power of the South. The passage of the new bill stabilized sectional bitterness at a new high. South Carolina, led by John C. Calhoun, threatened to secede over the "tariff of abominations." It was a taut, dramatic time. The personalities on the high political stage—Adams, Webster, Calhoun, Jackson—were not unlike jealous actors intent on hogging scenes.

The presidential campaign of 1828, the year of the tariff, further marked the undisguised enmity between North and South. Adams was the Northerner, cold, formal, legalistic and stone-hard in his moral opposition to slavery; Jackson the Southerner, boisterous and very, very human. The contrast was not the measure of the contrast between the two sections, but it served. During the campaign the differences were distorted, added to, magnified. Social morality, as pointed up by the ceaseless arguments over slavery, the class struggle, the sectional economic struggle, and private feuds that never should have been made public were all tied up in one package and delivered to the American people as a single political issue.

By some strange osmotic means the slaves sensed all this, just as they sensed the growing flagrancy of the North's disregard for the Fugitive Slave laws; just as they sensed the wonder and the terror in the names Gabriel Prosser and Denmark Vesey; and, in 1829, just as they sensed the unrestrained anger in their masters' whispers of the name David Walker.

This man, David Walker, a free Negro living in Boston, published his famous pamphlet, "Walker's Appeal, in Four Articles," in 1829. With unconscious irony it was addressed "particularly to the Coloured *Citizens*" of the United States. The "Appeal" was not directed to reason, though there was reasonable matter in it: it was directed to the passions, in the name of God. Beneath the surface of its religiosity unmeasured doses of poison gave off the odor of sulphur and brimstone. It was scurrilous, ranting, mad—but these were the temper of the times, when nearly every event was climactic and every utterance a shout of rage.

Never make an attempt to gain our freedom, or natural rights . . . until your way is clear—when that hour arrives and you move, be not afraid or dismayed, for be you assured that Jesus Christ the King of Heaven, and of Earth who is the God of Justice and armies will go before you. And those who have for hundreds of years stolen our rights, and kept us ignorant of Him and His divine worship, He will remove. . . .
Let twelve good black men get armed for battle and they will kill and put to flight fifty whites. . . . If you commence, make sure work, don't trifle, for they will not trifle with you. Kill or be killed. Had you rather not be killed than be a slave to a tyrant who takes the life of your wife and children? Look upon your wife and children and mother and answer God Almighty, and believe this that it is no more harm to kill a man who is trying to kill you than to take a drink of water when you are thirsty.

The "Appeal," like other pieces of inflammatory writing before and after, found its way to the South and undoubtedly into the hands of slaves. "Many people, otherwise conservative and slow to take alarm, were seized with panic." The Governor of North Carolina made the "Appeal" the subject of a special message to the General Assembly. The Governor of Virginia was likewise moved. Georgia petitioned Massachusetts to suppress it, but Massachusetts did not see fit to comply. In 1830 Walker himself, disdainful of the South or his life, or both, traveled to Richmond, Virginia, and there distributed his pamphlet. The Virginia police rounded up as many copies as they could find. Walker himself was arrested and was never seen again.

But the "Appeal" had done its work. 1830 was too late for North Carolina to pass laws against teaching slaves to read and write; too late for Virginia to make enactments against inflammatory literature and to tighten precautions against Negro assemblages, Negro preachers, Negro travelers. By 1830 Benjamin Lundy had been disseminating anti-slavery propaganda for a decade; west of the Appalachians the Reverend David Barrow and John Finley Growe had been militantly for abolition. William Lloyd Garrison was ready to step upon the stage. The anti-slavery movement, at first inseparable from the general movement for humanitarian reform, was fast becoming differentiated by the vigor of its leaders and the cohesion of its apostles. The extraordinary repressive measures which the South took in 1830 to meet the regathering of abolitionists' energies came too late to quell the bloodiest slave uprising of them all.

This occurred in Southampton County, Virginia, in 1831. Its prime mover was Nat Turner, a plowman by reason of his servitude, and a preacher and prophet by the grace of God. Turner came of refractory, mettlesome stock. Presumably to save him from slavery, his mother had attempted to murder him at birth. Shortly afterwards, Nat's father, after two previous efforts, made good his escape. Nat himself learned somehow to read and write, and grew up a passionate, intelligent but a somewhat remote and sullen youth. He was early given to hearing strange voices, whose admonitions he took to heart, and to seeing visions. Thus in 1828 he was suddenly transfixed by a "loud noise in the heavens" and there came to him a vision of the "Spirit" which told him that "the serpent was loosened, and Christ had laid down the yoke he had borne for the sins of men," and commanded him to take up the fight, "for the time was fast approaching when the first should be last and the last should be first."

But the time for this reversal of the order of things was not yet, and Turner kept the secret of this command for three years. He was by then a man of thirty-odd, persuasive and dramatic when he deigned to talk, theatrical in his movements, and, in spite of his hammered-down figure, impressive and austere of bearing. Visions came to him with influential regularity. In one of these he saw black spirits at war with white spirits around the blotted-out sun and amid the fury of the primal elements. A tempestuous voice spoke to him: "Such are you called to see, and let it come rough or smooth, you must surely bear it!" Turner felt himself to be an instrument in the awful hands of God. When he had yet another sign, he enlisted the support of four fellow slaves.

Unlike Gabriel Prosser, who was also a mystic, and Denmark Vesey, who was a cold-headed strategist, Turner put together no careful plan. He depended entirely, it seemed, upon divine guidance—some word, some sign. What he took for such a sign appeared in August, 1831, when for three days the sun looked "blue" and for three nights there was "blood on the moon." Nat Turner passed the word to his fellows that they would strike the following week.

On the afternoon of Sunday, August 21, they went into the woods. There were seven of them now. They stayed in the woods for several hours in a kind of spiritual communion. Only the oath to kill all the whites, spare none, bound them together. If Turner had any plans he did not reveal them.

Sometime before midnight, the seven crept out. They went first to the home of Nat's master, Joseph Travis. Nat climbed in a window. He was the first to strike. The five whites in the Travis house were killed—the baby because Nat remembered that "nits make lice." A few guns and some ammunition were taken. The maddened slaughter was begun, with resolution, though headlong, fitful. It went on through the night, the day, the next night. The insurrectionists gathered recruits as they went. Old and young, men, women and children were beaten, clubbed, hacked to death, beheaded, disemboweled in the hot blood of the cumulated wrath of madmen.

By the morning of the twenty-third, some of the fury had spent itself. Upwards of fifty white people had been killed. The military might of three states had been mobilized against the insurrectionists. It was the white folk's turn, and their vengeance, too, was mad. At least a hundred Negro innocents fell its victims. Fifty-two of the insurrectionists were captured almost at once, but Turner himself escaped. For six weeks, while the countryside swarmed with soldiers, he eluded pursuers. At last, on Sunday, October 30, the "Terrible Nat" was taken. On November eleventh, with the three remaining rebels, he was hanged. Of the fifty-three slaves brought to trial, twenty-one were acquitted, twelve transported, and twenty hanged.

The dead Nat Turner quickly became a legend compounded of glory and terror. The Negroes saw him as a hero; the whites as a depraved fiend. The panic he had aroused did not quickly abate. It welled up in newspapers and in letters. "It is like a smothered volcano," Mrs. Lawrence Lewis, of Virginia, wrote to the Mayor of Boston—"we know not when, or where, the flames will burst forth, but we know that death in the most horrid forms threatens us. . . ."

Yet the risk of "death in the most horrid forms" was easier to take than the loss of wealth. Under President Jackson the Indians were dispossessed of large areas of Georgia, Alabama and Mississippi, and planters poured into these good cotton lands. The price of slaves went up. The breeding of slaves for sale became a specialized business in the upper South. The absconding rather than the rebellion of slaves was the great problem.

For principally, in protest and rebellion, slaves ran away. Freedom was represented to them as a cruel illusion that could bring only repining, suffering, death. The North was a hell of "pauperism, oppressive exactions, rampant diseases," where Negroes went deaf, dumb, blind and insane. But slaves ran away. How many? It is impossible to tell. But their numbers were great enough to create the new occupation of slave catching and a new breed of dog (or a new use for an old breed), the "nigger hound." Advertisements for runaways in Southern newspapers were standardized, showing a Negro in flight, his worldly possessions done up in a napkin on his back. There was also a standard cut announcing a capture. It showed a Negro cringing under the hand of a white man; but this appeared ("in only a few enterprising papers") about once in twenty-five times for the other. "Absconding" was so common that it was called a disease, vouched for and diagnosed, and labeled "drapeto-mania" by a Louisiana physician. Slaves ran away toward freedom as if freedom were a place and that place heaven. The route was underground.

3

Running away to freedom was a lonely, lonesome business. Not all who tried it were successful. Many were caught by the professional slave hunter, whose trained hounds were said to have "the power to distinguish 'nigger-smell'" from the smell of whites. The notices describing runaways were very full and accurate. Thus one Jim Belle was advertised for in the Baltimore *Sun:*

Ran away from the subscriber on Saturday night, Negro man Jim Belle. Jim is about five feet ten inches high, black color, about 26 years of age; has a down look; speaks slow when spoken to; he has large, thick lips, and a mustache. He was formerly owned by Edward Stansbury, late of Baltimore county, and purchased by Edward Worthington, near Reisterstown, in Baltimore county, at the late Stansbury's sale, who sold him to B. M. and W. L. Campbell, of Baltimore city, of whom I purchased Jim on the 13th of June last. His wife lives with her mother, Ann Robertson, in Corn Alley, between Lee and Hill streets, Baltimore city, where he has other relations, and where he is making his way. I will give the above reward, no matter where taken, so he is brought home or secured in jail so I get him again.

Jim Belle was more fortunate than some others, for he made good his escape.

In the early days many must have died on the tortuous, unbroken trails across mountain and river, through forest and swamp. There was no well-worn, posted route: each must break a new one for himself. No one in those days dared return to tell others how it was. Escaping was as complete and as impenetrably silent an adventure as death, and it cut as deeply into individual destinies. There was the North Star to guide the fugitive, but the stars did not always shine. Nor did it matter very much, for dark nights or fair were of equal danger. The darkness made the going slow, but it was cover for the runaway; the moon and stars that gave him light could also show him to the enemy. And the enemy was legend; patrols, young toughs on a nocturnal lark, a stray white man, a barking dog, an unknown woods, a snake-infested swamp; heat and cold, hunger and thirst, fear and sometimes also lack of fear.

Some slaves who escaped but did not reach the place of freedom met up with other fugitives to form gangs of marauders. Camping in forest clearings, mountains and swamps, they made a living as best they could. A few of these clandestine bands established havens so well protected from intrusion that they "built homes, maintained families, raised cattle, and pursued agriculture." More than a thousand runaways had a stable community in the heart of the Dismal Swamp and "carried on a regular, if illegal, trade with white people living on the borders of the swamp." Sometimes—and perhaps, in the very nature of the circumstances, more often—these fugitives turned desperadoes. Such was that gang, led by a white man, "a notorious robber," that terrorized the eastern part of Virginia in the 1780's. Another gang waged guerrilla war with the police authorities of South Carolina and Georgia for eleven years after the Revolutionary War. North Carolina, Louisiana, Mississippi and Florida had serious trouble with maroons, who, as allies of the implacable Seminoles and the fierce Cherokees, were resourceful enemies. They plundered, burned, killed. In South Carolina their depredations were the subject of an 1816 legislative message.

A few runaway negroes, concealing themselves in the swamps and marshes continuous to Combahee and Ashepoo rivers, not having been interrupted in their petty plunderings for a long time, formed the nucleus,

round which all the ill-disposed and audacious near them gathered, until
at length their robberies became too serious to be suffered with impunity.
Attempts were then made to disperse them, which either from insuffi-
ciency of numbers or by bad management, served by their failure only to
encourage a wanton destruction of property. Their force now became
alarming, not less from its numbers than from its arms and ammunition
with which it was supplied. The peculiar situation of the whole of that
portion of our coast, rendered access to them difficult, while the numerous
creeks and water courses through the marshes around the island, furnished
them easy opportunities to plunder, not only the planters in open day, but
the island coasting trade also without leaving a trace of their movements
by which they could be pursued. . . . I therefore ordered Major-General
Youngblood to take the necessary measures for suppressing them, and
authorized him to incur the necessary expenses of such an expedition. . . .[7]

Not all the whites who helped escaped Negroes joined with them
in predatory assault. The Quakers did not. An undemonstrative,
God-fearing breed, their hatred of slavery was strongly tempered
with moral indignation. They were lovers of peace whose weapons
were words and whose power was the truth they lived by. Their work
in behalf of the slaves was fairly well organized by the 1780's, when
George Washington mentioned a society of Quakers who it seemed
had a hand in helping one of his slaves escape. It was because of
such activities that the first Fugitive Slave Law was passed in 1793.

It was a law made to be broken, and with stoical defiance the
Quakers proceeded to break it. Even more—they made of it a crusade.
The accidents of history and migration had brought means and men
into almost unbelievable congruence. Quaker settlements were relatively thick in Ohio, Delaware, Pennsylvania and New Jersey, states
bordering the slave states, and beyond these, individual Quaker
families were spaced like way stations through the West to Lake
Erie and through the East to Maine. From settlement to family to
the border of Canada the secret road was beaten out, prayed out,
and at night wheel-muffled vehicles hauled illegal cargo over it.

And not only Friends, but those of other faiths and of no religious
faith. Lewis Paine, of Georgia, was said to be antichrist, and John
B. Mahan was hard-shell Baptist, and Calvin Fairbanks was no
Quaker, yet these and thousands more gave food, clothing, shelter,
money and risked their necks. Indeed, some of them lost their necks.
But ever sharper was the cleavage drawn between North and South,

and with ever more tenacious fervor the crusade caught on.

The fugitives came up from Louisiana, Mississippi, Arkansas, Tennessee and Kentucky, and crossed the river into Ohio. At the Reverend John Rankin's station there they rested until a cryptic message could be sent ahead. "Your goods arrived today. Will be forwarded tomorrow." But it was always tomorrow *night,* under the cover of darkness, across stubble fields, through icy streams and ghostly woods. Black, brown, mulatto, "white mulatto," men, women, children—big-eyed with fright, at the mercy of their sharpened senses, in paralyzed suspension between joy and anguish. They came up from Alabama, Georgia, South Carolina, Virginia, Maryland, and into Delaware, from whence the good Friend Thomas Garrett sent them on to Isaac Hopper or William Still in Philadelphia, and these in turn put them on the line to New York, western Massachusetts and Canada.

But after a while to meet and send seemed not enough for the daring ones, for those whose zeal fed on danger. Thus John Fairfield, son and nephew of Virginia slaveholders, went boldly South and brought slaves out to freedom. First he freed his childhood body boy and took him to Canada. A short time later he was back, and then back again, disguised as preacher, drummer, poultryman, spiriting slaves from under the very noses of their Alabama, Mississippi and Louisiana masters. For twelve years he matched his daring and resourcefulness against the swollen police forces of the slaveocracy. Twice he was arrested and twice escaped; but at the last, taking part in a servile insurrection in Tennessee, he was killed by vigilantes.

There were others of equal courage. A "Captain F" (for Fountain) figures prominently in one account of the Underground Railroad. His looks "were not calculated to inspire the belief that he was fitted to be entrusted with the lives of unprotected females, and helpless children; that he could take pleasure in risking his own life to rescue them from the hell of Slavery; that he could deliberately enter the enemy's domain, and with the faith of a martyr, face the dread slave-holder." But looks were deceiving, for he did. And so did Captain William Bayliss, master of the *Keziah,* a steamer out of Delaware. After years of taking "articles" and "merchandise" north from Norfolk and Richmond, he was caught with "contraband." His ship was seized and auctioned off, and he was sentenced to forty years in prison. Not until federal troops took Richmond in 1865 was he released.

These were some of the spectacular ones, the "artists in the art of stealing freedom." If their stories read like romantic swashbucklers, the hard and sometimes brutal facts of the lives of the Reverend John Rankin, Levi Coffin, Elijah Lovejoy and Benjamin Lundy bring a balance to the completed tale and infuse it with the constant spirit of humanitarian reform. These were the sturdy artisans. Benjamin Lundy, who had "heard the wail of the captive," who had "felt the pangs of distress" and "the iron enter his soul," for years traveled up and down the country, generally afoot, stopping to run off another issue of *The Genius of Universal Emancipation* where-ever he found a printing press, and speaking wherever two or three would gather to hear him. Levi Coffin, reared in North Carolina, sacrificed the comforts of what would surely have been a highly prosperous life to do his duty as he saw it. Driven from pillar to post, Elijah Lovejoy was three times attacked and finally killed by a pro-slavery mob. But the strong, plain men multiplied; kept get-ting stronger. David Nelson and James Birney, Theodore Weld and Beriah Green, Arthur and Lewis Tappan, hundreds more.

The number of Negro "engineers" cannot be reckoned. How many fugitive husbands went back for wives and children? How many escaped sons went back for mothers and fathers? How many were moved by what Levi Coffin called the "higher law of being"? To ask, is to grant them that humanity which the South denied them and which had justified their enslavement in the first place. Things like loneliness and love and family feeling moved them, but also this something more, this higher, more selfless thing. Else how account for Josiah Henson, immortalized now as Harriet Stowe's Uncle Tom, who made thirty round trips between Canada and Kentucky and brought out two hundred slaves? And how account for Harriet Tubman?

4

If Harriet Tubman bore a charmed life, she needed it—early. As a slave girl in her teens, blocking a doorway to an overseer who was chasing a slave, she was laid low by the hurled force of a two-pound ingot of iron. She lay senseless for weeks, and the injury to her head left her with a disability from which she suffered the rest of her life. Without warning, suddenly, in the middle of a motion or a word, her eyes would roll, her face set blankly, her head drop to her chest, and she would plunge into a heavy stupor "from which even the lash in the hand of a strong man could not arouse her." For this reason she was accounted a harmless half-wit. But in 1849 she made plans to escape.

There were those who knew. After all, Harriet was not going merely to the next plantation. She might never come back, for escape was not simply departure; it was usually an irreparable break with family and friends. But one could not be demonstrative about it, one could not make a proper farewell. The necessity for the repression of emotion, the constant thwart to free communication were among the subtler cruelties of slavery, the psychological cost of which has not been totaled; but surely the shuffling hesitancy, the lazy-lipped speech, the evasiveness, the defensive lying and the instinctive distrust of white people are items that must be reckoned. More gifted slaves found not merely spiritual compensation but an adequate communicative substitute in singing. They made up songs, constantly improvising for finer shades of meaning, fresher expressiveness. Their songs became a melodic code. Roland Hayes, one of the world's great singers and a student of his people's music, tells us that many of the spirituals were drawn out of slave heads and hearts by the necessity for secrecy. To spread word of a secret meeting, someone might pour forth the modulated harmonies of "Steal Away." Because rhythm and phrasing and sly gesture could be varied without arousing suspicion, "Swing Low, Sweet Chariot" and "Git on Board, Little Chillen" might at one time be a call to a religious service, at another a message telling of a successful escape, or at still another an announcement of the imminence of an underground conductor. There were many songs about trains and hiding places and silence—the very language of escape, which some slaves learned instinctively.

So there were those who knew what Harriet Tubman meant on the day she sang:

> "When dat ol' chariot comes,
> I'm gwine to lebe you.
> I'm bound for the promise' lan'
> Frien's, I'm gwine to lebe you.

"I'm sorry, frien's, to lebe you,
Farewell! Oh, farewell!
But I'll meet you in de mornin',
Farewell! Oh, farewell!"

That night she was gone. Two of her brothers started out with her, but the way was far and strange, the dangers forbiddingly unknown, and the brothers turned back. Many dawns later Harriet stood on a hill on free soil. "I looked at my hands to see if I was de same person now I was free. Dere was such a glory ober eberything, de sun come like gold trou de trees, and ober de fields, and I felt like I was in heaven."

But if free land were heaven, she knew that she had left a hell behind, and her father and mother and husband, her brothers and sisters and friends were back there in it. "I was free, and dey should be free also; I would make a home for dem in de North, and de Lord helping me, I would bring dem all dere. . . . Oh, dear Lord, I ain't got no friend but *you*. Come to my help, Lord, for I'm in trouble."

So Harriet Tubman went back. She went back nineteen times in the next twelve years. She brought out whole families. She carried a pistol to persuade the faint-hearted who, turning back, might betray her party to recapture. "Dead niggers tell no tales; you go on or die." She carried paregoric with which to drug babies into silence. She carried God. She operated principally out of her home section of Maryland. Since the Fugitive Slave Law of 1850 made any place nearer than Canada a potential trap, she conducted her flights "cross Jordan" to the "real promise' lan'." Moses she came to be called.

Go down, Moses,
Way down into Egypt's land. . . .

And this Moses went down, matching her wits against the wits of the police power and against the cupidity of professional slave hunters. For the price on her head rose from $2,000 to $5,000 to $40,000—and that was a lot of money to men who considered themselves well paid at $100 a capture. By cunning subtly blended with intuition, both of which slavery had sharpened, she eluded snares. She had an uncanny prescience. She began to space her visits—and this was wise because she needed funds. Having seen a party of fugitives safely through, she would take a job in the North and devote her spare time to anti-slavery meetings and activities. Once in Troy, New York, she wrested Charles Nalle, a recaptured slave, from the very hands of the police. In Syracuse she fought in a riot. But such things were but skirmishes on the flanks of her great campaign. When she had saved enough of her wages to finance another expedition, she would head South again. She brought out more than three hundred slaves.

When the inevitable war came, Harriet Tubman sailed into it, expertly tacking from nursing to scouting to soldiering. She took a shooting part in the Combahee River campaign, a series of minor military actions which she got the credit for originating and conducting. But her reputation as an engineer-conductor on the Underground Railroad lost none of its lustre. In 1863, Franklin B. Sanborn, a Boston newspaper editor, declaring that the "true romance of America" was "in the story of the fugitive slaves," went on to say that the extraordinary career of Harriet Tubman had the "power to shake the nation." All sorts of people, including Wendell Phillips and Lucy Stone, Gerrit Smith and Thomas W. Higginson, spread her fame, a fact which made her life exceedingly dangerous before the war. Some of her contemporaries attributed supernal powers to her. Letters from England, Scotland, Germany and France inquired for her. Around her name sprung up a cult almost worshipful, and she —small black, fibrous, one side of her forehead bashed in from the blow in her childhood—became a living legend. But she was real enough, "too *real* a person not to be true."

And real too was Belle Baumfree, and of, to say the least, a different mold. Escaping from her Dutch master, she first made a steep descent into a libidinous mysticism. No extreme of carnal experience seemed too much for her. Fornication and adultery were proved against her, and once she was suspected of murder. Clearing herself of this last, she underwent a great conversion, renamed herself Sojourner Truth in token of it, and ever afterwards bore a reputation for uprightness, for singular devotion to the anti-slavery cause, and for courage. For three decades she went through the North and West preaching freedom. She was tall, gaunt, grim-visaged, with the deep resonant voice of a man, and she drew curious and sometimes hostile crowds. Once in Indiana she was stopped in the middle of a speech with demands that she prove herself a woman by exposing

her breast to some of the ladies present. Superbly angular like a structure of steel, Sojourner stepped close to the edge of the rostrum, and
indignation broke in her Dutch-accented voice. "I will show my
breast to the entire congregation," she shouted. Then she grew calm.
"It is not my shame but yours that I should do this. Here then," she
said, ripping loose the cloth, "see for yourselves." This was the same
woman who, in Salem, Ohio, interrupted one of Frederick Douglass'
gloomiest orations to ask, "Frederick, is God dead?"

Sojourner Truth did not confine herself to the anti-slavery cause.
When the World Anti-Slavery Convention met in London in 1840
and refused to admit eight women delegates, Sojourner undertook
to speak for women's rights. Later still she spoke for prison reform,
labor reform and temperance. Harriet Beecher Stowe called her
"Sybil," for she was a "seer" into the dark complexities of that roiling
era. By 1850 a book had been written about her and she had been
prominently featured in two more.

Meantime other figures were crowding in from the wings onto
the brightly lighted stage. Every anti-slavery society in the North
had a Negro, usually a fugitive slave, as a featured speaker. Some
societies had several. Not all of these were as effective as Sojourner
Truth. A few, indeed, were riders, frauds, impostors in a work in
which deception was easy. In a time so clamorous and a movement
so fanatical, a hollow voice here and there among the many raised
in identical shouts was hard to detect. Some fugitive slaves and some
who had never been slaves were petty self-seekers. But such as these
were thrown into shadow by the sincere, gifted and sometimes
desperate men, who came in numbers during the 1840's.

By then Henry Highland Garnet, long since escaped from Maryland, was straining nearer the absolute belief in violence that eventually made him the radical of radicals. William Wells Brown, done
with his apprenticeship to the abolitionist printer, Elijah P. Lovejoy,
was an agent of the Western Massachusetts Anti-Slavery Society.
Having purchased his freedom, Lunsford Lane was unique among
anti-slavery workers. But so, too, were John Russworm, the first
Negro to graduate from an American college (Bowdoin), and Alexander Crummell, who had studied at Cambridge University, and
James McCune Smith, a medical graduate of Glasgow and a practicing physician in New York. By 1840, Richard Allen and Absalom
Jones had converted the Free African Society into the African

Methodist Episcopal Church, and the ranks of black Christian abolitionists were soon to be swelled by the addition of Samuel Cornish,
Frances Ellen Watkins, Frances Coppin, Benjamin Rush, and
Charles Ray. Out of these men and women came strength and
idealism and, above all, the testimony without which the spirit of
abolition might have died and the proof of the Negro's educative
capacity never been discovered.

They organized churches and were the preachers. They established
schools and taught in them. Having had a start in fraternal organization when a Negro, Prince Hall, was inducted in the Freemasons in
1775, they set up fraternal orders. Their first newspaper, *Freedom's
Journal* (hopeful title!) began publication in 1827, and by 1850 there
were a dozen, including the famous *North Star*. Most of these were
short-lived, for free Negroes, never exactly affluent, were having their
ups and downs—somewhat more of the latter. Still they were making themselves heard and felt. Dozens of books narrating their ex-
slave lives could be found on sale at anti-slavery meetings. They were
writing letters (to the New York *Tribune,* the Brooklyn *Eagle,* the
London *Post*), and books of travel and novelettes, and in the 1850's
the first play by a Negro, *The Escape; or A Leap to Freedom,*
appeared. Much earlier the North Carolina slave, George Moses
Horton, had produced a volume of poetry, *Hope of Liberty*. Verse
gushed from Frances Ellen Watkins. Martin R. Delany, who had
studied medicine at Harvard, was sometime a newspaper editor,
and later became a major in the Union Army, wrote:

> Were I a slave, I would be free,
> I would not live to live a slave;
> But boldly strike for liberty—
> For Freedom or a martyr's grave.

These lines were far from the peak of literary accomplishments,
but they expressed the pitch of an attitude. Most of the people who
read them in Delany's paper, *The Mystery,* had struck for liberty.
Freedom was not easy, to be sure, and the job competition with Irish
and German immigrants was constantly more bitter; still, out of
their wages as handymen and domestics and carpenters and bakers,
out of their earnings as stock hands and tailors and confectioners
they could always pinch a little for the cause. They formed their

own anti-slavery organizations, and had arguments over policy, and personality clashes, and moments of jealous rivalry. But after all, they had a single aim and on the whole they pushed together for it. They raised such a ruckus as sometimes to make the North uneasy and always to keep the South aware that up there in the North were several million dollars' worth of escaped slaves.

In 1838, Frederick Douglass stole away to freedom, and the ranks of Negro abolitionists were about to get their unquestioned leader.

6

HOUSE DIVIDED

•••

FREDERICK DOUGLASS WAS born a slave in Maryland in or about 1817. His father was his master, but this made no difference in the treatment he received. Indeed, during the three years he lived on Captain Anthony's place he was "so pinched with hunger" that he fought with the dogs for scraps and followed "the waiting girl when she shook the table cloth, to get the crumbs and small bones flung out for the dogs and cats." He was happy to be sent, at the age of ten, to Baltimore to live with Hugh Auld, a relative of his master's.

Here as a houseboy and as laborer in Auld's shipyard, he learned to read and write. At first his mistress taught him, but Auld soon put a stop to this. But the mischief had been done, "the first and never-to-be-retraced step had been taken. Teaching me the alphabet had been the 'inch' given, I was now waiting only for the opportunity to take the 'ell.' " He took the ell by various ingenious ways, and his appetite for learning was stimulated by the scraps it fed upon. He grew thoughtful, silent. Sneaking into nooks and corners, he spelled through whatever he could come across—Webster's *Speller,* the *Columbian Orator.* He read—whenever he could steal a copy—the Baltimore *American,* which occasionally reprinted enough anti-slavery criticism to arouse the South. "And as I read, behold! The very discontent so graphically predicted by Master Hugh had already come upon me. I was no longer the gleesome boy. . . . Light had penetrated the moral dungeon where I had lain, and I saw the bloody whip for my back, and the iron chain for my feet, and my *good kind* master, he was the author of my situation. . . . I wished myself a beast, a bird, anything rather than a slave. . . ."

When he was sent to a new master and the old plantation life at the age of seventeen, Frederick Douglass was morose, unmanageable. But for this there were cures and professional "nigger-breakers" to effect them. The treatment was simple and severe: work, starvation, the lash. Edward Covey, the slave breaker to whom Fred was sent, gave it in double measure. He worked the recalcitrant boy to the point of stupor, starved him on the thinnest gruel, whipped him —or tried to—to senselessness. But Fred would not be broken. Indeed, after a few months, when he had taken all he could, he defended himself against Covey so stubbornly that the slave breaker never again tried the lash on him.

Still it was another three years before Fred could escape. An earlier attempt had been thwarted in the interval, and he had been sent again to Baltimore. Some years older and more knowing now, more aware, in this second experience of city living, he came to understand a "phase of slavery which was destined to become an important element in the overthrow of the slave system." That phase was the conflict of slavery with the interest of white mechanics and laborers. Its day as an important element in the overthrow of the system was as yet far off. The impression was strong among the laboring whites that slavery alone prevented them from sinking to the social and economic level of the blacks. The master class encouraged enmity between the two, and in the cities of the South poor white and poorer black, slave and free, sometimes met in bitter conflict. Fred was once the victim of such strife. In the shipyard where he was employed, he was brutally beaten by a gang of white mechanics.

He escaped his master shortly afterwards. Disguised as a sailor and carrying an official-looking but wholly spurious paper ("with the American eagle on it"), he fled to New York. From there he went to New Bedford, where he began to order his life around the occupation of handyman.

For in New Bedford he could not work at his trade of ship calking. Northern native white labor was wary. It had known hard times, and it was just then getting organized to meet new economic conditions. It was not sure of its own strength. Striking, its most effective weapon, had been declared illegal in 1835. Two years later a depression brought on divisive, cut-throat competition for jobs, which wiped out previous social and economic gains. Recovery was slow. Not until 1840, when President Van Buren made ten hours a legal day's work on government projects, did labor win a victory.

But this, too, seemed threatened by incoming hordes of foreign laborers. And did not free Negro labor constitute a greater bane? It was not strange that pro-slavery, anti-Negro propaganda had penetrated to the wharves and shipbuilding docks of coastal New England. Northern shipping had once thrived on the slave trade. The area had its share of slavery sympathizers, and these nourished carefully the racial concepts. The Negro could live on less and therefore required less, and this was a danger to free white labor. What the white man demanded two dollars for doing, the Negro would do for one. And what did he know—or care—about the principles of unionism, when he could underbid organized labor? What did he care about labor's social program? About tax-supported public schools for instance?

The fears of whites doubtless had substance. The Negro could do with less, for he had had to. He cared nothing about the principles of labor organization: he did not know what they were. So Fred, who by this time had named himself Frederick Douglass, took the proscriptions in his stride and did for a livelihood only the things a colored man could do in peace. He "sawed wood, shoveled coal, dug cellars, moved rubbish from back yards, worked on the wharves, loaded and unloaded vessels, and scoured their cabins."

But this was not to last long, for already he was reading the *Liberator* and slowly learning the dialectic of revolution. He had heard Garrison lecture in Liberty Hall in New Bedford, and he was finding his own voice among the colored people of the community. New England's anti-slavery group was small then and close-knit, like a consecrated brotherhood—which indeed, it was. The quarrels that later shook it, the factional schisms that rent it were still hidden in the wave of the future. Such a brotherhood is as sensitive and as alert as a wild thing, its head constantly to windward, vigilant for friends as well as enemies. If Frederick Douglass thought that his speeches to Negro neighbors in the schoolhouse on Second Street stopped there, he was mistaken. Besides, had he not also whispered to every sympathetic white ear "on the wharves and elsewhere the truth which burned in [his] breast"? Yet no one was more surprised than he when, in the summer of 1841, William Coffin asked him to address an anti-slavery convention in Nantucket.

By his own account, Douglass did not do so well with that speech. His knees turned to jelly, his voice quaked, his lips went thick and dead. But he was heard and seen. He was twenty-four, a tower of a mulatto man with strongly marked features—long nose, firm, straight mouth—and a head of bushy hair which his contemporaries described as leonine. William Lloyd Garrison and John Collins, who were there, must have been impressed, though perhaps more by his appearance than his speech. At any rate, when the convention closed, the Massachusetts Anti-Slavery Society urged him to become their agent.

The fugitive slave's value as an anti-slavery agent at first lay largely in the curiosity he aroused. People wanted to see and hear a runaway slave, a thing, a property, a chattel that had the appearance of a human being and could talk. Douglass, as he put it—not quite accurately—"had the advantage of being a *brand new fact,* the first one out." When he made the circuit of eastern Massachusetts, curious crowds gathered to hear him tell his slave story. He gave it to them simply, for the officers of the society gravely admonished him to be factual. "Give us the facts," John Collins told him; "we will take care of the philosophy"; and William Lloyd Garrison added, "Tell your story, Frederick."

It is probable that in the first fall and winter of his lectureship, telling his story was all that Douglass could bring himself to do. But he soon came to feel that audiences would tire of it, especially now that other fugitives were in the field. William Wells Brown was over in western Massachusetts. Samuel Ringgold Ward was telling *his* story in Connecticut and New York. Moreover, Douglass was reading, thinking, growing. He needed room. Though the desire to follow his own head was strong, it was not just simple willfulness that made him begin to ignore Garrison's admonition. He felt a compulsion to go beyond the facts, to light them up, to reveal the deeper truth. But the warnings of his white anti-slavery associates had sprung from practical considerations. Douglass did not look like a slave, nor act like one, and by 1844 he had sloughed off the characteristics commonly attributed to one of his status. Much reading had given him a flexible vocabulary. His voice had a crisp, commanding roll. It was hard enough to believe him a "runaway nigger," even though his story rang with truth and the evidence of his bondage coiled in ropy scars on his back. It was still harder to credit when he propounded abstract arguments and presented them logically. "People won't believe you ever was a slave, Frederick, if you keep on this way," Friend George Foster told him. And so it proved.

One of Douglass' shrewd, outspoken Yankee listeners summed it up. "He don't tell us where he came from—what his master's name was—how he got away—nor the story of his experience. Besides, he is educated and is, in this, a contradiction of all the facts we have concerning the ignorance of slaves." There was nothing for it but to run the ultimate danger of recapture by telling all, by calling names of people and places, by giving dates. This he did in writing, against the advice of his friends, and shortly afterwards, escaping the immediate consequences of his willfulness, sailed for England.

Though it was not then apparent, Douglass' apprenticeship to the Massachusetts Anti-Slavery Society, to Collins, Coffin, Phillips and Garrison was over. The little break that was finally to mean the severing of all but the tie of purpose had come. In approach, in the direction of his thinking, in political philosophy, Douglass was to take a different course from Garrison who, throughout the 1840's, was the outstanding policy-maker of the anti-slavery movement. While Garrison was to hold fast to abolition alone, Douglass was to see abolition as merely the first step toward the end of enlarging all human rights. Garrison was not to be moved from his conviction that the relation of the free states to the slave states was criminal and full of danger, that the Constitution was a "covenant with death," an "agreement with hell," and that therefore the North should break the constitutional bonds of union with the South. Douglass believed that the preamble to the Constitution governed the meaning of the whole. Garrison said, "No union with slaveholders," but Douglass would change it to read no union with slaveholding. Garrison denied the use of political means to effect abolition; Douglass went in for political action. While one was to preach non-resistance to slavery and state it as his conviction that servile rebellion was morally inadmissible, the other was to come to the opposite point of view, lend at least moral support to John Brown, and at last, in 1849, declare that he would "welcome the intelligence tomorrow, should it come, that the slaves had risen in the South, and the sable arms which had been engaged in beautifying and adorning the South were engaged in spreading death and destruction there."

The differences between the points of view of these leaders represented no more than the individualism—fashioned by differing experiences—of sincere and gifted men.

Douglass' two-year visit in England, where he went everywhere lecturing, gave him an international reputation. He had the room for lack of which he had complained after the first months of his anti-slavery work in America. Though he returned ever and again to the topic which after all was his main concern, his English speeches ranged the field of social problems. He spoke on world peace, on temperance, on universal manhood suffrage, on women's rights. His intelligence on these issues was cause for wonder. William Hewitt, the British author, remarked: "He has appeared in this country be-fore the most accomplished audiences, who were surprised, not only at his talents, but at his extraordinary information." One in-cident marred his stay. When English friends raised money to pur-chase his freedom, some American abolitionists brought up the objection that purchasing the freedom of a slave was a concession to evil, to the hated legalized right of property in man. They saw it as a violation of anti-slavery principles, and "a wasteful expenditure of money" besides. Douglass' answer to these objections was that he considered his purchase simply "in the light of a ransom, or as money extorted by a robber."

Douglass had nothing but respect in England. There he had grown. Returning to America in 1849, he again suffered from lack of room, the more troublesome now in view of his new importance. Many American newspapers maligned him; audiences abused him, demonstrated against him. There was something viciously personal in it. In Boston, the "cradle of abolition," and in Harrisburg, the boos of audiences silenced him. In Norristown, he was stoned. There was small consolation in knowing that those who plagued him were the hired hoodlums of pro-slavery sympathizers.

By now Douglass had come to believe that he should not only work for his people but with them. Given the premise on which he stood, Garrison could not have been expected fully to appreciate this at-titude. But Douglass was interested in more than emancipation for the slaves. If, as Booker Washington asserts in his biography, Doug-lass was by temperament a politician and "more or less an opportun-ist," he was also far-sighted and increasingly sensitive to what was being thought and said by the most liberal minds of the day. So he had looked forward beyond emancipation to the day when "the doors of the school-house, the workshop, the church, the college" should be thrown open "as freely to our [Negro] children as to the children of other members of the community." To be sure, Garrison might have envisioned such a day, but the fact remains that he did not. Fanatical concentration on abolition blinded him to all else; led to friendly and then to somewhat strained disagreement with the colored anti-slavery agent. For months their relations were taut and uncertain, for both men were reluctant to make a break.

An idea, long past the gestation stage, was making Douglass increasingly restive. He wanted to start a paper of his own. Whether friends urged him to it, or whether he was inspired by the examples of Lundy and Lovejoy, or Garrison himself no one knows. He had expressed his wish while still in England, and friends there raised $2,500 to help him fulfill it. Rationalization was easy after that. "I already saw myself wielding my pen . . . in the work of renovating the public mind, and building up a public sentiment which should . . . restore to 'liberty and the pursuit of happiness' the people with whom I had suffered both as slave and freeman."

Still he held off for weeks after his return. He listened to Garrison and to Phillips, who enumerated their objections. The paper, they said, was not needed. It would interfere with Douglass' usefulness as a lecturer, a function for which he was peculiarly endowed. Besides, were not the risks great? A half dozen Negroes had founded papers and failed. Less persuaded by these arguments than made reluctant to foster the breach they certainly forecast, Douglass consented to the compromise of writing a weekly column for the already established *Anti-Slavery Standard*.

Meantime he had begun to address Negro audiences, to join exclusively Negro organizations and to preside at their meetings and conventions. Until now he had simply been a spokesman of the cause close to Negro hearts; not the leader. But in identifying himself with every phase of Negro life, in realizing anew the necessity for such identification, the idea of starting a paper of his own seemed to Douglass more than ever right.

"From motives of peace" and so as not to interfere with the local circulation of the *Liberator* and the *Anti-Slavery Standard*, Douglass moved from Boston to Rochester, New York, late in 1847. The first number of his paper, the *North Star*, was published on December third of that same year.

2

So at last the break had come, as it must have come sooner or later. Garrison was not a practical man. His appeal was to the con-science. He wanted to effect the moral regeneration of the people. He fought slavery on grounds that the slaveholders had long since abandoned, and it was like fighting a ghost—a whole host of them—possessed of very material weapons. Raucous but effective politicians, the slaveholders were beating Garrison to the punches that counted most. They were a wealthy minority, with leisure to give to public affairs and motives of self-interest to arouse them. They had won a victory in the Missouri Compromise of 1820. In 1836, sensitive to and tired of the petitions to Congress against slavery, they had estab-lished the "gag rule," which did not at all prevent Congressman Hammond, of South Carolina, from bellowing hotly, "I warn the abolitionists, ignorant and infatuated barbarians as they are, that if chance shall throw any of them into our hands, they may expect a felon's death." By 1840 John C. Calhoun was the fashioner of Southern thought and a fiery advocate of Southern expansion. Work-ing with Robert Walker, the Senator from Mississippi, Calhoun forged a political alliance between the cotton men of the South and the land-hungry farmers of the West. Their ambitious drift was ap-parent by the middle of the decade: they wanted Texas annexed. They wanted New Mexico, Arizona and California. The election of James K. Polk in 1844 assured the success of the first part of their plan. Texas came in, a mighty addition to slave power and slave territory. For the rest, we went to war with Mexico.

But in the face of all this Garrison remained iron-firm in his determination to have nothing practical to do with politics. He re-mained not only a non-voter and a non-unionist, but, until the 1850's, a non-resister of Southern aggression as well. This stand, like so much that is noble, was futile. It was a tilting at windmills that were not even there. That Garrison continued to rely on moral suasion was because he *had* achieved some results with it; he had won adherents. If he remained undaunted by the Herculean proportions of the task remaining to be done, it was because he was a man of abiding pa-tience.

Negro abolitionists had no such patience. Many of them were ex-or escaped slaves, and they were goaded by anger and urgency, for the poisoned virility of the South threatened to burst its geographical bounds and reengulf them.) In Pennsylvania the black abolitionists had committed themselves to political action in 1838 when they protested against a proposal of the Pennsylvania "Reform Convention" to disfranchise free people of color. Their leader, Robert Purvis, declared: "We do not believe our disfranchisement would have been proposed, but for the desire which is felt by political aspirants to gain the favor of the slaveholding States. . . . We take our stand upon that solemn declaration, that to protect inalienable rights 'governments are constituted among men . . .' and proclaim that a government which tears away from us and our posterity the very power of consent is a tyrannical usurpation which we will never cease to oppose." [1]

Even when they were non-resisters in theory, the Negro freemen backslid in practice and stormed their hot applause for every violence done by slaves against slaveholding. But by the 1840's they were openly abandoning even the theory of pacifism. Speaking before the National Convention of Colored Citizens in 1843, but addressing himself to slaves, Henry Highland Garnet gave voice to the ascendant attitude.

"However much you and all of us may desire it, there is not much hope of redemption without the shedding of blood. If you must bleed, let it all come at once—rather die freemen than live to be slaves. . . . Brethren, arise, arise! Strike for your lives and liberties. Now is the day and the hour. Let every slave throughout the land do this, and the days of slavery are numbered. You cannot be more oppressed than you have been—you cannot suffer greater cruelties than you have already. . . . In the name of God, we ask, are you men? . . . Awake, awake; millions of voices are calling you! . . . Let your motto be resistance! resistance! resistance! No oppressed people have ever secured their liberty without resistance." [2]

Douglass was somewhat less rash. Once, in 1841, he had declared, like Garrison, that "we ought to do just what the slaveholders don't want us to do; that is, use moral suasion. They care nothing about your political action, they don't dread the political movement; it is the *moral* movement, the appeal to men's sense of right, which makes them and all our opponents tremble." It was in this same spirit that Douglass opposed Garnet's defiance two years later. But before the decade was out, even before he had set up his press in Rochester,

Douglass had begun to move away from Garrison's position on the Constitution and on violence. After a visit to the hot-eyed, grim-visaged John Brown (in 1847), who revealed to him his plan for a slave rebellion, Douglass' "utterances became more and more tinged by the color of this man's strong impressions. Speaking at an anti-slavery convention in Salem, Ohio, I expressed this apprehension that slavery can only be destroyed by blood-shed, when I was suddenly and sharply interrupted by my good old friend Sojourner Truth with the question, 'Frederick, is God dead?' 'No,' I answered, 'and because God is not dead slavery can only end in blood.' My quaint old sister was of the Garrison school of non-resistance, and was shocked by my sanguinary doctrine, but she too became an advocate of the sword." And the advocacy of the sword spread in ever-widening circles.

As for politics, Frederick Douglass worked actively for the Liberty Party in the campaign of 1848 and became a member of its national committee. But politics was a game about which he had much to learn. Though the issues were starkly drawn along sectional lines in the campaign of that year, party factionalism was rife, political ambitions vaulting. Sectionalism, newly vitalized by the Mexican War and its consequences, rode the nation like a fire-breathing hag. The Democratic Party was split three ways over a question growing out of slavery—the Wilmot Proviso, which prohibited slavery in the territories. The "regular" Democrats, opposed to it, nominated Lewis Cass at their convention at Baltimore. The reforming "Barn Burners" held a convention of their own at Utica, pledged themselves to the support of the Wilmot Proviso, and put forth James Van Buren as their nominee. But the Barn Burners' opposition to slavery did not go far enough for Northern Democrats, and these, augmented by all but the die-hards of the radical Liberty Party, held a convention at Buffalo, changed their name to Free Soilers, and also nominated Van Buren.

Douglass was pretty much confused by all this, as indeed he had an excuse for being. If the moderate radicals and the extreme radicals had come together on more than just a nominee; if they had struck a compromise on party policy; if . . . But there are no ifs in history. "Old Rough and Ready" Zachary Taylor, the candidate of the Whigs, rode to victory on a minority popular vote.

Crucial events and the spreading contagion of the anti-slavery

fever were forcing Douglass into wider avenues of thought, realms
of more desperate action. Many men were being so forced. Not that
they were typical. Quite the contrary. Douglass was not the archetype
of Negro anti-slavery leaders; he was simply the greatest. Ultimately
his was the voice, the brain, the direction, but he was not always
the first to take a new course. Robert Purvis and Samuel Ringgold
Ward understood the potential effectiveness of political action before
he did. While Henry Garnet was shouting militant abolition, Douglass was still preaching pacifism. He came to a policy of aggression
slowly and with even greater tardiness did he seek to implement such
a policy with action. He was not an extraordinarily perceptive man,
but once he had seen the wisdom of an idea or of a line of conduct,
he followed it with tenacity, with courage, and sometimes with
brilliance. His outstanding trait—indeed, his besetting virtue—was
fidelity to purpose and to men of similar purpose. So, for instance,
he never uttered a word of obloquy against Charles L. Remond, who
was jealous and did spiteful things; nor against Garrison who, following the break in their personal relations, whetted his sharp
tongue on Douglass' character. John Brown must have sensed this
loyalty, for on his first meeting with Douglass he revealed to the
one-time slave his dangerous plans for a widespread slave revolt.
Negroes sensed Douglass' fidelity too, for he attracted them as a
magnet attracts steel filings, and they "rallied around him and lived
and labored in intimate association with him."

It was not until he moved to Rochester that Frederick Douglass
took an active part in the spectral movements of the Underground
Railroad. Then his house became the terminal of one of its eastern
routes. It was an activity he could ill afford, for his paper ate up all
the funds he earned from lectures. But Lake Ontario was only seven
miles away, and on the other side lay Canada, and it was not easy
to refuse what must have seemed at first so little aid. After all what
was a little food for several days, outfits of clothing for (once at least)
seven people, medical attention, and a small sum of money for boat
fare or for bribes? Nevertheless it is true that some conductors, while
convinced of the moral righteousness of helping slaves escape, could
not afford to give their services free. They were not all Thomas
Garretts, the station operator at Wilmington, Delaware, who at sixty
lost everything he had to the cause. They were not all Daniel Dray-
tons, willing to forfeit livelihood and liberty.

Douglass doubled his speaking schedule to earn the extra funds. Once he had seven fugitives under his roof; at another time eight; at another eleven. He had "difficulty in providing so many with food and with sufficient money to get them on to Canada." The risks, too, were especially great for him. Internationally known as an abolitionist, his home was constantly watched, and his every movement was the focus of suspicion.

3

Meantime the national political pot had never ceased its furious boil. The ambitious scheme of Southerners to multiply their political power was temporarily blocked by a plexus of questions. Were the provisions of the Constitution effective over the territories recently acquired from Mexico by war and negotiation? What of the western boundary of Texas? What of the addition of California to the list of states? What of the Oregon Territory, of Utah Territory and New Mexico? Though they might masquerade as something else, all were questions of slavery—the warp and woof of every political consideration. And what about the Fugitive Slave Law, the flouting of which had irritated Southerners for nearly half a century? The financial loss from runaways was costing millions annually, and the South wanted a more stringent law for these more stringent times.

When Congress met in December, 1849, these and other questions divided that body like a hop scotch pattern. If there was danger in this division, there were men who welcomed it. Speaking for South Carolina and the South, John C. Calhoun, only months before his death, again threatened secession as he had done over the tariff question twenty-one years before. Mississippi now declared herself in similar terms. Impatient of the issue, the Virginia House of Delegates resolved to resist any attempt by the federal government to prescribe the right of citizens to carry their human property into territory acquired by the nation. All of this had about it the air of desperate frustration that seeks relief in violence. And on the other side, too, there was a similar extremism in and out of Congress. It showed itself in the suddenly stepped-up activity of the Underground Railroad; in the practical nullification of the Fugitive Slave Law of 1793 by Northern courts; in the added vitriolic content of the anti-slavery writings of Garrison, Whittier and Holmes. Northern representatives in Congress were as touchy as Southern. Had not Salmon P. Chase, of Ohio, proved it? Was not William H. Seward, Senator from New York, whose intimacy with the President was an affront to the South, even then urging upon Zach Taylor the immediate admission of California as a free state and seconding the General's threat against the Texas expansionists?

But while there were men who welcomed disunion, there were others who wished to avoid it at all costs. President Taylor at bottom was one of these. Henry Clay, the great compromiser, wanted to try one more compromise. Indeed, now an old man, he had come back into public life for no other purpose than to split the difference that would unite the nation. Daniel Webster was to be his able minister— and earn thereby the calumny and scorn of the North.

Congressional tempers were raw. More than sixty ballots were taken before a Speaker of the House was elected, and before the session could get fairly under way not a man in Congress but could sniff the red brew of fraticidal war.

Clay opened the debate. Like all compromises, his was an evasion of principles without a definition of policy. But he was merely seeking to gain time for a hoped-for lasting and peaceable working out of the emotion-ridden problem. He knew that his proposals were a flimsy expedient, a patch on a leaking balloon that might, with luck, stay afloat a year, or five years, or ten. Yet the Compromise was a masterpiece of its kind, and old Henry Clay presented it skillfully. To mollify the North he proposed that California be admitted as a free state; that the slave trade be abolished in the District of Columbia; and that Texas forego her claim to an extended western boundary. For the South he denied the right of Congress to control the slave trade within states and between states; proposed that Utah and New Mexico become territories with the restriction of the Wilmot Proviso (thus leaving the decision on slavery up to the people of those territories); and urged a harsher fugitive slave law. To these proposals John C. Calhoun, the fire-eater, had nothing to add except the ready warning that the South would secede unless the North consented to some such terms as Clay had suggested.

Then, on March 7, 1850, Daniel Webster rose. Surely the times were out of joint, for he was about to make the greatest speech of his career in support of the South. Webster had been a Northern champion, a Northern sectionalist. His reply to Hayne, though it had foreshadowed this speech of twenty years later, was a brilliant defense of New England. But now he spoke "not as a Massachusetts man, nor as a Northern man, but as an American. . . . I speak today," he said, "for the preservation of the Union. Hear me for my cause." After a debate that lasted well into the summer, his cause was saved—but only temporarily. No compromise could long withstand the successive waves of fury, of sectional interest and pride, of frustration, and of reality that now began to pound. How unsatisfactory the compromise was to both sides (and perhaps even more to the South than the North) was soon demonstrated. At a convention of the Southern states in 1850, South Carolina influenced Mississippi, Georgia and Alabama to declare for secession. The attacks upon Webster in the North were unrestrained, almost hysterical. Whittier wrote of the "surprise and grief" with which he read Webster's speech, and he saw, he said, "with painful clearness its sure results—the Slave Power arrogant and defiant, strengthened and encouraged to carry out its scheme for the extension of its baleful system, or the dissolution of the Union, the guarantees of personal liberty in the free states broken down, and the whole country made the hunting-ground of slave-catchers." It seemed to him—and to Phillips, and to Garrison (for the time)—like the plunge of a section and a people and a principle to a depth beyond moral sounding and recovery.

Though the full political implications of what happened seemed lost on him, Frederick Douglass reacted in much the way of other abolitionists. The passage of the Fugitive Slave Law of 1850 was a "stunning blow." By its provisions those who engaged in Underground Railroad activity, even to the extent of giving food to a fugitive, were subject to five years in prison or a fine of $5,000. Other terms, while equally stringent, were vindictive and cynical, aiming at revenge at the same time that they sought to make enforcement easy and attractive. Senator Mason of Virginia, who framed the bill, reasoned that the righteousness of the "moral North" could be penalized out of existence or bought. The law set up a system of rewards for the capture of fugitive slaves. It stipulated a penalty of $1,000 against the United States Marshall who refused or neglected to arrest an alleged fugitive when called upon to do so. Runaways could be arrested without warrant and taken before a commissioner or a judge, who need require as proof of the charge only a sworn statement claiming right of property by the alleged owner. Finding for the claimant entitled the commissioner to a larger fee. A fugitive could not testify in his own behalf, nor have a trial by jury.

Negroes in the North went into panic. No longer sure of the validity of their titles to themselves, they stampeded out of the country, beyond the pale. As Douglass said, "even colored people who had been free all their lives felt very insecure in their freedom, for under this law the oaths of any two villains [the capturer and the claimant] were sufficient to confine a free man to slavery for life." The effects of the law were deep and disruptive. Much of the economic stability, striven for so patiently against great odds and represented in homes and jobs and families, was lost. Courage had been kept alive through social solidarity, but now that sense of union was gone. Whole settlements of Negroes fled. Three days after the signing of the bill, Holland tells us, many colored people left Boston and "the pastor of the Colored Baptist Church in Rochester fled with every other member, except two, out of a hundred and fourteen, to Canada." Many Negro abolitionists, themselves fugitives, sought sanctuary on British soil. Samuel Ringgold Ward, one of the most brilliant, went to Canada and in Canada he died. Henry H. Garnet stole way to England. The courage utterly gone out of him, Bishop Daniel Payne of the African Methodist Church, moaned, "We are whipped, we are whipped! and we might as well retreat in order."

Douglass did not retreat, and there were those who called him foolhardy. Indeed, perhaps he was, for he went on with desperate energy speaking at meetings, denouncing the Fugitive Slave Law and its supporters, trying to pump up the courage of disheartened freemen. He continued to collect funds to help fugitives cross into Canada. He harbored fugitives in his home, and once, in the very year of 1850, he had eleven fugitives at one time, and John Brown, already a dangerous man to be associated with, came and made a speech to them. Even had he foregone these activities, Douglass' own safety would have been far from certain. His purchase, he explained, "was of doubtful validity," since it had been made under circumstances that left his owner no choice. For some time friends guarded his house in Rochester against the possibility of a raid by "nigger catchers" who were everywhere active and who were kidnapping even free Negroes and taking them South to slavery. The reign of terror, which Whittier had predicted, seemed to have come.

But it grew more clear every day that the North was not long to be coerced into the service of slavery. The very excesses of the slave hunters confirmed the North's old scale of human values. Yankee stubbornness and pride and something more metaphysical took over. Even some Northerners who were by habit or from self-interest cold or only lukewarm in their anti-slavery sentiments felt the Fugitive Slave Law of 1850 to be an infringement of their liberty of conscience. Not that the conservatives had vanished from the scene. Textile manufacturers, shipowners, bankers whose profits came from the South were there in plenty, and they were still powerful. Only more powerful was the indignation of Bostonians when the slave "Shadrach" (Frederick Jenkins) was taken as a runaway and slated for return to Dixie. The citizens of Boston rescued him and spirited him away to Canada. At the subsequent trial of the alleged culprits, the case against them was dismissed. Within six months of its passage, Bostonians had flouted the new law. Within another three months, inspired and led by such respected men as Thomas Wentworth Higginson, Theodore Parker, Wendell Phillips, and Leonard Grimes, they tried it again, this time without success. The police powers of the government were too strong, and Thomas Sims, the seventeen-year-old slave whose freedom was at stake, was returned to Georgia and there gloatingly, publicly whipped. But Massachusetts had set a flaming example. New York State and Pennsylvania soon followed it.

4

Meantime neither section was able to turn completely from the course each had set itself, though it must be said that an element in the South tried to. This group may have been moved by politics rather than policy; still it was actively for the Compromise, even if it meant overworking the breach of some of the Compromise's provisions. These conservatives had no wish to make the enforcement of the Fugitive Slave Law the point upon which the decision as to union or secession turned. Actually, of course, enforcement was the least moot point, involving as it did the prestige of law and the dignity and authority of federal government. From the group of Southern conservatives developed a movement strong enough in 1851 to sweep into the governorship of Tennessee William B. Campbell, a conservative who was pledged to the union of the States. Mississippi, too, went for the Compromise. In Georgia the radical Southern

Rights Party nominee for governor was defeated by Howell Cobb, a unionist. North Carolina returned to the United States Congress one Edward Stanly, who was accused of Northern sympathies. These men professed to believe that an adjustment of the differences between North and South was possible. They wanted the South to settle down and accept the Compromise as workable and lasting.

And for a time it did seem workable. Millard Fillmore, who had risen to the Presidency after the death of Zachary Taylor, was careful to congratulate the country "upon the general acquiescence in the compromise measures which had been exhibited in all parts of the Republic." But this, as events soon proved, was wishful thinking. In word and deed Northerners—and not only irrepressible abolitionists—openly expressed their defiance of the law. Emerson, Whittier and Holmes continued their attacks upon it. Thoreau was prepared to go to jail rather than pay taxes to a government that sanctioned slavery. The Fugitive Slave Law, declared young Rutherford B. Hayes, was for barbarians rather than Christians. In Syracuse, New York, another fugitive slave, Jerry McHenry, was snatched from the authorities and sent on to Canada. And as a crowning touch, the weight of Northern sentiment for the indicted rescuers, including the abolitionists Gerrit Smith and Samuel May, was so great that prosecution was deemed useless.

Though these events convinced the South that the North did not mean to honor the Compromise, the political and emotional balance between the two sections was so nearly equal as to result in temporary stalemate—or so it seemed from the sudden strange quiescence, lull. Yet this was only seeming, for tensively and carefully beneath the surface a gigantic test of strength went on. Nothing that contributed to the surge toward war was really adjourned. The undercurrent was irreversible. Quietly but grimly the South went on with its old line, its old dream, its old quest for unassailable power. The North, or rather abolitionists in the North, went on with their baiting, their taunts and baleful recriminations. For all this strain and play for advantage, the Negro was the cause. Negligible as an active participant in both policy and politics, he rode and ruled the divided temper of the nation like a nightmare. His influence in just being here was all-pervasive.

In 1852 the emotional weather was right for a thunderclap, and the thunderclap came. It came disguised as a book with the innocently bucolic-sounding title of *Uncle Tom's Cabin.* The book had been running for a year in the anti-slavery *National Era,* a coterie paper with a restricted public. Appearing between covers of its own, the effect of the novel was instantaneous, startling, and it weighted the emotional balance heavily on the side of abolitionists. Three hundred thousand copies were sold within a year. It was almost immediately dramatized and began a run of performances that took it to many thousands. It leaped language barriers and was published in German, Polish, Chinese, French and Italian. It was like a running tongue of flame, scorching the conscience of the world. A sincerely conceived but often maudlin attack on slavery, *Uncle Tom's Cabin* strained men's emotions to a point all but unbearable. It pictured with unabashed pathos the cruelest sufferings of slaves, the blackest evils of slavery, and the degeneracy of slaveholders. With all its exaggerations, it was obviously true, composed as it was of incidents out of real life.

The South's reaction was shock—not at the truth, which it knew full well, but at the world's reaction to it. The North hugged her self-righteous satisfaction and offered to produce the living people from whose stories Mrs. Stowe had drawn. Uncle Tom was a living man—and he could vouch for Little Eva. Simon Legrees were common enough. And as for the flight, the bloodhounds . . . The South's disclaimers served but to enforce the impression of veracity the book made. No novel has ever had so great an influence on the hearts and minds of men. Because of it discussions of American slavery became world-wide and the slaveholder the target for universal opprobrium.

Before Harriet Beecher Stowe sailed to present herself to the English public that "just must see her," she invited Frederick Douglass to visit her in Andover, Massachusetts. She was full of ideas and enthusiasm. She was gracious, dynamic, sincere, and perhaps a bit bewildered. She had, she thought, done something for the slaves by writing her book; but what about the free colored people? She wanted to do something for them too. Did Mr. Douglass have anything to suggest? What she wanted was "to have some monument rise up after *Uncle Tom's Cabin*" to "show that it produced more than a transient influence." In England she expected to have a considerable sum of money put at her disposal, and this could be used for the benefit of the free Negroes. What about an industrial school?

Mr. Douglass thought it a very good idea indeed. Mrs. Stowe clapped her hands delightedly. Could Mr. Douglass set forth his views at length and in writing so that she would have the word of the most outstanding Negro leader to back her up? Mr. Douglass would. He did. Mrs. Stowe sailed happily for England.

When she returned some months later, she informed the disappointed Douglass that she had given up the idea of a school for free colored people. The fight was still for freedom of the slaves. The money she had collected in England must go for the cause, and this was not now so bright as it had been when she went away.

5

That the cause had been darkened by the aggressive machinations of the slaveocracy became apparent in 1854. In January of that year the smart and ambitious Senator from Illinois, Stephen A. Douglas, introduced a bill to organize the territories of Kansas and Nebraska. The measure was loaded in favor of the slaveholding South, for it provided for the repeal of the Missouri Compromise. Although vigorously attacked by Chase and Sumner and other men of like persuasion, the bill passed both houses and President Pierce, Northern tool of the slaveholders, quickly signed it. The Missouri Compromise, which for thirty years had served to maintain the political balance between North and South was broken, and broken too, in effect, was the Compromise of 1850.

The Southern aristocrats were jubilant. They had combined the Whig and Democratic parties to wield an influence out of all proportion to their numbers and out of all agreement with the principles of democratic rule. In and out of Congress, they had fought with cynical and arrogant realism. To argument, they had opposed action; to principles, politics; to humanitarian appeals, demands for the reopening of the African slave trade. The Kansas-Nebraska Act was triumph indeed. Since it provided that slavery in these territories should be decided by territorial vote, an area of nearly half a million square miles was thrown open to slavery—or to freedom, depending upon whether slavery or anti-slavery people got there first with the greatest numbers. It was, as Frederick Douglass remarked, "an open invitation to a fierce and bitter strife."

The strife was not to be long in coming. In truth, the country had

climbed upon the toboggan already nosed in for the plunge to
catastrophe. And the brakes were off. Momentum gathered day by
day, hour by hour. "From this time there was no pause, no repose,"
wrote Frederick Douglass. There was certainly none for him. As the
Negro leader, his position was unique. He was called upon to divide
his energies between abolition and bettering the lot of the free Negro.
Many of those who might have helped him—Garnet, Ward, Payne—
were gone to Canada or to England. Others were lying low, frightened that they might be snatched back into slavery. Douglass went
everywhere speaking, advising, collecting funds. In 1854 he was the
principal guest and speaker at the anniversary of the American Anti-
Slavery Society. The next year he traveled west to Ohio and Iowa,
skirting the borders of the slave empire. He ran his paper. He had
frequent and disturbing contacts with John Brown. He received
fugitives and sent them on to Canada. He worked with the Emigrant
Aid Society, organized to help freedom-lovers to settle in the Kansas
Territory. In the beginning of the presidential campaign of 1856, he
was active for Gerrit Smith, the candidate of the Radical Abolitionists; but soon realizing the waste of energy in a campaign so hopeless, he went over to the Republicans, a new and strong party whose
candidate was Colonel John C. Frémont and whose platform Douglass liked. That platform proclaimed that it was "the duty of Congress to prohibit slavery in the Territories," pledged itself uncom-
promisingly against slavery, and demanded that Kansas be immediately admitted to the Union as a free state.

Meanwhile the New York *Times'* flat assertion "that the repeal
of the Missouri Compromise has done more than any other event
of the last ten years to strengthen anti-slavery sentiment" [3] was proving true. Northerners realized that if the provisions of the Kansas-
Nebraska Act were fulfilled, the system of the South would engulf
them, leaving them politically powerless, economically dependent
and morally bankrupt. The slave system, Northerners felt, was inimical to their interests and their free institutions. It was two years
yet before Lincoln, paraphrasing the Gospel according to St. Mark,
was to put it into words, but already a majority of leaders on both
sides knew—bitter as the knowledge was to some—that "a house
divided against itself cannot stand."

The struggle now was without pretense of conciliation. Each side felt insecure, and insecurity compelled the most vigorous offense and defense, ward and parry, short of war. Sectional hatred rose to a shrill crescendo. While the South poured men and their slaves into Kansas, the North hustled emigrants in too. The Northerners established themselves at Topeka and Osawatomie; the Southerners at Atchison and Leavenworth on the shores of the Missouri. Few of either side were genuine homesteaders. In Platte City the Southern settlers formed a defensive association for the purpose of ejecting "any and all" emigrants who should come there through the help of Northern emigrant societies.

Trickery and fraud took over. Territorial elections were rigged by first one side and then the other. The score: an impossible tie. John Brown, the wild-eyed, the clear-headed, the apotheosis of fanaticism, who had never believed that slavery would be overthrown but by force, gathered his sons and went to Kansas. Always close to the surface during the turbulent fifties, violence broke out at last. Douglass, who saw Brown on the latter's "repeated visits to the East to obtain necessary arms and supplies," became a broker of violence, a middleman of terror.

The fact that Brown could get Yankee guns and bread proves the temper of the North. The bloody work the man did in Kansas was cheered and excused in the East. "The horrors wrought by his iron hand cannot be contemplated without a shudder," said Douglass, "but it is the shudder which one feels at the execution of a mur- derer. . . . To call out a murderer at midnight, and without a note of warning, judge or jury, run him through with a sword is a ter- rible remedy for a terrible malady." [4] Only one great anti-slavery leader found no satisfaction in Brown's Kansas exploits. Garrison called them "misguided, wild, and apparently insane," but later— without surrendering his own position, indeed in a way solidifying it—he was to observe that:

. . . the sympathy and admiration now so widely felt for him, prove how marvelous has been the change affected in public opinion during the thirty years of moral agitation—a change so great indeed, that whereas, ten years since, there were thousands who could not endure my lightest word of re- buke of the South, they can now easily swallow John Brown whole and his rifle into the bargain. In firing his gun, he has merely told us what time of day it is. It is high noon, thank God! [5]

But the anti-slavery spirit had grown to encompass even more than Garrison knew. Shortly after the Kansas bloodshed, at a rally of anti-slavery people in Boston's Tremont Temple, the great abolitionist editor was naïve enough to inquire from the rostrum how many of those present were non-resisters. His answer was a solitary "I." On Garrison's clock it may have been high noon, but on the clock of national destiny it was nearer midnight.

6

And Washington, the face of the clock the whole world watched, indicated palpably how fast time was going. When Senator Charles Sumner of Massachusetts arose to speak on May 19, 1856, debate had rumbled on, like the angry mutter of distant thunder, for a matter of months. Now for the better part of two days, while one half of the country bristled with rage and the other half bridled with self-righteousness, Sumner was a vitriolic Jeremiah castigating the Southern power and the men who wielded it and the men who were its dupes. Franklin Pierce, the President, Stephen A. Douglas of Illinois, but most of all Senator William Butler of South Carolina, were the subjects of Sumner's acidulous ire.

Before entering upon my argument, [Sumner said,] I must say something of a general character, particularly in response to what has fallen from Senators who have raised themselves to eminence on this floor in championship of human wrong: I mean the Senator from South Carolina. . . . Of course he has chosen a mistress to whom he has made his vows, and who, though ugly to others, is always lovely to him,—though polluted in the sight of the world, is chaste in his sight: I mean the harlot Slavery. . . . But the Senator touches nothing which he does not disfigure—with error, sometimes of principle, sometimes of fact. . . . He cannot open his mouth, but out there flies a blunder. . . .[6]

Inexcusable as this invective was, it was no more so than the action of Preston S. Brooks. Three days after Sumner's speech, this relative of Butler's strode into the Senate chamber and, giving no hint of his intention, using a cane as a cudgel, beat the Massachusetts Senator into bloody unconsciousness. The next day the press of the nation was in full blast. There was condemnation from the North, reflecting the mind of that section. The attitude of the South was expressed in an editorial in the Richmond *Enquirer*.

In the main, the press of the South applaud the conduct of Mr. Brooks, without condition or limitation. Our approbation, at least, is entire and unreserved. We consider the act good in conception, better in execution, and best of all in consequence. The vulgar Abolitionists in the Senate are getting above themselves. They have been humored until they forget their position. They have grown saucy, and dare to be impudent to gentlemen! Now, they are a low, mean, scurvy set, with some little book-learning, but as utterly devoid of spirit or honor as a pack of curs. . . . They must be lashed into submission. Sumner, in particular, ought to have nine-and-thirty early every morning. . . . There is the blackguard Wilson, an ignorant Natick cobbler, swaggering in excess of muscles, and absolutely dying for a beating. Will not somebody take him in hand? Hale is another huge, red-faced, sweating scoundrel, whom some gentleman should kick and cuff. . . . These men are perpetually abusing the people and representatives of the South, for tyrants, robbers, ruffians, adulterers, and what not. Shall we stand it?

This editorial appeared on June 12, three weeks after the event, when in ordinary times the cooling off of passion and the reassertion of reason might have been expected. But these were not ordinary times. Men had come to that dangerous emotional state in which any incident no matter how small could drive them from propriety. It was not only in the nature of slavery never to rest in obscurity, as Frederick Douglass remarked, but it was not in the nature of the forces opposed to slavery to rest in silence and inaction. So after murder was done in Kansas—by both sides, more murder. A linked, sequential series of incidents, a kind of chain reaction. The citizens of Wisconsin declared the Fugitive Slave Law repealed and battered down the door of the courthouse in Milwaukee and rescued a fugitive slave. There were house burnings and lynchings and hangings in effigy. In Osawatomie, more murder.

Yet the ordinary round of daily living went on. Institutions functioned and men met, discussed, agreed, disagreed and resolved exactly as if their deliberations could avert the tragedy that impended. The year, 1856, was an election year, and men threw themselves into politics with vindictive energy. The Know-Nothing Party nominated Millard Fillmore, who was committed to a policy of merely restricting slavery. The Democrats, upholding all the provisions of the 1850 Compromise and again declaring Congress powerless to deal with slavery, nominated James Buchanan. The Republicans again put forward John C. Frémont. For anti-slavery men the choice was easy. Only the young Republican Party was unequivocally committed against slavery. Though hopefully fought by the Republicans in the North, the result of the campaign was never in doubt. Buchanan was elected. The planters felt safe for four more years.

The institution of the law ground on too. Off and on for more than a decade it had been grinding out the case of one Dred Scott, and now the United States Supreme Court was about to deliver an opinion, "the shock of which jarred the two sections of the nation farther apart."

Dred Scott had made persistent legal efforts to obtain his freedom. His master, an army surgeon, had taken him from Missouri to Illinois and thence into a part of the Louisiana Territory in which slavery had been prohibited by the Missouri Compromise. Brought back to Missouri, Scott sued for his freedom. The lower court found in his behalf, but Dr. Emerson, the master, appealed to the state Supreme Court and the judgment was reversed. Sold to John Sanford in 1853, Scott again sued, this time in the United States Circuit Court, and when the decision went against him, he appealed to the Supreme Court of the United States. In 1857 the decision came. Scott, the five-to-two majority decreed, being a slave, was not and had never been a citizen and could not bring legal suit.

But the matter did not rest here; it went way beyond. Congress, averred the written opinion, had no power to prohibit slavery in the territories. Sectional feelings blazed higher than ever. The South had done it again, or so it was felt because the majority of the Court's justices were Southerners. And this was certainly the consideration behind Senator Seward's bill to reorganize the Supreme Court along more "representative lines." Many people in the North were suspicious of collusion between Buchanan and the Court. "The Court," Seward maintained, "did not hesitate to please the incoming President . . . by pronouncing an opinion that the Missouri prohibition was void. . . ." From this opinion there was no appeal, for the Court was the final judge of the extent of the powers of the federal government. There was a storm of denunciation and protest, but it was useless and more than useless. For were not the dire consequences already apparent? Of articulate abolitionists only Frederick Douglass did not see them, or refused to see them.

We are told that the day is lost, all lost; and that we might as well give up the struggle. The highest authority has spoken. The wisdom of the Supreme Court has gone out over the troubled waves of the national conscience. . . . But my hopes were never brighter than now. I have no fear that the national conscience will be put to sleep by such an open, glaring, and scandalous tissue of lies. . . . The Supreme Court of the United States is not the only power in this world. . . . Judge Taney may do many things, but he cannot perform impossibilities. He cannot bail out the ocean, annihilate this firm, old earth, or pluck the silvery star of liberty from our Northern sky.

Douglass alone had hope, not for some miraculous reversal of the Court's decision, some backward turning of the wheels of destiny; but he only knew that his "star of liberty in the northern sky" was no mere figure of speech.

7

Douglass had long been in close association with John Brown, a man "divinely sent" to wipe slavery off the earth. Brown had made a very deep impression upon Douglass, whose heart vibrated to the iron string of the revolutionist's fanaticism. Brown's mission seemed "the only apology for his existence. . . . He would walk the room with agitation at the mention of slavery. He saw the evil through no mist, haze, or clouds, but in a broad light of infinite brightness, which left no line of its ten thousand horrors out of sight." He did not believe that moral suasion would ever liberate the slaves, or that "political action would abolish the system." Eventually he had brought Douglass around to an acceptance of this view. What Brown had wrought in Kansas did not seem enough, for his granite soul demanded "all done, well done." Kansas was a rehearsal.

For he had a plan some quarter of a century old, and by 1858 he felt that the time had come for its execution. With the help of twenty-five men, already in Iowa training for their mission, he would build a stronghold in the mountains of Virginia. From there he would operate against the slave power, by stealth if possible, openly if necessary. If by the former, then his object would be to steal slaves and send them North to freedom; if by the latter, then his purpose was to foment revolution. Douglass pointed out difficulties, argued against the scheme. How would Brown provision his men? What about bloodhounds tracking them down? Once found out, would it not be easy to surround and strangle his mountain fastness?

Brown brushed these objections aside. All through January and February, 1858, while he lived in Douglass' home, he wrote letters soliciting funds from other abolitionists. Theodore Parker, F. B. Sanborn, George Stearns and Gerrit Smith tried dissuasion, but Brown was adamant, and since he must go ahead—well, there *was* some money for the cause. Through the spring and summer Brown traveled from anti-slavery cell to anti-slavery cell collecting funds which he converted into arms and provisions. That winter, just for practice, he and his men made an excursion into Missouri and set free a handful of slaves.

Meantime Frederick Douglass busied himself in the usual ways. He spoke in twenty cities in Illinois, Michigan and Wisconsin in 1858. His editorials expressed satisfaction over the split in the Democratic Party and surprised gratification over the way an unknown lawyer named Abraham Lincoln debated Stephen A. Douglas into a political position from which there was no escape. Yet as the weeks went by, Frederick Douglass grew a little concerned. Did not this Kentuckian from Illinois talk out of both sides of his mouth? Did he not say at one time that he hated slavery because of its "monstrous injustice" and at another that he could not blame the slaveholders? And what did he mean by saying that he would not know what to do about slavery even if he had "all earthly power"? Was this just the man's honesty, which legend already was calling rugged and incorruptible? Douglass' friend, Sojourner Truth, said Lincoln was all right; but there was another friend, Harriet Tubman, and she had strong doubts. Still, the invective and vilification being levelled at Lincoln from the South meant something. The South hated and feared this "rail-splitter," this "third-rate lawyer."

Douglass went on speaking and speculating and thinking aloud. He went to New York City and delivered a eulogy on William Jay, an early abolitionist. He went to Geneva, New York, and spoke on the anniversary of the emancipation of the slaves in the West Indies.

Then in August, 1859, he had a preemptory letter from John Brown urging a rendezvous. It was a dangerous summons to obey. Douglass was a marked man. He could go nowhere without being recognized. The very solicitude of his friends might betray his whereabouts. Moreover John Brown had a price on his head for

the blood he had spilt in Kansas, and if Douglass should be implicated in this more daring plot . . .

The two men met in an abandoned stone quarry outside Cham-
bersburg, Pennsylvania, on Saturday, August 30. Brown's appearance
had changed, his salient features sharpened. He was thinner,
straighter, and like a granite shaft which the suns and rains and
snows of Kansas had weathered faintly yellow. Under shaggy brows,
his eyes burned like fires in a thicket. But this was not all: his plans
had changed too—drastically. As he talked, his grimly assertive
speech bare for all its biblical imagery, Douglass listened with aston-
ishment and dismay. The old man no longer wanted merely to harass
the slaveholders by stealing slaves. He would seize the arsenal at
Harpers Ferry. He would capture leading citizens and hold them
as hostages. He was after blood, a death blow to be struck or received.

All night Saturday and most of Sunday Douglass argued, but
Brown was already possessed of his doom. He was incapable of seeing
the consequences of defeat, or of counting such consequences dire. He
wanted to be a martyr. No thrust of reason reached him; no threat
of injuring the very cause for which he would gladly die. A squad
of his men were even then reconnoitering the mountains of Virginia.
Others, watchful and silent, were there in the quarry with him.
When at last Douglass rose to go, John Brown put his arm around
him. "Come with me, Douglass," he said. "I will defend you with my
life. I want you for a special purpose. When I strike the bees will
begin to swarm, and I shall want you to help hive them."

On October sixteenth he struck, but the bees did not begin to
swarm. With eighteen men, four of whom were colored, he captured
the government arsenal, the rifle factory, and the armory at Harpers
Ferry. He took prominent citizens prisoners, freed fifty slaves, and
prepared to hold the town as long as might be.

Panic seized the South, for this was that evil most feared of all—
slave revolt. And treason! President Buchanan sent federal troops to
Harpers Ferry and called out the militia of the District of Columbia.
The state of Virginia armed and called on other states for aid. Even
after Brown's capture, fear, fed by rumor, continued to mount. It
was said that Brown's raid was only the first in a series of planned
revolts which would break out in Maryland, North and South
Carolina. The South kept men in a state of semi-mobilization.

Extraordinary precautions were taken to guard the prisoners, for it was also said that attempts would be made to rescue them. Virginia's Governor Wise claimed that positive information of such an attempt had come to him from Pennsylvania and Ohio.

The newspapers of the North belittled these fears and were nearly of one voice in calling Brown "mad," "demented." *Freedom's Champion,* a paper published in Kansas, declared that Brown's was an "insane effort to accomplish what none but a mad man would attempt." Other anti-slavery papers were equally condemnatory.

Meantime among Brown's confiscated personal effects were found letters from prominent abolitionists. These implicated Frederick Douglass, George Stearns, Gerrit Smith, Joshua Giddings, Thomas W. Higginson and Theodore Parker. The South was determined to avenge itself. Theodore Parker was already safe in Italy. Uttering blunt defiance, Higginson remained in Massachusetts, where a historic family name and powerful friends protected him. George Stearns and Samuel Howe fled to Canada. Aided and urged by friends who feared that once in the hands of the slave power his life would be worth considerably less than a nickel, Douglass fled Rochester just six hours ahead of the United States marshals President Buchanan sent to arrest him.

One other person was accused of complicity in John Brown's scheme of rebellion. She lay low until the spring of 1860 when, while the New York *Herald* was "exposing" her as a long-time conspirator and Underground Railroad conductor, she engineered a raid to rescue a captured fugitive slave in Troy, New York. There was a price of $40,000 on her head. "The law tracked her for days . . . the wrath of the pro-slavers demanded her arrest, her trial, even her blood." [7] But Harriet Tubman was not to be caught, and her work was not to stop. The Underground kept right on running, and slaves kept right on finding their way to freedom.

7

THE BLACK AND THE WHITE

● ●

WHAT WAS THIS freedom once they had got it? Well, it was a precarious thing, a sometime thing, a completely unpredictable quantity. Besides being a feeling and a hope, in truth, felt some, it was not much —dependent as it often was upon man's conscience and man's whim.

And this, it seems, had been so always. It is true of course that now and then in colonial times there emerged Negroes for whom freedom was whatever they could make of it. Some of them acquired it when their periods of indentureship were over, and, where the laws were equally administered, some of these did well. In 1651, for instance, black Anthony Johnson imported five indentured servants, and on their headrights received a grant of two hundred and fifty acres of land. Behind him came a troop of industrious Negroes who bore his name and lived as free men on the shores of the Pungoteague River. They were woodsmen, carpenters and planters. They owned land, had white indentured servants and white wives, and were respected yeomen in the community.

But even then, and though the Johnson kind endured—increased, in fact—the fortunes and the status of free Negroes were declining. The change came inevitably on the grossest and most logical motivation. No devious, compulsive and unending metaphysics here. It was simply that, as the economic system took root first in the single crop tobacco, and later in the single crop cotton, slaves became valuable items of wonderfully sentient property. And it followed, then, that, granting the master class a conscience—and it did have one—the free Negro became a reminder of that conscience's troubled state, as well as a real menace to the institution of slavery. Nor did it take long, once the South's economic bearing was fixed, to reach this sound

conclusion. The very increase in the number of free Negroes between 1775 and 1800 led naturally to it; and when the South threw
off the hypnotic spell of the Revolution, it had been proved that the
free Negro was a menace. The proof did not grow less in the years
to come. The free Negro was a contradiction in terms. According
to Van Evrie, he was a "social monstrosity." "Free negroism," he
wrote, ". . . is not a condition . . . which the higher law of nature
grants. . . . There are, then, only two possible conditions for the
negro—isolation or juxtaposition with the white man—African
heathenism or subordination to a master." [1]

By the 1820's this was the accepted point of view in the South, and
it was more and more supported by custom and statute.

While admitting that black men had the right to freedom, the
North was thrown off social balance by their presence. Manumitted
slaves, freed on the condition that they leave their home districts, and
fugitive slaves—unless they went to Africa—had no place to go but
North. Here they were completely unabsorbable; pools of noxious
oil on water. Trade unions, spurting for tighter, more effective organization in the 1820's and '30's, proscribed them. There were few
places for Negroes in the Northern economy. Sapped of initiative,
habituated to dependence, in freedom they were prone to become
public charges. Those who did slip into jobs depressed wages, and
thus incurred the common white laborer's ill will. Moreover, German
and Irish immigrants began to displace Negroes in the menial service
occupations of porters, waiters and coachmen.

Thus the beginning of a cycle that came full with the Northern
concept of the Negro as a sluggard, inherently stupid and indigent.
It was the same concept that, with the addition of bloodthirstiness,
had framed the Indian; the same that, even then in the 1830's and
'40's, was fixing rigidly about the Mexicans in the Southwest and
to a lesser extent about the Irish in the Northeast—for cultural
chauvinism and racism are twins. The editor of the New York
Tribune must have known that all of these attributions were ra-
tionalizations of race and culture prejudice. But the Indians were a
"vanishing" race, and the Mexicans were in faraway Texas, and the
Irish eventually would be assimilable. The Negro however was right
under the eye, and it was he, Greeley knew, who was conspicuously
denied the rights which theoretically belonged to all men and
then was reproached for not being thrifty and enlightened and

virtuous. Fanny Kemble, writing of the free Negro of the North, knew this too. "They are not slaves indeed, but they are pariahs, debarred from every fellowship save with their own despised race, scorned by the lowest ruffin in your kitchen. They are free, certainly, but they are also degraded, the off-scum and the off-scouring of the very dregs of your society." [2]

And in the North, too, this image was set in custom and limned in law. No phase of the free Negro's life but what it was not burdened with interdictions. He did not have the protection, either from the stringency or the misapplication of the law, or from the whim of the individual white man, that slaves might hope for from their masters. The effort was to keep him contained, to keep his social world in strictest isolation and his economic life just this side of total pauperism. He was allowed service jobs and common labors, when he could find them. Though many Negroes had been taught trades in slavery, mechanical pursuits were closed to them in the North, and even apprenticeships in industry were impossible to obtain. Dr. Charles Wesley's occupational tables are revealing enough. Of 3,337 free Negroes in New York City in 1850, 1,578 were laborers (including deck hands) and 808 were servants. In that same year in Boston the working Negro male population numbered 935, of whom 135 were common laborers, 46 barbers and hairdressers, and the rest personal servants and domestics.

But even these jobs were too few to go around among those who wanted them, and it must be said that not all Negroes did. It must indeed be reckoned that some fled slavery to escape from work. Where they came from, work was dishonorable, degrading; as witness the fact that slaves did most of it, and slaves were despised; as witness the fact that poor whites found in abstinence from work the one condition that lifted them above the slaves. So for some—and probably a good number (the figures can only be inferred)—freedom was license to loaf. In spreading slums near the waterfront in Philadelphia and Cincinnati, in teeming courts and alleys in New York and Boston, Negro men lived on the paltry earnings of their women. Many were without pride or ambition, and were content to wallow in indolence. Many turned mean and vicious, creating problems for the police and a race-conscious shame for their better-minded brothers. Crime was said to be endemic among them. Diseases of poverty, filth and immorality prowled and death stalked. The South could and did point a finger of triumphant scorn at the free Negro in the North and purr a self-righteous "I told you so." Freedom for the Negro in the North, the South could say, was cruel, wicked and inhumane. And the indictment could be proved by the testimony of Negroes themselves.

Frederick Law Olmsted relates second-hand the case of the Negro who bought his freedom from his Virginia master and moved to Philadelphia. After only a few weeks he returned to his former home and, when asked why, replied, "Oh, I don't like that Philadelphy; an't no chance for colored folks dere. . . . I couldn't git anythin' to do, so I jist borrow ten dollars of my broder, and cum back. . . ." Nor did a "very intelligent colored man," a minister, of whom Olmsted heard later, like New York any better. "Niggers were not treated well there—there was more distinction made between them and white folks than there was here." This was not true, as in the circumstances it could not have been true, of course; but it expressed the potency of class awareness which free Negroes in the North could not escape and which drove not a few to the extremity of reenslaving themselves.

There was not much the free Negro anywhere could do about the restrictions imposed upon him. He had no political voice at all in most of the South—South Carolina and Maryland being exceptions for a while—and such voice as he had once enjoyed in the North faded to less than a whisper in the years between 1810 and the Civil War. In New York and New Jersey a property qualification stopped him from voting. Ohio excluded Negroes from the exercise of the ballot in 1803, Connecticut in 1818, Rhode Island in 1822, and Illinois at about the same time. Though strongly protested by the intelligent Negroes of Philadelphia, Pennsylvania restricted voting to whites in 1838, and Indiana and Iowa did likewise less than a dozen years later.

Having no political power, and indeed as a consequence of not having it, free Negroes enjoyed few of the general rights and privileges and services for which nevertheless they paid taxes. They had no police protection. Negroes were hounded out of Portsmouth, Ohio, in 1830, and out of Cincinnati three times between 1827 and 1841. They were the victims of mobs in Pennsylvania in 1834, and again in 1835, and once again in 1839, when the citizens of Pittsburgh put the Negro neighborhood to the torch. When a free Negro sailor was arrested for using "impertinent" language in Wilmington, North Carolina, the patrol ordered him whipped by a slave, and Guion G. Johnson's *Ante-Bellum North Carolina* cites a Wilmington paper as asserting that "it was never better done. This may be Judge Lynch's Law, but we think it a very good one." Then it added significantly: "Nor has the patrol stopped here. They have extended their services into the tribe of free Negroes who have swarmed here from other sections and squatted in the purlieus of the city, and already have and now are in the act of abating much of that nuisance."

Legal prosecution of free Negroes in theory was often persecution in fact. Crimes of violence committed against free Negroes were seldom punished with the severity they deserved. Robbery, mayhem, murder, rape—the punitive bars against these outrages just were not put up for the protection of the free Negro. Add to this the fact that nowhere in the South, nor yet in Ohio, Indiana and Illinois, could he give testimony against a white man, and you have the stage set for the enactment of those travesties in which justice played a clown.

Nor was this all, for congruency demanded that the crimes of free Negroes against whites be punished in strictest severity either within or without the law. In North Carolina, in 1827, for instance, "William Kansell, a free lad of color," was sentenced to be hanged for burglarizing the house of "a lady of great respectability of five dollars' worth of candy." And he was hanged too.

2

Still the number of free Negroes continued to increase, though slowly after 1830, in New Jersey, Pennsylvania and Kentucky. There were significant additions to the free Negro population in Michigan, Illinois and Ohio between 1840 and 1850. In spite of the Iowa law of 1839, which demanded a "fair certificate of actual freedom" and a bond of $500 of every Negro who wished to settle there, the state's free Negro population rose from 172 in 1840 to 1,069 in 1860. The half million black free men that the census of 1860 reported, lived in their settlements in Ohio and Michigan, and in concentrated masses in Southern cities like Baltimore, Richmond, Charleston, Mobile and New Orleans; and in Philadelphia, New York, New Haven and Boston. Cities seemed to attract them. In cities they found a measure of protection in anonymity. In cities they found greater opportunities for wage work. In cities they found people and organizations to help them.

And the help was often far-seeing and disinterested, for there were still those upon whom the propaganda made little impression, those in whom it had been impotent to wither the roots of faith and the vine of practice. Nor is it necessary again to mention the Quakers, though they kept and contributed to schools and gave of their resources to establish free Negroes on land of their own. The Reverend Charles Avery was no Quaker, and he willed $300,000 for the establishment of a college for free Negroes. Even the American Colonization Society seemed for a time to shape its policy simply from a consideration of the Negro's welfare. But if freedom in Africa was sweeter than the hope of freedom in America, few Negroes wished to prove it. Though several states gave African colonization legislative support and though the federal government backed the plan with funds and sent Reverend Samuel Bacon and John Bankson to Africa as official agents, only ten thousand Negroes ever sailed, and most of these died of hardships. When, in the 1830's and '40's, the Colonization Society came into sharp dispute and it was declared that the object was more to get rid of than to help the freedman, opposition to colonization grew bravely vocal in the meetings and conventions which Negroes called from time to time.

For free Negroes in the North did hold meetings. (In the South they could not.) Every circumstance tended to force them to come together for mutual protection and benefit. Otherwise they could not have met the demands of the times. It is important, too, that though their grouping was economic and social and later political, it was primarily ethnic and to a great extent emotional.

Fraternalism had been started among them back in pre-Revolutionary War days when fifteen Negroes of Massachusetts were taken into the British military order of Freemasons. Some years later, Prince Hall, one of the original fifteen, received permission to set up a chapter of colored Masons. In 1787 we find this pioneer order petitioning the legislature "to provide educational facilities for colored children," and Prince enjoining his brothers in these words: "Let us lay by our recreation, and superfluities, so that we may have that to educate our rising generation, which was spent in these follies. Make you this beginning, and who knows but God may raise up some friend or body of friends as he did in Philadelphia, to open a school for the black here, as that friendly city has done." [3] The Boston lodge was wide awake on matters of general welfare too. When Shays' Rebellion broke out in 1786, Prince Hall wrote the Governor of Massachusetts tendering the help of the men of the lodge. "We, by the Providence of God, are members of a lodge that not only enjoins upon us to be peaceable subjects to the civil power where we reside, but it also forbids our having concern in any plot or conspiracies against the state where we dwell."

African Lodge, Number 495 of Boston, soon mothered others. The Grand Lodge of Massachusetts was founded in 1792, and by 1825 there were chapters of colored Masons in Rhode Island, Pennsylvania, New York, Maryland and the District of Columbia. If these and the less formal fraternal organizations, which abounded, made romantic ceremony of visiting the sick and burying the dead, then they also made realistic sense in their approach to the practical demands that faced them. They established savings banks and insurance groups; they invested in real estate and supported schools and churches. Out of a community of interests grew craft guilds of mechanics, coachmen, calkers and other workers. The Colored Knights of Pythias were originally more a labor union than a lodge, and all of them—the Grand United Order of True Reformers, the Knights of Tabor, and the International Order of Good Samaritans —stressed protective and racial uplift activities. Many of these fell or were dragged into bankruptcy, but others survived and flourish still.

Secret societies meant much to Negroes, but the brotherhood of religion meant infinitely more, and it was from this that they derived their greatest satisfaction. Religion took them out of themselves, fired their imaginations, transported them from a hostile world to one of ineffable peace, where their peculiar endowments were not stifled by either the curse of slavery or the harsh demands of freedom. Long before there was any formal church organization among them, Negroes poured out into song and prayer, sermon and spiritual— this last above all—the resources of their rich religious natures. A mixture of superstition and naïve faith their theopathy may have been, as certainly by definition it was, but it gave them a directness of spiritual communion beyond anything known to formal religion.

And not all white people, masters and superior though they were, scorned to share in this communion. At least a half dozen Negroes preached regularly to congregations of whites before the Civil War. The famous evangelical bishop, Francis Asbury, ordained his Negro companion, Henry, and often used him to preach in his stead. Lemuel Haynes, offspring of an African father and a white mother, pastored various churches in Vermont from 1788 to 1812. Even in the South white congregations listened to powerful Negro preachers. Ballagh, the historian of slavery in Virginia, cites the case of Preacher Jack, who was "instrumental in the conversion of many whites" and to whom "the most refined and aristocratic people paid tribute." John Chavis and Ralph Freeman, one born free and the other slave, did all the services of the ministry for white worshippers until in the 1830's the law put an end to Negro preaching in the South and for thirty years, following the Vesey and Turner rebellions, forced the Negro church underground.

In the North the organization of Negro churches continued in the pattern laid down by Richard Allen. Both the African Methodist Episcopal and the African Methodist Episcopal Zion denominations, now the most powerful Negro religious bodies in America, came about as a result of the indifference, if not the antipathy, of the white ministry to the black man's spiritual needs. Refused the rites of ordination and consecration by the established churches, the stripling A.M.E.Z. church ordained its own deacons and elders, formalized their own orthodoxy and, after twenty years of missionary endeavor, founded a national body. That this body set up rivalry with Allen's A.M.E. church, which was already rivaled by independent congregations of black Baptists, made for rapid growth. Soon there were churches representative of all the Protestant sects in New York, Boston, Cincinnati, St. Louis and in all the way places where there were a handful of colored freemen. No other institution has produced so many effective leaders among Negroes.

And no wonder; for no other institution was so exclusively and indisputably theirs. They were forced to make their own decisions, solve their own problems, steer by their own lights. They learned independence. They got training in leadership. Scarcely a Negro of ability and accomplishment in the years down to the Civil War but what an important part of his development was fostered by the church. Frederick Douglass, later something of an agnostic, tried his first oratorical flights before a small congregation of blacks in New

Bedford. Henry Highland Garnet and Samuel Ringgold Ward were preachers. Before he learned to read and long, long before he turned to writing as a career, William Wells Brown preached the gospel. The first Negro newspaper, *Freedom's Journal,* was started in 1827 by Samuel E. Cornish, a preacher. The only colored newspaper surviving today from pre-Civil War days, *The Christian Recorder,* was founded by the church. Harriet Tubman was a religious mystic, and so was Sojourner Truth. The A.M.E. denomination alone had 286 churches and eighty thousand members by 1860, while Negro Baptists numbered half a million and a million more were divided among other colored Methodists and the Episcopalians and Catholics.

But the rare food of Catholicism and Anglicanism was poor fare for the voracious Negro spirit. The formalism, the ritualistic coldness of these sophisticated faiths were glittering pretties among which the humble and unlearned moved with sad and bewildered loneliness. The God of the Negro was not an abstraction, an idea, or even just a promise. He was a personal, intimate God with whom a "little talk" could make things right. In His eyes the Negro had status— or so the colored people believed—and the tribulations that beset them were a sign of God's ultimate favor. In His own good time, He would humble the mighty, raise up the lowly, and strike a just balance between earthly suffering and heavenly reward. If this faith was naïve, it at least was the basis of those spiritual experiences out of which has come a wonderful music, up to now America's most distinctive contribution to the culture of the world.

3

But, after all, the Negro's religion was a withdrawal from reality. In a sense, his organized church was this too. Into both he could retire from the unequal competition of the material world. "You can take all *this* world, but give me Jesus," Negroes were fond of singing in their meetings; and actually the physical fact of the building of Negro churches was an exercise in renunciation. An undue proportion of the freemen's resources went into them. In Pennsylvania, New York and Massachusetts alone the value of Negro church property was well over half a million dollars by 1850. That this represented a considerable denial of the flesh cannot be doubted, and at least one Negro leader questioned the wisdom of such abnegation. "Howbeit, that was not first which is spiritual, but that which is natural," Frederick Douglass found an applicable quotation.

Nor was he the first to realize that religion alone was no impervious armour against the slings and arrows of the freemen's outrageous fortune. We have already seen that Prince Hall, the fraternal organizer, was interested in Negro education. Quakers, North and South, themselves pragmatically religious, had all along recognized the Negro's need for practical instruction, and they made education a regular part of the program of abolition. So active in the teaching of Negroes were the Quakers of Virginia that the law of the state excluded them from the teaching profession back in the seventeenth century. The Quakers of North Carolina were teaching the Negroes the three R's as early as 1731, and they continued to do so clandestinely even after the law forbade it. The instruction they gave was intended, as Benjamin Lay exhorted, "to bring up the Negroes to some Learning, Reading and Writing and the learning of some Honest Trade and Employment." A good many slaves who were hired out as mechanics had been taught by Quakers.

On the other hand, the literate Negro who was free was considered a menace in the South. Had not Denmark Vesey, the South Carolina revolutionary, got dangerous ideas about universal freedom and human equality from reading? Was not David Walker a compelling example of what the free Negro would do with his learning? John Chavis, educated, it is believed, at Princeton, was an exception that proved the rule. For a while, beginning in 1808, sons of the "best families" in North Carolina studied side by side with Negro boys in Chavis' school. When objections to this arose, Chavis did not demur, but opened "an evening school for the purpose of instructing children of Colour." Asked to discontinue this after a few months, again he did not demur. There was no use breasting the rising tide of opposition to the teaching of black freemen. Reading, writing and arithmetic were as dangerous in the heads of free Negroes as guns in the hands of slaves.

Nevertheless, the education of free Negroes went on in the South, though often in an unorganized, hit-and-miss fashion. The objection to it was only token in Baltimore, where a Negro church-sponsored school ran more or less openly. There were three Negro schools in the District of Columbia by 1807, and here, as in many other places, self-sacrificing whites taught in them and maintained them. In the

Gulf states area, Mississippi, Florida and Louisiana, it was not unusual for wealthy white fathers to send their mulatto children to be educated in France. New Orleans was the home of many of these, and around them grew up a distinct society on the French' pattern, devoting itself to literature and the arts as wealth and leisure allowed. This society did nothing of great creative moment, but its tradition contributed to the artistic development of Archibald Motley, the painter, and Richmond Barthe, the sculptor, both well-known today.

In the West and North there was no concentrated opposition to the education of Negroes. When the Negro Masonic Lodge of Boston petitioned the selectmen for a school for colored children, the selectmen moved almost at once. By the end of that year, 1796, such a school was founded. It was not free, nor the first, nor the best, as even Boston realized; but in 1820 the city opened a Negro school it could be proud of. Meanwhile the indefatigable Northern Quakers, who had started societies "for the Free Instruction of the Orderly Blacks and people of Color" in 1789, were still carrying on, and various non-Quaker groups and individuals carried on with them. Among them they established Negro schools in Wilmington, Delaware, Philadelphia, New York, New Haven and Portland. Their activity so prodded the sluggish consciences of Ohio, Indiana and Illinois as to stimulate these near-South states to make gestures in the direction of Negro education. Except in the African Free School in New York, instruction cost money, but it was carefully designed to meet the special needs of the pupils. Besides reading, writing and arithmetic, the girls were taught sewing and other domestic arts, the boys carpentry or kindred skills.

These educational experiences were a distinct benefit. Out of the gray and faceless mass slowly arose an articulate few—a greater few indeed than anyone had reason to expect—and they hurled their weight against the wall of slavery, against the degrading social concepts that also made a wall, and against the indifference that so many good men were subject to. This articulateness came out especially in the conventions which free Northern Negroes held intermittently from 1817 to 1850 and after the latter date almost yearly down to the Civil War. From the platforms of these meetings they spoke their minds on such subjects as African colonization (in opposition to which the first convention was called), slavery, of course, Negro suffrage, legislation, moral reform and education. Such leaders as James McCune Smith, John Vashon, James Forten, James Purvis, Martin Delany and Frederick Douglass found in them their largest Negro audiences. Increasingly also they found whites. S. S. Jocelyn, the Tappan brothers and Gerrit Smith seldom failed to attend a Negro people's convention after 1828, and William Lloyd Garrison was led to abandon the cause of African colonization by what he learned at the National Negro Convention in Philadelphia in 1831.

Negroes were getting and using training in other ways too. Though a rough, stumbling literacy was sufficient qualification to speak for the anti-slavery societies, once connected with such an organization, the Negro was likely to find it, as Maria Weston said, common school and high school and university. Ambitious graduates of the Anti-Slavery Society platforms became orators, lawyers, authors, editors. Writing and editing seemed to be the goal of a disproportionate number of free Negroes, and perhaps the reason for this was not far to seek. Frederick Douglass held that "a tolerably well conducted press in the hands of persons of the despised race would, by calling out and making them acquainted with their own latent powers, by enkindling their hope of a future, and developing their moral force, prove a most powerful means of removing prejudice and awakening an interest in them."

At any rate, *Freedom's Journal,* the first Negro newspaper, was not long alone in the field. More than a dozen Negro newspapers lived and died in the years between 1827 and 1850. Most of these were published along the Atlantic seaboard, where the free Negroes were concentrated, but Pittsburgh, Cleveland, Cincinnati and San Francisco could boast short-lived papers. None of them had the quality or influence of *Frederick Douglass' Paper,* but, like it, they kept the "anti-slavery banner flying" and had as their objective the "moral, social and political improvement of the free colored people."

If their newspapers were for their improvement, the books that many Negroes wrote were for something else again. A goodly number of the "slave narratives" can be discounted, either because they are pure fiction or because, edited by overzealous abolitionists, they stray willfully into polemics. What remains, however, is a body of writing meaty with human experiences, redolent of the American earth, innocent of tricks and clean with truth. Letters, history, fiction, essays, drama, biography and autobiography—more than a hundred titles in more than a half dozen categories appeared between 1810 and 1860.

Most of these works have, as they ought, the naïve directness of true folk stuff. For all of its unfortunate overcast of factual misrepresentation, *Father Henson's Story,* by that Josiah Henson who was the model for Uncle Tom, is one of these. So are the first two autobiographical works of William Wells Brown, the *Narrative* of Frederick Douglass, and those episodes of her life told by Harriet Tubman to Mrs. Sarah H. Bradford. Other books, like Douglass' *My Bondage and My Freedom,* Jermain W. Loguen's *Life,* Brown's *The Rising Son* and William Nell's *Colored Patriots of the American Revolution,* attempt to evaluate the Negro's place in American history and the American culture. Still others are works of creative imagination, for which Negro writers had a tradition going back to Phillis Wheatley and Jupiter Hammon and continuing through the North Carolina slave, George Moses Horton. The first Negro novel, *Clotel; or The President's Daughter,* and the first Negro play, *The Escape; or a Leap for Freedom,* both by W. W. Brown, may be worth very little as literary art, but they help make up the sum of those abilities and achievements which the popular race concept denied.

And this was perhaps the real significance of the lives of many free Negroes.

The labors for the anti-slavery organizations in which dozens spent their native energies could just as well have been done by others. There were enough exhibits A, enough impassioned orators, enough daring conductors on the Underground Railroad. Instead of debilitating himself in a cause already sufficiently manned, John Russworm, the first Negro graduate of an American college (Bowdoin, 1825), would have served his people better had he used his talents in another direction. The brilliant graduate in medicine from the University of Glasgow, James McCune Smith, might have been a distinguished medical practitioner and a pioneer actuary had he followed up his research on the *Influence of Climate on Longevity, with Special Reference to Life Insurance.* Martin Delany, graduate of Harvard Medical School, J. W. C. Pennington, honored by the University of Heidelberg with a Doctor of Divinity, Charles Reason, a professor of belles-lettres at white Central College in New York state, might have added immeasurably to the estimation in which

Negroes were held if the work for which they were trained had not been incidental to the "cause" which racked their minds.

4

But the cause was winning—not so much perhaps through the strength of its adherents as because of the weakness of slavery and the slave oligarchy. That this weakness was apparent only to the most perspicacious is understandable. With the election of James Buchanan in 1856, the South had actually chosen eleven of the country's sixteen Presidents. Of twenty-eight Supreme Court justices, seventeen had been Southerners. The South had long held dominance in Congress. The Compromise of 1850 and the Kansas-Nebraska Act of 1854 were superbly engineered borings to new sources of political and material power. The Dred Scott Decision seemed a stranglehold on Negro freedom. The beautiful but futile heroics of John Brown, his sons and his Negro followers at Harpers Ferry, though they moved to wonder and admiration, increased the conservative North's fears of radical abolition. Not a few Southern papers noted that the suppression of Brown's revolt was the work of a Southern-born army officer, Colonel Robert E. Lee. The United States Army and Navy too were dominated by Southerners.

All this was apparent, though actually this was only seeming strength. Weakness was shown, in the first place, by the very galvanic desperation with which the South had pushed for Clay's Compromise and the Kansas-Nebraska Act. Moreover, the passage of this latter measure robbed Southern Whigs of the necessary support of Northern party members. By the end of 1854, the Whig Party was so moribund that two new parties, the Know-Nothing and the Republican, could rise like new suns on the horizon. The "course of empire" drifted westward, inevitably drawing off Southern manpower and resources. Westering railroads helped this process. Forecasts of the congressional apportionment of 1856 indicated a loss to the South of no less than six congressional seats. Though it seemed to recover quickly after the panic of 1857, the South was on the road to economic ruin. Her credit was overextended, she supported a staggering imbalance in trade, and every year found more and more cotton land unfit for cultivation.

Morally and spiritually, the South had been fatally stricken since the Revolution. The effect of the psychological factors in slavery upon Southerners is incalculable, but certainly these factors were as responsible as the economic ones for the creation of that tragic class known as "poor whites." As for the masters, slavery "tended to inflate the ego of most planters beyond all reason; they became arrogant, strutting, quarrelsome knights; they issued commands; they made laws; they shouted their orders; they expected deference and self-abasement; they were choleric and easily insulted. Their 'honor' became a vast and awful thing, requiring wide and insistent deference." [4]

These were the qualities of heart and mind that made the epithet "Hotspurs" so appropriate to men like Jefferson Davis, of Mississippi; William Miles and Milledge Bonham, of South Carolina; Howell Cobb, of Georgia; and the drunken and lecherous Louis Wigfall, of Texas. These were the uncontrolled emotional impulses that led South Carolina to secede in December, 1860, and Mississippi, Alabama, Florida and Louisiana to follow a few weeks later. Aroused by the activities of the Knights of the Golden Circle and prodded by Robert Toombs, Georgia voters, too, threw in on the side of the rebels. Demoniacal pride, hypersensitiveness and rash behavior were symptoms of the psychic trauma that made civil war inevitable. And when old Edwin Ruffin—as fine a study of arrogant madness as ever convulsed the world—fired on Fort Sumter, war came.

8

"—AND FOREVER FREE"

● ●

THERE WAS CONFUSION, and it was ideological. Abraham Lincoln at first did nothing to clarify matters. A national figure since the famous debates with Stephen A. Douglas, he had declared that "a house divided against itself cannot stand. I believe this government cannot endure . . . half slave and half free." But also he had admitted that even if all earthly power were granted him, he "should not know what to do as to the existing institution" of slavery. This admission had been generally overlooked by the time he reached Washington.

His first inaugural address was cautious and conciliatory and satis-fied almost no one. When it was made, seven states had already seceded and formed a Southern Confederacy, whose emissaries, en-couraged by the outgoing Buchanan, were even then at the nation's capitol prepared to negotiate economic treaties with the United States. No matter what Lincoln said, or did not say, the South had driven too far along her course to turn back. Plain Northern Repub-licans simply waited; but Frederick Douglass stated the attitude of the abolitionists when he confessed "to a feeling allied to satisfaction at the prospect of a conflict between the North and the South."

A conflict of arms was exactly what the patient Lincoln wanted to avoid. It was evident also that he followed the wishes of the generality in the North by trying to shun slavery as an issue. But an issue it was. The South made it so. Alexander H. Stephens, Vice President of the Confederacy, set it forth in unequivocal terms. "The new Constitution [of the Confederacy]," he said, "has put at rest forever all the agitating questions relating to our peculiar institution —African slavery as it exists among us—the proper status of the Negro in our form of civilization. This was the immediate cause of the late rupture and the present revolution." And in Montgomery, Alabama, the impassioned rebels were telling their government that unless they "sprinkled blood in the face of the people. . . . they [the people of the South] will be back in the old Union in less than ten days."

Certainly this was Lincoln's hope. But the Southern Hotspurs killed it. When Major Anderson refused to surrender Sumter, General Beauregard ordered the fort reduced. The reluctant Lincoln had no choice but to declare the Confederacy in a state of rebellion and to call for seventy-five thousand "three months' men" to put it down.

If up to this time the President's policy was wavering and muddy, he now gave it resolution and clarity. He would save the Union. In July, 1861, the United States Senate averred that "this war is not prosecuted upon our part. . . . [with] the purpose of overthrowing or interfering with the rights or established institutions of those [rebellious] States, but to defend and maintain the supremacy of the Constitution. . . . to preserve the Union, with all dignity, equality, and rights of the several states unimpaired; that as soon as these objects are accomplished the war ought to cease."

They were objects toward the accomplishment of which nearly all elements of the North and West could unite, for as these two sections saw it, slavery was an extremely peripheral matter. A popular jingle of the time expressed the attitude that was current above the Mason-Dixon line and west of the Ohio River:

> To the flag we are pledged, all its foes we abhor,
> And we ain't for the nigger, but we are for the war.

They were for the war because keeping the Union whole made for the certainty of markets, the stabilization of trade and the assurance of profits.

On the other hand, the Confederacy seemed not to worry overmuch about the severance of economic ties with the North. The South was certain that the North needed her and that within "six months at the most" the North would sue for peace on the Confederacy's own terms. Moreover, the South was convinced that foreign markets— and especially English markets—would support her economy, even through war.

Though President Lincoln must have known that the result of the war necessarily would be either the complete abolishment of slavery or the affirmation of slavery's right to remain and spread, he continued to try to steer a middle course, at least until 1862.

Meantime, the progress of the war was inexorably forcing his hand. Some of the country's most daring and expert soldiers, among them Robert E. Lee and Joseph E. Johnston, had resigned their federal commissions to fight on the side of the South. Fifty thousand Southerners had been mobilized and issued quantities of arms seized by the rebels from United States arsenals. Southern diplomats were in Europe trying to wheedle support for the Confederacy. Virginia, North Carolina, Tennessee and Arkansas—states that had wavered between loyalty to the Union and adherence to the South—had thrown in their lot with the latter.

Realizing their tremendous stake in the outcome, Negroes presented themselves for military service with the North. They asked for a modification of the law so that they might be permitted to fight. The denial of this privilege was ironic. Having fought the Revolutionary War for the white man's liberty, Negroes could not now fight for their own. But they were persistent in their efforts. They importuned the War Department. In New York they formed a military club and studied the Manual of Arms and drilled until the police disbanded them. Frederick Douglass sought permission to recruit a Negro regiment. Such friends of freedom as Horace Greeley, William Lloyd Garrison, Charles Sumner and Moncure Conway urged upon the President a commitment to the use of Negro troops. They went further: they urged that he commit himself to emancipation. But Lincoln demurred, and stubbornly. Even in the face of realities, which, had they been boldly exploited, might have shortened the war, he continued to demur.

2

One of these realities was the disaffection of the slaves. The South counted on the slaves for manpower in field and factory and, if need be, in actual battle. One Southern editor boasted that the "institution of slavery in the South alone enables her to place in the field a force much larger in proportion to her white population than the North, or indeed any country which is dependent entirely upon free labor. The institution is a tower of strength to the South, par-

ticularly at the present crisis . . . [and] is really one of the most
effective weapons employed against the Union by the South."

But this "tower of strength" was built on a foundation of sand.
True, some slaves remained loyal, "but," even a Southern historian [1]
has admitted, "in the light of contemporary evidence, [they] must be
considered exceptional." Measures had to be instituted for holding
slaves in line. Slave patrols were increased; slave codes were given
added stringency. To keep slaves from escaping, masters drove them
deep into the back country, far from battle lines. The Confederacy
passed the "Twenty-Negro" law, exempting one white man for every
twenty slaves on a plantation. Most of the Southern states had slave
impressment laws by 1862, and in 1863 the Confederate government
passed a general impressment law.

For the truth of the matter was that slaves were escaping in greater
numbers than ever. They were escaping to the Union lines, at a
cost, estimated for North Carolina alone, of a million dollars a
week. This, of course, was to the North's advantage, although the
Commander-in-Chief and many of his officers in the field did not
seem to realize it. Union Officers regularly relinquished absconded
slaves to importunate masters. The historian, George W. Williams,
cites an address delivered to the people of Virginia by a Union officer.
"I desire to assure you," said Colonel Pryor in the first months of
the war, "that the relation of master and servant as recognized in
your state shall be respected. Your authority over that species of
property shall not in the least be interfered with. To this end I assure
you that those under my command have peremptory orders to take
up and hold any Negroes found running about the camp without
passes from their masters." [2]

Whether dictated out of deference to proprietary rights or by a
sense of military chivalry, it was a stupid policy under the circumstances. Yet Sherman, Hooker and Burnside all followed it.

General Benjamin ("Peg-leg," the Negroes called him) Butler was
more realistic. He did not have to be told that the South was employing slaves as laborers on military fortifications, as cooks, as carriers of supplies and in other military capacities. Even had he not
known this, he was too intelligent not to see that so long as the
Confederacy kept them under control, the slaves would be an over-
balancing advantage to the South in a protracted war. Behind his
lines, idle, without any organized means of sustenance, ragged,

hungry, homeless, they were a nuisance as they were. Why should he not use them? Since there was no certain policy, General Butler determined to force one. "Are these men, women and children slaves?" he demanded of the Secretary of War. "Are they free? Is their condition that of men, women and children, or of property, or is it a mixed relation?" Without waiting for an answer, he declared fugitive slaves contraband of war and put them to work in the Union cause. Simon Cameron upheld him. "Persons held by rebels, under such laws, to service as slaves, may, however, be justly liberated from their constraint, and made more valuable in various employments, through voluntary and compensated service, than if confiscated as subjects of property."

By means of the slave grapevine, the word got around, and slaves flocked to the Union lines in such numbers that Georgia called upon the Confederate authorities "to halt in some way the flight of property worth from $12,000,000 to $15,000,000."

The sanctuary which these thousands of fleeing blacks sought was not always sure.

Often the slaves met prejudices against their color more bitter than any they had left behind. . . . Their condition was appalling. There were men, women and children in every stage of disease or decrepitude, often nearly naked, with flesh torn by the terrible experiences of their escape. Sometimes they were intelligent and eager to help themselves; often they were bewildered or stupid or possessed by the wildest notions of what liberty might mean—expecting to exchange labor and obedience to the will of another, for idleness and freedom from restraint. Such ignorance and perverted opinions produced a veritable moral chaos. Cringing deceit, theft, licentiousness—all the vices which slavery inevitably fosters—were hideous companions of nakedness, famine, and diseases. A few had profited by the misfortunes of the master and were jubilant in their unwonted ease and luxury, but these stood in lurid contrast to the grimmer aspects of the tragedy—the woman in travail, the helplessness of childhood and of old age, the horrors of sickness and of frequent death. Small wonder that men paused in bewilderment and panic, foreseeing the demoralization and infection of the Union soldier and the downfall of the Union cause.[3]

What to do with these refugees was the question, but there was no standardized answer. Union commanders, who were of all shades of opinion and of all degrees of feeling from indifference to good will, did whatever expediency seemed to require or attitude to dictate. In Missouri, General Frémont issued a decree abolishing slavery; but Halleck, who followed him there, permitted no fugitives within or behind his lines. General McClellan was also adamant on this point, and, farther, forbade the Army of the Potomac to sing "John Brown's Body."

Reports of the suffering of refugees aroused humanitarian groups in the North and West. Societies for the relief of freedmen sprung up everywhere. By the fall of 1861, the American Missionary Association had sent agents to administer relief behind the Union lines in the peninsula area of Virginia and in South Carolina. The Society of Friends, the Western Freedmen's Commission of Cincinnati, the Women's Aid Association of Philadelphia, the National Freedmen's Relief Association solicited funds and sent representatives—teachers and social workers—south, where at last far-seeing officers like Grant, Hunter and Saxton were organizing freedmen for the cultivation of abandoned lands, the harvesting of cotton and rice, and the raising of crops to feed themselves and the Union armies. By 1863, the former slaves, "catching a learning" between hours of labor, were considered indispensable to a Union victory.

3

The blacks were to give more than labor and sweat. Their brothers in the North, though discouraged by the attitude of official Washington, chafed to be on the field of battle. Abolitionists pressed for the enlistment of Negroes as a recognition of the cause of freedom. British workmen, led by Karl Marx, pressed. However, Lincoln felt that he could not listen. The border states were edgy. An indication that the war was for the purpose of freeing the slaves would surely have decided Maryland, Missouri and Kentucky for the Confederacy. As Lincoln saw it, this would spell the Union's doom. So he could not be moved when Frederick Douglass reproached him and the North that "they fought with one hand, while they might strike more effectively with two; that they fought with the soft white hand, while they kept the black iron hand chained and helpless behind them; that they fought the effect, while they protected the cause."

But the necessitous day was dawning. Rebel arms were doing all that they boasted, more than they dared—and with an audacity that was maddening. Moreover, the South enlisted black men early. That these troops did no important fighting early or late is beside the point. Wearing the gray and bearing the Stars and Bars of the Confederacy, 1,400 free colored men of the South passed in review before Southern officers in a parade in New Orleans in 1861. Other thousands armed with hoes and mattocks and pruning hooks labored in Dixie's fields so that whites might go into battle.

The pressure to make use of Negroes was slowly building up. Down in South Carolina, General David Hunter felt it and responded. Wrestling with a mission he lacked the forces to accomplish, his repeated requests for more troops brought the repeated answer that he must do with what he had. General Hunter lost patience. In defiance of his superiors in Washington, he organized a regiment of ex-slaves in the spring of 1862. "They are sober, docile, attentive, and enthusiastic," he reported; "displaying great natural capacities in acquiring the duties of the soldier. They are now eager beyond all things to take the field and be led into action." But the General was ordered to disband them.

Meanwhile, the free Negro in the North was finding the competition with whites for jobs intensified. White labor was restive, and this restiveness was encouraged by a part of the press that was hostile to Lincoln and prejudiced against Negroes. All the elements in a nasty situation were quite apparent. Irish and German immigrant laborers were warned that Negroes accepted lower wages—which they did; that Negroes broke strikes—which they did; that Negroes were replacing white men—which they were. If Negroes were emancipated, as rumor had it they were bound to be, then the economic security that white labor had struggled to obtain would be further jeopardized by waves of freed blacks seeking homes, seeking jobs. And if the ultimate goal of the war *was* emancipation, as the radicals were saying it most certainly was, then it was a "niggers' war" and the "niggers" should be made to fight it.

The surface swellings, which broke out in street brawls between Negroes and whites, were poulticed here and there, but the corruption was not drained off and it built up like gangrenous matter in a wound. When, in 1863, President Lincoln signed a draft law which exempted the rich, the working class whites turned in fury on the only creatures more defenseless than themselves. A whole Negro section of Detroit was ravaged and burned. In Cleveland, a hundred blacks, including women and children, were killed. A wave of race hate rolled on for four days in New York, consumed a Negro orphanage, drove five thousand Negroes from their jobs and homes, and left many score dead.

And Southern daring meanwhile and all the while was winning battles. Employing the lightning fast raid, rebel troops were darting and zigzagging northward over roads that seemed to lead to victory. Rebel ships found holes in the federal blockade. Rebel spies were everywhere active. In proportion as the rebel arms were effective, the will to victory in the North grew weaker. Indeed, a large and influential section of the North wanted peace, peace even on the South's own terms. Horatio Seymour, Governor of New York, was one of the spokesmen for this point of view; so was Franklin Pierce, ex-President of the United States; so was the publicist James Gordon Bennett. Faction-ridden, emotionally divided, what the Union needed was some audacity of its own, some bold stratagem, at once political and military. The drafting of the Emancipation Proclamation was a poor excuse for this. It was like a telegraphed blow to a boxer.

As early as 1861 Lincoln had begun to talk of emancipating and colonizing slaves, paying a reasonable indemnity to their owners. By 1862 he had advanced this idea so far as actually to send a shipload of ex-slaves to Ile à Vache, off the coast of Haiti. That same year he abolished slavery in the District of Columbia and in the territories. No one was surprised, then, when a general emancipation proclamation was drafted and issued in September, 1862. But no one was really pleased either. It decreed "that on the first day of January in the year of our Lord, one thousand eight hundred and sixty-three, all persons held as slaves within any state, or designated part of a state, the people whereof shall then be in rebellion . . . shall be then, thenceforward, and forever free."

The reason for the South's displeasure of course was obvious, but why should Garrison in the North warn the abolitionists that their work was "still to impeach, censure, and condemn"? Why should Frederick Douglass be disappointed? Because they saw the "one hundred days of grace" as a loophole through which slavery could slip practically untouched. What, for instance, if the war ended in October, or November, or at midnight on the twenty-ninth of December? What was to prevent the rebellious states from coming to heel within those three months and thus, no longer under interdiction, keep their slaves? Why had the slaveholding states still in the Union

—Maryland, West Virginia, Kentucky and Missouri—been excluded from the terms of the proclamation?

The Negroes and the abolitionists in the North lived through those three months like people in a beleaguered camp, awaiting doom or deliverance. The suspense was unbearable. On New Year's Eve there was scarcely a Negro church or lodge hall but that it was crammed with those who had much to hope and pray for. Many who gathered were themselves escaped slaves. Many more had relatives still in chains. All night they watched and waited, and the next day, when the proclamation freed three million slaves, repressed feelings exploded in a swelling chorus of jubilation. Old and young, white, cheek by jowl, with black, marched in triumph through the frost-ringing streets of Philadelphia, New York, Cincinnati, Cleveland. Boston's Music Hall was packed far beyond the limits of safety. So was Tremont Temple. In the one, a chorus of one hundred voices sang Mendelssohn's "Hymn of Praise" and Handel's "Hallelujah Chorus" and Oliver Wendell Holmes' "Army Hymn." Ralph Waldo Emerson recited his "Boston Hymn." In the other, other Brahmins joined with ex-slaves to cheer the absent Abraham Lincoln, the weeping William Lloyd Garrison, who sat in the balcony. Frederick Douglass led the singing of

> Blow ye the trumpets, blow . . . the year of jubilee has come. . . .

And it had come for some slaves in the fields too.

"A Yankee soldier tole somebody in Williamsburg dat Marse Lincum done signed de Mancipation. Was winter time an' moughty cold dat night, but ev'ybody commences gittin' ready to leave. Didn't care nothin' 'bout Missus—was goin' to de Union lines. An' all dat night de niggers danced an' sang right out in de cold. Nex' morning at daybreak we all started out wid blankets an' clothes an' pots an' pans an' chickens piled on our backs, 'cause Missus said we couldn't take no horses or carts. An' as de sun come over de trees de niggers all started singin':

> 'Sun, you be here an' I'll be gone,
> Sun, you be here an' I'll be gone,
> Sun, you be here an' I'll be gone,
> Bye, bye, don't grieve arter me.

> 'Won't give you my place, not fo' your'n,
> Bye, bye, don't grieve arter me;

'Cause you be here an' I'll be gone,
Bye, bye, don't grieve arter me.' " [4]

But all slaves could not sing "I'll Be Gone." Hundreds of thousands of them in areas far removed from the fighting did not know of the proclamation for many months; some for three years.

4

The proclamation provided for the admission of Negroes into the Union Army. Oddly enough, whereas Negroes not fighting had been the cause of much bitterness in the North, the decision to permit them to enlist aroused an equal bitterness. James Gordon Bennett saw the recruitment of Negroes as "a pretty fair start for miscegenation," that prime bugaboo. Hundreds of white men were said to be deserting from the Army, thus giving some validity to the opinion that white men would not serve on the same footing as Negroes. Another opinion was that ex-slaves could not be made into soldiers; that they could not or would not fight. The parts that Negroes had played in the Revolutionary War and in the War of 1812 were forgotten.

Negroes mustered in, even though their pay was seven dollars a month to the white soldiers' thirteen. Recruiting in Massachusetts for a regiment of Negroes, Frederick Douglass harangued them: "Men of Color, to Arms! . . . I have implored the imperiled nation to unchain against her foes her powerful black hand. Slowly and reluctantly that appeal is beginning to be heeded. Stop not now to complain that it was not heeded sooner. . . . Action! Action! not criticism, is the plain duty of this hour. . . . From East to West, from North to South, the sky is written all over, 'Now or Never!' Liberty won only by white men will lose half its lustre. 'Who would be free must themselves strike the blow.' "

If it was Lincoln's hope that, as Karl Marx had said, a single regiment of Negro soldiers in Union arms would have a shattering effect upon the South, he was mistaken. The Confederates were psychologically prepared—had, in actual fact, anticipated the Union. In the month before the Emancipation Proclamation went into effect, Jefferson Davis ordered that all Northern officers captured in command of Negro troops should be put to death and that "all Negro slaves captured in arms be at once delivered over to the executive authorities of the respective states to which they belonged and be dealt with according to the laws of said States." In every case the penalty for rebellion was death—and bearing arms for the Union was rebellion, as the South viewed it.

The record does not show that this countering policy slowed down Negro enlistment. From the slave states 125,000 Negroes took up arms for their freedom; the North supplied 80,000 more. The record does not show either that the discrimination practiced by the Union Army sapped the morale of Negro troops. The 54th Massachusetts Regiment, under the famous Colonel Robert Gould Shaw, went a year without pay in protest against the wage differential—but it served, and suffered. It was literally annihilated in the assault on Fort Wagner.

Wagner loomed, black, grim and silent. There was no glimmer of light. Nevertheless, in the fort, down below the level of the tide, and under the roofs made by huge trunks of trees, lay two thousand Confederate soldiers hidden. . . . Behind the 54th came five regiments from Connecticut, New York, New Hampshire, Pennsylvania and Maine. The mass went quickly and silently in the night. Then, suddenly, the walls of the fort burst with a blinding sheet of vivid light. Shot, shells of iron and bullets crushed through the dense masses of the attacking force. I shall never forget the terrible sound of that awful blast of death which swept down, battered or dead, a thousand of our men. Not a shot missed its aim. . . .

The column wavered and recovered itself. They reached the ditch before the fort. They climbed on the ramparts and swarmed over the walls. It looked as though the fort was captured. Then there came another blinding blaze from concealed guns in the rear of the fort, and the men went down by scores. The rebels rallied, and were reinforced by thousands of others, who had landed on the beach in the darkness unseen by the fleet. . . . The struggle was terrific. . . . Our men rallied again, but were forced back to the edge of the ditch. Colonel Shaw, with scores of his black fighters, went down struggling desperately. Resistance was vain. The assailants were forced back to the beach, and the rebels drilled their recovered cannon on the remaining survivors.[5]

The next day, the Confederate commander sent word of Colonel Shaw: "We have buried him with his niggers."

Negro troops fought at Port Hudson, at the Battle of Nashville and at Millikens Bend. The mad massacre they suffered at Fort Pillow brought shame to Southern arms. When the Confederate

troops under General Forrest compelled the surrender of the outnumbered Union force, no Negro prisoners were taken. Disarmed, they
were shot, bludgeoned to death, bayoneted, burned alive, crucified.
So flagrant was the cruelty inflicted on Negro soldiers that Frederick
Douglass urged President Lincoln to retaliate. If Jefferson Davis
shoots or hangs colored soldiers "in cold blood," Douglass said, "the
United States government should, without delay, retaliate in kind
and decree death upon Confederate soldiers in its hands as prisoners."
But Lincoln thought it a "terrible remedy, and one . . . difficult to
apply." Only after repeated protests did Jefferson Davis agree, in
1864, that Negro soldiers were to be treated as prisoners of war.

Before the end, Negro troops fought in every theatre and under
almost every command. They served as spies and scouts, slithering
back and forth through the Confederate lines with a wiliness born
of slavery and their knowledge of the countryside. According to the
record, acknowledged by the Provost Marshal General to be in-
complete, 36,847 Negro soldiers died in battle and of disease. This
figure represents a ratio half again as large as that for white United
States volunteer troops. On one of many desperate days before the
close of the war, Lincoln declared: "Abandon all the posts now gar-
risoned by black men; take two hundred thousand men from our
side and put them in the battlefield or cornfield against us, and we
would be compelled to abandon the war in three weeks."

No one knew this better than the Confederate generals. But the
South was faced with a problem in metaphysics and pride. Many
slaves and free Negroes had been pressed into menial services with
the rebels, and some of these were even permitted to wear the Confederate gray. But to put guns in their hands! To declare some black
men free to die in battles fought that other black men might remain
forever slaves! Still, there were those who urged just this, who saw
as the alternative a defeat so utter that no small rag of pride would
remain to flutter in the winds of memory. The Confederate Secretary
of War was bombarded with letters. Generals in the field wrote him.
Governor Allen of Louisiana wrote: "Put into the [Confederate]
army every able-bodied Negro as a soldier!" Jefferson Davis opposed
the idea at first. The impressment of forty thousand Negroes as
menials, yes; but as soldiers—why that "would be scarcely deemed
wise or advantageous by any."

But the necessitous day was dawning for the Confederacy too. It was heralded in the defeats of the summer and fall of 1863. Lee was routed from Gettysburg. Vicksburg fell to Grant, Port Hudson to General Banks, and in December the rebels were blasted out of Nashville. That year there were fifty thousand desertions from the Confederate Army. "We should away with pride of opinion," stormed Sam Clayton of Georgia, "away with false pride, and promptly take hold of all the means God has placed within our reach to help us through this struggle. . . . Some people say that Negroes will not fight. I say they will fight. They fought at Ocean Pond, Honey Hill and other places. The enemy fights us with Negroes, and they will do very well to fight the Yankees."

Tennessee, Georgia and Louisiana called Negroes to arms, and both the Carolinas and Mississippi resolved to do so. In January, 1865, General Robert E. Lee wrote to the Confederate Senate through Andrew Hunter, one of its members:

We should not expect slaves to fight for prospective freedom when they can secure it at once by going to the enemy, in whose service they will incur no greater risk than in ours. The reasons that induce me to recommend the employment of Negro troops at all render the effect of the measures I have suggested upon slavery immaterial, and in my opinion the best means of securing the efficiency and fidelity of this auxiliary force would be to accompany the measure with a well-digested plan of gradual and general emancipation. As that will be the result of the continuance of the war, and will certainly occur if the enemy succeeds, it seems to me most advisable to do it at once, and thereby obtain all the benefits that will accrue to our cause.[6]

In March, the Confederate Congress passed an act calling for the recruitment of three hundred thousand blacks, with each state supplying a quota not to exceed twenty-five per cent of the male slaves.

But time was far gone. Grant's siege of Richmond was fulfilling its intended purpose. Richmond and Petersburg were evacuated by the rebels on the night of April second. The government fled to Danville. President Lincoln entered the former capital of the South on April fourth. Meantime the Army of the Potomac was chasing Lee through the foothills of Virginia. Sailors Creek was fought and won on April sixth. Three days later, at Appomattox, Lee, outmanned, outwitted, outstayed, surrendered.

Curiously enough, the last skirmish of the war came a month later at Palmetto Ranch, Texas, and it was fought by Negroes.

"The 62nd United States Colored Infantry, in this fight, probably fired the last angry volley of the war, and Sergeant Crocket of that regiment (three days after Jefferson Davis's capture) received the last wound from a rebel hostile bullet, and hence shed the last fresh blood in the war resulting in the freedom of his race in the United States. The observation irresistibly comes, that on the scene of the first battle of the Mexican War—a war inaugurated for the acquisition of slave territory—and of the *first* battle participated in by Lieutenant-General (then Second Lieutenant) U. S. Grant, almost exactly nineteen years later, the last conflict took place in the war for the preservation of the Union, and in which slavery was totally overthrown in our Republic." [7]

So finally the military phase of the war was over, but peace had not come. One issue was settled clearly: states could not secede from the Union. All else was confused. There was the Thirteenth Amendment, hailed with bonfires and with cannonade in 1864, giving freedom to the slaves; but freedom was no fact. And what to do with the four million blacks suddenly thrown resourceless into the body politic? Peonage and tenantry, said the South. Land and the ballot, said the North. And what to do with the rebellious states? Treat them with moderation, Lincoln had early urged, outlining his reconstruction policy, under the provisions of which Louisiana was already back in the Union. Lincoln knew that the South faced the heartbreaking difficulty of rebuilding her entire economy, of adjusting to a new and unwanted way of life. The North faced the equally difficult duty of making victory a ministrant to peace, of "binding up the nation's wounds."

"The sun will rise," a statesman said, but with Lincoln's death a few days later, the sun seemed to have set forever.

Part Two

9

THE WHITE

●●

LINCOLN HAD FELT his anguished way to a benign policy of Southern reconstruction through a forest dark with political hazard and clamorous with bitter complainings. At first he seemed to think that the chief problem in the South could be solved by logistics. Transport the Negroes, he had said, to some place that would be their own. In 1862 he advised a committee of Negroes that between black and white there was a "broader difference than exists between almost any other races. . . . Your race suffers very greatly, many of them, by living among us, while ours suffers from your presence [and] this affords a reason why we should be separated." He believed that North and South could not live in peace until the country was "rid of Negroes."

That same year, he sponsored a bill in the House calling for $200,000,000 to purchase and colonize a half million border-state slaves. A few months later he engaged with an adventurer to begin the work of transporting and transplanting freed Negroes. Though this practical-seeming approach was so unrealistic as to indicate an aberration, Lincoln harbored it all through the war. Not until General Ben Butler pointed out the complete and simple impossibility of it did Lincoln give it up.

By that time he had begun an approach to the problem from another side. As the rebellious states fell one after another before the onslaughts of Sheridan, Sherman and Grant, Lincoln set up temporary military authority in each of them. The plan which he outlined to Congress in 1863 called for the replacement of this military by civil authority so soon as in each state one tenth of the number of citizens who had voted in 1860 swore allegiance to the United States. But—and the stipulation was important—formal recognition would not come until the state had made constitutional provisions for the Negroes' freedom. Lincoln had no thought of indiscriminately enfranchising the freedmen. He did not believe that the Negro was ready for the ballot—and he was right. The great unlettered mass of Negroes could not have distinguished between a ballot and a billet-doux. But in a letter to the reconstructed Governor Allen, of Louisiana, the President expressed the hope that some Negroes, "as, for instance, the very intelligent," would be given the vote.

Lincoln's private hopes, however, seemed to run counter to his published policy, and groups of immoderates in the North were far from satisfied. There were powerful men in Washington and north of it who, for a variety of reasons, wished to see the South utterly prostrate. Some wished to see the South made safe for Republicanism. Others wished to exploit her—land for railroads, cheap industrial sites, cheap labor. Still others, moved perhaps by basically humanitarian reasons, but mistaking vengeance for justice, simply thought it right that the South should pay for two centuries of unspeakable cruelty to slaves. The tempers of all these factions came out on the floor of Congress. The President's reconstruction plan met opposition. There was a bitter fight between Lincoln and Congress over the Wade-Davis Bill, which made more stringent the qualifications for a state's reentry into the Union. This bill did not provide for Negro suffrage either, but to many it was better than anything yet proposed, and even Charles Sumner, certainly no moderate, finally voted for it.

The free Negroes of the North were shocked. Since the beginning of the war, Frederick Douglass had preached that there "was no chance of bettering the condition of the freedman, until he should cease to be merely a freedman and should become a citizen." Now he declared that "if the Negro knows enough to fight for his country, he knows enough to vote." Northern Negroes backed this view at a great convention held in Syracuse, New York, in the fall of 1864. All the Negro leaders were there—Jonathan Gibbs, who was later Secretary of State and Superintendent of Education in reconstructed Florida, Henry Highland Garnet, Dr. William McCune Smith, George T. Downing, Peter H. Clark—but Douglass dominated it. The resolution drawn up was largely in his words.

The weakness of our friends is strength to our foes. When the *Anti-Slavery Standard,* representing the American Anti-Slavery Society, denies that the Society asks for enfranchisement of colored men, and the *Liberator* apologizes for excluding colored men of Louisiana from the ballot-box, they injure us more vitally than all the ribald jests of the whole pro-slavery press. . . . Do you, then, ask us to state in plain terms, just what we want of you, and just what we think we ought to receive at your hands? . . .

We want the elective franchise in all the states now in the Union, and the same in all such states as may come into the Union hereafter. We believe that the highest welfare of this country will be found in erasing from its statute-books all enactments discriminatory in favor or against any class of its people, and by establishing one law for the white and colored people alike. . . .

We may conquer Southern armies by the sword; but it is another thing to conquer Southern hate. Now what is the natural counterpoise against this Southern malign hostility? This is it: give the elective franchise to every colored man of the South who is of sane mind, and has arrived at the age of twenty-one years, and you have at once four millions of friends who will guard with their vigilance, and if need be, defend with their arms, the ark of Federal Liberty from the treason and pollution of her enemies. You are sure of the enmity of the masters,—make sure of the friendship of the slaves; for, depend upon it, your Government cannot afford to encounter the enmity of both.[1]

But there was stubbornness as well as native charity and wisdom in Lincoln, and he held on to moderation.

Thus things rocked along through the war years. Having freed the slave, his jobless, homeless, landless status was a burden and a hindrance, and the government was obliged to provide for him. Various types of land allotment and work relief were tried under a number of departments. In spite of administrative confusion and the absence of a coordinated policy, the results were often heartening. These efforts were gradually consolidated, and in 1865 the Bureau of Refugees, Freedmen and Abandoned Lands, generally known as the Freedmen's Bureau, took over.

What it took over was no game of tiddlywinks. Indeed, the bureau itself came into being over the opposition of those who did not want to see the government foot the bill; of those who feared that the bureau would tempt venality; and of those who thought that the colored people were able to take care of themselves and that it was not necessary "to secure the property of one race that another shall be destroyed."

But if the Bureau came into being against odds, they were as nothing to those it faced in its brief life. To begin with, it had no certain, established income, but was supposed to depend on "chance accumulations." It had to use the fixed, rigidly conventionalized procedure of the military to fashion complex and "delicate social reform." And social reform looked—and finally was in fact—impossible of attainment.

2

For Southern reactionism and Southern bourbonism, far from being dead, were not even scotched, and insofar as Lincoln's policy looked forward to the economic and political rehabilitation of the South, there was nothing guaranteed to kill them. "Home rule" meant planter rule, and the planters as a class were grimly committed to the establishment of an adequate substitute for slavery. They opposed any practical amelioration of the Negro's social and political condition that might provide a step upward toward equality. They opposed his ownership of land; they opposed his education; they opposed his use of the ballot. This opposition, though effective, was more or less hidden until Lincoln's death. When Johnson was elevated to the Presidency, it came out into the open.

Johnson was a well-meaning but a violent, headstrong and limited man, full of contradictions. He had proved all these qualities, first as Congressman, then as Senator and finally as Military Governor of Tennessee, which state he brought back into the Union. As a Congressman, he had voted for the annexation of Texas and Cuba in order that slavery might expand, yet the subject which sent him into apoplectic rage was the "odious and dangerous aristocracy" which slavery made possible. As a Senator, his hatred of this same aristocracy led him to declare for emancipation, but at the same time, he held that the government should remain strictly the white man's government. Becoming Chief Executive, though formerly pledged to Lincoln's conciliatory policy, Johnson made violent speeches which thoroughly frightened the South. Within a week of taking the oath of office, he was telling a delegation of Indiana citizens that the Confederate leaders "must not only be punished, but their social power must be destroyed" and that "every Union man and the government should be remunerated out of the pockets of those who have inflicted this great suffering upon the country."

It seemed to be Johnson's idea—or at least men like Senator Sumner and Chief Justice Chase got such an impression—to include Negroes in the suffrage. Sumner, who saw Johnson many times in the days immediately following Lincoln's assassination, wrote to John Bright that the President "accepted this idea [of Negro suffrage] completely." In May, however, Johnson issued his North Carolina Proclamation. If Sumner, Stevens and Southern-sympathizer Seward are to be believed, it was a brazen about-face. It dashed the hopes of those who thought that freedom without the ballot was a farce. It declared for a general amnesty, repudiation of the Confederate war debt, and the disfranchisement of only a handful of Southern whites, including those worth $20,000 or more. It made no mention of Negro suffrage. Headed by Frederick Douglass and George T. Downing, a delegation of Negroes protested to President Johnson in person.

Years later, Frederick Douglass was to write in his *Life and Times* that the first time he was pointed out to Andrew Johnson, the expression "which came to his face was one of bitter contempt and aversion. Seeing that I observed him, he tried to assume a more friendly appearance." Much later still, Claude G. Bowers was to write that Douglass' own attitude was "one of studied insolence." Howbeit, the President was at first equivocal, and then he fell back upon the opinion that to give the Negro the suffrage would only increase interracial enmity.

"Now," he said, "the question comes up whether these two races, situated as they were before, without preparation, without time for passion and excitement to be appeased, whether the one should be turned loose upon the other at the ballot box with this enmity and hate existing between them. The question comes up right here whether we do not commence a war of the races."

Douglass thought this an evasion, and said so. Then, disappointed, he and his delegation withdrew.

Apparently the aspect of the question which troubled the President was of no moment to Negroes. Colored groups in Louisiana, Tennessee and Virginia had petitioned for the right to vote early in the winter of 1865. Sparked by an energetic Negro dentist, Dr. Thomas Bayne, hundreds of Virginia Negroes came together to:

. . . promote union and harmony among the colored portion of this community, and to enlighten each other on the important subject of the right of universal suffrage to all loyal men, without distinction of color, and to memorialize the Congress of the United States to allow colored citizens the equal right of franchise with other citizens . . . to give publicity to our views all over the country, and to assist the present administration in putting down the enemies of the government, and to protect, strengthen, and defend all friends of the Union.[2]

Demonstrations continued and petitions multiplied and grew more urgent all through that fateful year. "Traitors," one Negro resolution declared, "shall not dictate or prescribe to us the terms or conditions of our citizenship, so help us God!" But if by traitors they meant those who had fought on the side of the Confederacy, then theirs was an empty boast and their will had already been violated. President Johnson recognized Francis H. Pierpont, notoriously anti-Negro, as Governor of Virginia. A month later, he appointed Benjamin F. Perry Provisional Governor of South Carolina. Perry had held office under the Confederacy, and he soon reinstated many of those who had held office with him. The constitutional convention of the state was packed with former Confederate military and civil officers. All over the South the story was the same. Home rule—planter rule—white rule.

And to enforce rule, laws were fashioned which became as notorious as the earlier Black Codes. They were not strictly uniform laws, for each state had its own, but they were as nearly so as the same purpose could make them. Keep the nigger in his place! Everywhere the Negro was disfranchised. Everywhere restrictions were placed on his choice of residence and work. He could not migrate into South Carolina except he entered bond of $1,000 for his good behavior and support. In Louisiana he had to make labor contracts within ten days of the start of the year, and he could not "leave his place of employment until the fulfillment of his contract, unless by the consent of his employer." The same law provided that "all difficulties arising between the employer and the laborers . . . shall be settled, and all fines be imposed by the former." Every civil officer in Mississippi was *obligated* and any white man *could*—that is, had the definite authority to—arrest any "freedman, free Negro, or mulatto" *suspected* of having left the service of an employer. Any South Carolina white man could arrest any Negro for a misdemeanor. Virginia's

Vagrancy Act empowered state officers to arrest idlers, or those pur-
suing no "labor, trade, occupation or business." General A. H. Terry
saw this as a means to "reduce the freedmen to a condition of servitude worse than that from which they have been emancipated, a
condition which will be slavery in all but its name."

Under the law, Negroes could not own firearms without permission. They could not deal in spiritous liquor. They could not intermarry with whites. Their testimony in court was generally confined
to cases involving other Negroes. They were subject to a curfew.
In some places free speech and the right of assembly were denied
them. Morse, the biographer of Thaddeus Stevens, sums up fairly:

> In most of the states the laws established a condition . . . in one im-
> portant respect far worse [than slavery]; for in place of the property in-
> terest, which would induce the owner to preserve and care for his slave,
> there was substituted the guardianship of penal statutes; and the ignorant
> black man, innocent of any intention to commit a wrong, could be bandied
> about from one temporary owner to another who would have no other
> interest than to wring out of him, without regard to his ultimate condition,
> all that was possible during the limited term of his thraldom.

The atmosphere out of which the black codes materialized like
malignant genii was recreated by Carl Schurz. A German who came
to America after the revolution of 1848, Schurz had considerable
intellectual and spiritual weight to throw on the side of liberalism.
Sent south through what Claude G. Bowers calls "a serious tactical
blunder" on the part of President Johnson, the German reported his
findings to the President and later to the public through the press.

> Wherever I go—the street, the shop, the house, the hotel, or the steam-
> boat—I hear the people talk in such a way as to indicate that they are yet
> unable to conceive of the Negro as possessing any rights at all. Men who
> are honorable in their dealings with their white neighbors, will cheat a
> Negro without feeling a single twinge of their honor. To kill a Negro, they
> do not deem murder; to debauch a Negro woman, they do not think forni-
> cation; to take property away from a Negro, they do not consider robbery.
> The people boast that when they get the freedmen's affairs in their own
> hands, to use their own expression, "the nigger will catch hell."

Many stories document Schurz. Roscoe Lewis in *The Negro in
Virginia* records some; B. A. Botkin in *Lay My Burden Down*

records others. There was the old, illiterate Negro who, having bought a shack and a piece of land, felt secure in their possession until the sheriff came to evict him. Then he discovered that in exchange for his hard-to-come-by cash he had been given a deed that read: "And as Moses lifted up the serpent in the wilderness, so have I lifted fifty dollars out of this old nigger's pocket." And there was the comely mulatto girl caught without a "pass." The price she had to pay for continuing to her home was carnal submission to the three white men who apprehended her.

Whippings, kidnapping and murders were done with impunity.

3

It was in this atmosphere of almost carnival vindictiveness that the Freedmen's Bureau took over, or tried to take over, the conduct of the Negro's affairs. At the bureau's head was General Oliver O. Howard, a former Union soldier noted for his humanity. There was confusion at first, some of it striking a note of comedy in the grim discord of tragedy and loss. " 'Scuse me," a former slave is reported to have inquired, "is dis where de Freedmen's Bureau is?" Told that it was, "I'd like to git a bureau, one wid a mirror on it, if it ain't too much trouble," he said. But nothing was quite that simple, and bureaus were the least of the Negroes' needs. In Virginia alone more than a quarter of a million of them were homeless, thousands needed medical care, and hundreds of "worked-out" slaves were totally dependent.

Relief, then, was the first task the bureau set itself—and not only among Negroes, but among poor whites, many of whom, bewildered by the complete shattering of the accustomed social order, were more wretched than the Negroes. In two years the bureau supplied twenty-one million rations to fifteen million Negroes and five million whites, furnished clothing, set up homes for the aged and infirm, and was brood hen to a host of homeless waifs.

But relief of this sort was not enough. Negroes were soon protesting their concern for fair treatment in the matter of work. At a mass meeting in Charleston, South Carolina, Negroes spoke for "a fair and remunerative reward for labor." The Negroes of Alabama complained that many of them were "in a condition of practical slavery, being compelled to serve their former owners without pay and to call them 'master.'" It was the same in Mississippi and Florida and Texas.

The bureau tried to extend its work as the need seemed to warrant. The "forty acres and a mule" for every freedman, rumors of which had gone through the South, did not materialize. Thaddeus Stevens in the House and Trumbull, Fessenden and Sumner in the Senate, pushed for measures that would give Negroes ownership of land, but such projects, however fair they may have seemed to the radicals, were patently impossible, and agitation for them scattered and collapsed. The Bureau did settle a few of the destitute on abandoned and confiscated lands. All that opposing circumstances allowed, was done for the material welfare of the blacks. In two years forty-six hospitals were founded in fourteen states. The death rate among Negroes dropped seventeen per cent in 1865 and fifteen per cent lower in 1869. The bureau found jobs for hordes of laborers. To protect the unlettered from the worst abuses of the new Black Codes, the bureau set up arbitration boards and courts and undertook to supervise labor contracts.

When the South said that the Negro was not ready for the ballot, she was right, but her motives were wrong. They were the same motives that led to the black codes; that fixed farm wages at the level of nine to fifteen dollars a month (payable "if the crop allowed"); that created peonage; that suppressed Negro craftsmen and fostered enmity between them and white workers. They were the same motives that—once the aristocrat-South had been done almost to death, its organized and autocratic power broken—led to the establishment of the political unit known as the Solid South— a unit in which the ideal of noblesse oblige all but vanished and savagery was enthroned. They were motives not only of succor in the present, but of success for the reestablishment of an already romanticized past. And by the very conditions of that past, the Negro could not, and now must not, make progress and prosper as a freeman.

In the North there were those who wanted the Negro to succeed, and if education was the prerequisite for success, then education he should have. Philanthropic and religious agencies like the American Missionary Association, the Baptist Home Mission Board and the Presbyterian Synod were already in the field. The schools they founded and the teachers they sent got substantial aid from the Freedmen's Bureau. In 1867 practically every county in every state in the South had at least some small center of learning. Howard University was established in this period, and Armstrong founded Hampton, Cravath founded Fisk, and Ware went to Atlanta. When the first post-war decade closed, there were more than nine thousand teachers (a goodly number of them colored), four thousand schools and a quarter of a million pupils.

Education, however, was not an unmixed blessing. In the first place, it was not very thorough. In the second place, there was just enough of the wrong kind to encourage a Negro middle class that quickly grew out of touch with their fellows. And in the third place, there was not enough of the right kind of education to promote an understanding of the social, economic and industrial revolution that was taking place. Though the emerging Negro middle class felt the tremendous impact of the revolution on their daily lives and acquired a degree of resiliency to it, they were as lost for a means of helping to control and direct it as were the poor whites. Moreover, an education did not lighten the burden of obloquy and bitterness under which the Negroes suffered. Rather, it increased it. "Negroes were disliked and feared," says Dunning, "almost in exact proportion to their manifestation of intelligence and capacity."

It soon became apparent that the reactionary leaders of the South were bent upon returning to power—and not only to power in the South, but on the national political scene. They kept the Negro disfranchised. They made the Black Codes work. They defeated a congressional bill to make the Freedmen's Bureau permanent. They defeated Trumbull's Civil Rights Bill. They laughed to scorn the Fourteenth Amendment. Angered by the South's unrepentance and moved, too, by considerations bearing upon the whole complex of socio-economic change, political radicals of the North entered into a contest of strength with the South. With Thaddeus Stevens, Ben Wade, Henry Wilson and Charles Sumner on the one side, and President Johnson, Montgomery Blair, T. A. Hendricks and Michael Kerr on the other, the fight was sharp, acrimonious and uninhibited by rules either of parliament or propriety. It ended in "victory" for the North and the passage of the Radical Reconstruction Act of 1867.

The bill divided the South into five military districts, called for constitutional conventions in the ten still unreconstructed states and provided that constitutional delegates be elected by universal suffrage, without regard to race or color. It declared that the state constitutions must stipulate a suffrage that excluded only former rebels and those who refused to swear allegiance to the United States, and it further provided that no state could be readmitted to the Union until it had ratified the Fourteenth Amendment.

The South blanched at these provisions, for, by means of them, 672,000 Negroes were enfranchised "as against a total possible white electorate of 925,000. But some 100,000 of these whites had been disfranchised and 200,000 more disqualified for office." The South's spokesmen argued that the South was required to do what the North had not done: only eight Northern states in all permitted Negroes to vote. The contention availed nothing. Nor did the South's attempt to boycott the constitutional conventions. There were sufficient numbers of political hopefuls, carpetbaggers and scalawags in the South to give the conventions more than a touch of white. It is true that in five of the ten states, the number of registered Negro voters exceeded the number of whites, but only in South Carolina did Negroes have a majority of convention delegates. In Louisiana they were exactly fifty per cent; in Texas ten, and everywhere else white majorities of from sixty to ninety per cent were in control.

If what followed was informed by vengeance and marked by corruption and greed, it is clear that the Negroes could not be held entirely to blame.

4

But they were blamed. "Congress did a momentous thing, and committed a great political error, if not a sin, in the creation of this new [Negro] electorate. It was a great wrong to civilization to put the white race of the South under the domination of the Negro race. The claim that there is nothing in the color of the skin from the point of view of political ethics is a great sophism." [3]

The first point of this indictment—that the white race was under the domination of the black—is completely contrary to figure, to fact and to spirit. (The second point needs no comment.) Beverly Nash, ex-slave and a leading figure in the only state constitutional convention that had a Negro majority, did not sound like a dominator when he told his fellow delegates:

"We recognize the Southern white man as the true friend of the black man. You see upon the banner the words, 'United we stand, divided we fall,' and if you could see the scroll of the society that banner represents, you would see the white man and the black man standing with their arms locked together as the type of friendship and the union we desire. It is not our desire to be a discordant element in the community, or to unite the poor against the rich. . . . The white man has the land, the black man has the labor, and labor is worth nothing without capital. We must help to create that capital by restoring confidence, and we can only secure confidence by electing proper men to fill public offices.

"In these public affairs we must unite with our white fellow citizens. They tell us that they have been disfranchised, yet we tell the North that we shall never let the halls of Congress be silent until we remove that disability. Can we afford to lose from the councils of state our first men? . . . Can we put fools or strangers in their positions? No, fellow citizens, no! Gloomy, indeed, would be that day. We want in charge of our interest only our best and ablest men. And then with a strong pull, and a long pull and a pull altogether, up goes South Carolina." [4]

Negro constitutional delegates like those in Virginia, who were influenced by the mad and self-seeking James W. Hunnicutt, were few. With their intuitive understanding of what was required of them, and with their genius for reality, Negroes were not likely to body forth the emotions of hatred and vengeance, even if they were, under the circumstances, expected to feel them.

And if they cannot be held entirely to blame for the evils of the times, it is plain also that they cannot be exclusively praised for the good. And there was good. The enduring provisions in the state constitutions of the South are its monuments—public school laws, the abolition of property qualifications for voting and office holding, the ratification of the Fourteenth and Fifteenth Amendments.

Still, the Negro was there. He was highly visible. He could be focused upon. If for no more than consistency's sake, he was the scapegoat. Was there ignorance? He was its root. Corruption? He was its source. Waste? He was the sewer through which it flowed. Hatred? He was its conductor.

Actually, precious few Negroes understood the grim struggle for power and control that characterized Reconstruction. Capital opposed labor, black opposed white, oligarchy opposed democracy, land monopoly opposed capitalistic control of profits, cooperate financiers struggled against those who would enlarge civic welfare. Honesty took an extended holiday not only in the South, but in the North, whence came more than one man eager to emulate the notorious Boss Tweed. Votes could be bought, jurors and judges bribed, legislators perverted, and the whole machinery of government could be powered by venality.

Because the Union League, which had done great work for the North during the war, and the Freedmen's Bureau reduced the struggle to the simple terms of exchange that the Negro could understand, and because these organizations represented to him the benevolence of "Mr. Linkum," they had tremendous influence among the ex-slaves. Though they started as welfare and protective agencies, since 1863 both had become increasingly the instruments of the political-minded. The personnel of the bureau had many opportunists among it. The Union League, under the blush of humanitarianism, wanted nothing so much as a knitting up of political strength in the Republican Party. Field workers of the bureau were everywhere, and every Southern county harbored at least one chapter of the League. By 1868, the two agencies together controlled the Negro vote and for twenty years thereafter there was no reconstructed state that did not have Negroes sitting in its highest councils and playing some part in directing its weightiest affairs. Virginia had twenty-seven in its first reconstructed legislature, North Carolina nineteen, South Carolina eighty-seven, Georgia thirty-two, Alabama twenty-seven, Mississippi seventeen and Florida nineteen.

Some of these mistook duty for privilege and privilege for license, but most were of the highest moral calibre, upright and intelligent. No damning word was ever said of Jonathan Gibbs, graduate of Dartmouth, who served honorably and well as Florida's Secretary of State and, later (1872–1874), as Superintendent of Public Instruction. P. B. S. Pinchback, Acting Governor of Louisiana for a month in 1873, was irreproachable through a long political career. And so was Francis Cardozo, educated in law in London, who was State Treasurer of South Carolina from 1872 to 1876. Sixteen Negroes, representing seven states, sat in the National Congress between 1869 and 1876, and their reputations were spotless. Hiram Revels, who graduated from Knox College, was a chaplain in the Union Army before he was elected to Jefferson Davis' seat in the Senate. A Nast cartoon of the day shows Revels at his desk surrounded by Carl Schurz, Charles Sumner, Henry Wilson and Oliver P. Morton, while

Jeff Davis, dressed like Iago, skulks in the corridor.

If, as Rhodes says, the Negroes in the national Congress "left no mark on the legislature of their time," neither were any of them involved in the scandals that seethed like a witches' brew in the political cauldron. If they were not singularly perspicacious, neither were they corrupt, and the example of their rectitude was a shining light for their fellows serving as judges, sheriffs, jailors, committee-men and election officials in the counties, towns and villages back home.

5

The South was outraged by Negro office-holding and maddened by the presence of the Negro troops sent to insure obedience to the will of the radical reconstructionists. Moreover, the South was certain that the freedmen were lazy, congenitally base and immoral, and that they would destroy the very basis of civilization as their emancipation had destroyed its superstructure. "The nigger, sir, is a savage! He will not work." But there was evidence to the contrary.

In 1866, for instance, the Freedmen's Bank of Charleston had deposits of only $18,000, but four years later it had deposits of $165,000, and three years later still, nearly twice the latter amount. Robert Somers, an Englishman who journeyed South, averred that:

> The testimony borne of the Negro is that they work readily when regularly paid. Whenever I have consulted an effective employer, whether in the manufacturing works of Richmond or on the farms and plantations, such is the opinion, with little variation, that has been given. . . . That the Negroes are improving, and many of them rising under freedom into a very comfortable and civilized condition, is not only admitted in all the upper circles of society, but would strike even a transient wayfarer like myself in the great number of decent colored men of the laboring class and of happy colored families that one meets.[5]

Except that Negroes worked and worked hard under freedom, how account for the increased cotton acreage, the lengthening of railroad miles, and the increased production of coal and pig iron? And except that his education was preparing him for the responsibilities of citizenship, how account for Beverly Nash, Oscar Dunn, Alonzo Ransier, Blancke K. Bruce, James Rapier and a dozen more, all of whom were high state officials and of whom it was said that "their public conduct would be honorable to any race"?

But a completely contrary opinion prevailed among the white Southern majority. In the smash-up of all the old values, the majority clung tenaciously to the convictions that had once justified slavery. The Negro must be controlled. His labor must be got at a price that meant his virtual reenslavement. His person must be made subject to the will of white masters. His voice must be drowned, his vote nullified, his ambitions repressed. That these things were not so was gross insult to gross injury, harder to bear than the defeat of war. And how not to bear it? How circumvent the radicals whose only object was to render the white South helpless and rear brute savages to the place of power? What measures could be employed to counter the measures of the Northern madman who protected the Negro's ballot with bayonets, who passed the Enforcement Act, who tried to insure the triumph of abolition by pushing through Congress the Fifteenth Amendment? In all the Southern land, who knew a way out of the "Egyptian night"?

This was propaganda pitched on its most alluring level, and the more ignorant whites, who had never been allowed to forget their implacable Negro-hate, were seduced by it. They could not see that what the planters hoped to circumvent was an alliance of white and black labor and the possibility of a political domination that would put this labor alliance in position to control land, the source of the South's wealth. It was already clear by 1870 that the Negro-lower-white-class push for social legislation—public schools, public health and public relief—in the reconstructed governments entailed the use of public funds and a continuing increase in taxes. And it was clear, at least to Negro leaders, their friends in Congress and the Southern planters, that political power unwedded to economic sufficiency was nothing. Frederick Douglass had said this time and again. Thaddeus Stevens and Charles Sumner had preached it in Congress. Speaking in 1869, Isaac Myers, the Negro labor leader said, "American citizenship for the black man is a complete failure if he is prescribed from the workshops of the country." He urged a brotherhood of labor that would recognize no color, no sex, "no north, south, east, west." Had his hopes been fulfilled, there would have been laid the foundation for an order of things as equitable and forward-looking as the dreamiest social idealist could have wished.

It was, of course, just such an order of things that the planter class feared. They were hysterically insistent upon the Negro's asocial ignorance, his political corruption. They made the South ring with protests against the "subversion of the social order, whereby an ignorant and depraved race is placed in power and influence above the virtuous, the educated, and the refined." "Let every man at the South, through whose veins the unalloyed Caucasian blood courses, who is not a vile adventurer or carpetbagger, forthwith align himself in the rapidly increasing ranks of his species, so that we may the sooner overwhelmingly crush, with one mighty blow, the preposterous wicked dogma of Negro equality! We must render this either a white man's government or convert the land into a Negro man's cemetery." [6]

Not only was the poor-white South seduced by this mating call. Particularly sensitive to the cries of corruption, because corruption had been unmasked in its own bailiwick, the North listened, hesitated, and was at last convinced that the Democrats in the South were engaged in a desperate struggle against primary evils. The industrial interests of the North pretended to believe this too, and, to protect and increase the value of their Southern holdings (having bought governors and judges and juries to obtain them in the first place) were not averse to cooperating with the Southern Democrats. A return to home rule seemed in order. In 1872, President Grant's recommendation to wipe out all the political disabilities of former Confederates became a law. In that same year, the Enforcement Acts, which had served as a not-too-effective brake on secret orders, expired. The South was ready for its white home rule, if the South could establish it.

The next dozen years proved that she could.

6

The reign of organized terror that Southern minds conceived and Southern men promoted has been romanticized either by giving it the aspect of a sad but stern necessity, or by attributing its beginning to a larksome spirit of fun. Mrs. Susan Lawrence Davis did the former. In the preface to her *Authentic History of the Ku Klux Klan,* Mrs. Davis says that her book was written "in justification of the men and measures adopted which led to redemption of the Southern states . . . and as a glowing tribute to the lofty principles and heroic chivalry of the Ku Klux Klansmen of the 'Invisible Empire' who stood ever ready to see justice done."

Claude G. Bowers does even better. He weds the idea of stern necessity to the spirit of fun.

The night before Christmas in 1865, six young men, who had seen service in the war, were seated about the stove in a law office in a small brick building in Pulaski, Tennessee. Penniless, with poor prospects, with poverty and depression all about, a pall of sadness rested on the little town that Christmas Eve. "Boys," said one of the young men, "let's start something to break the monotony and cheer up our mothers and girls. Let's start a club of some kind." It was agreed, and plans were made to be perfected at another meeting. This was held in the home of a leading citizen, where many merry initiations were to be had that winter. In considering a name for the club, someone suggested "Kublio," from the Greek word meaning a band or circle; another proposed adding "Klan" because all the members were of Scotch-Irish descent; and a third offered "Ku"—Ku Klux Klan. Since the object was fun, why not costumes to deepen the mystery? Agreed—and the young men joyously raided the linen closet and brought forth stiff linen sheets and pillowcases. It was a period of much masquerading and the costuming was a natural instinct. And why not ride horses?—and disguise them, as well, with sheets. Yes, and ride out into the black night. . . . Thus for the first time the Ku-Klux rode, and every one was merry. . . .[7]

And what fun they had! And how many other secret organizations joined in it!—The Knights of the White Camellias, the White League, the Southern Cross, the Regulators, the Adjusters. And the record?

"After us colored folk was 'sidered free and turned loose, the Ku Klux broke out. Some colored people started to farming, like I told you, and gathered the old stock. If they got so they made good money and had a good farm, the Ku Klux would come and murder 'em. The Government builded schoolhouses, and the Ku Klux went to work and burned 'em down. They'd go to the jails and take the colored men out and knock their brains out and break their necks and throw 'em in the river.

"There was a colored man they taken, his name was Jim Freeman. They taken him and destroyed his stuff and him 'cause he was making some money. Hung him on a tree in his front yard, right in front of his cabin.

"There was some colored young men went to the schools they'd opened by the Government. Some white woman said someone had stole something of hers, so they put them young men in jail. The Ku Klux went to the jail and took 'em out and killed 'em. That happened the second year after the war.

"After the Klu Kluxers got so strong, the colored men got together and made the complaint before the law. The Governor told the law to give 'em the old guns in the commissary, what the Southern soldiers had used, so they issued the colored men old muskets and said protect theirselves. They got together and organized the militia and had leaders like regular soldiers. They didn't meet 'cept when they heard the Klu Kluxers was coming to get some colored folks. Then they was ready for 'em. They'd hide in the cabins, and then's when they found out who a lot of them Klu Kluxers was, 'cause a lot of 'em was kilt. They wore long sheets and covered the horses with sheets so you couldn't recognize 'em. Men you thought was your friend was Klu Kluxers, and you'd deal with 'em in stores in the daytime, and at night they' come out to your house and kill you." [8]

"We lived in a log house during the Ku Klux days. They would watch you just like a chicken rooster watching for a worm. At night we was scared to have a light. They would come around with the dough faces on and peer in the windows and open door. Iffen you didn't look out, they would scare you half to death. John Good, a darkey blacksmith, used to shoe horses for the Ku Klux. He would mark the horses with a bent nail or something like that; then after a raid, he'd go out in the road and see if a certain horse had been rode; so he began to tell on the Ku Klux. As soon as the Ku Klux found out they was being give away, they suspicioned John. They went to him and made him tell how he knew who they was. They kept him in hiding, and when he told his tricks, they killed him.

"When I was a boy on the Gilmore place, the Ku Klux would come along at night a-riding the niggers like they was goats. Yes, sir, they had 'em down on all fours a-crawling, and they would be on their backs. They would carry the niggers to Turk Creek bridge and make them sit on the banisters of the bridge, then they would shoot 'em offen the banisters into the water. I 'clare them was the awfulest days I ever is seed. A darkey name Sam Scaife drifted a hundred yards in the water downstream. His folks took and got him outen that bloody water and buried him on the bank of creek. The Ku Klux would not let them take him to no graveyard. Fact is, they would not let many of the niggers take the dead bodies of the folks nowheres. They just throwed them in a big hole right there and pulled some dirt over them. For weeks after that you could not go near that place, 'cause it stunk so far and bad." [9]

"On Sunday before the election on Monday, they went around through that county in gangs. They shot some few of the Negroes. As the Negroes didn't have no weapons to protect theirselves, they didn't have no chance. In that way, quite a few of the Negroes disbanded their homes and went into different portions of the state and different states. Henry Goodman, my grandfather, came into Hot Springs County in this way." [10]

A congressional investigation in 1871 confirmed all this and much more. Paul L. Haworth says that "in reference to South Carolina, the report of the joint select committee of the two houses of Congress in 1872 contains such a mass of revolting details that one cannot decide where to begin their citation or where to stop."

As an answer to the report, Congress passed the Klu Klux Enforcement Law, but this, like an earlier law, was generally ineffective. Violence continued, growing more red and ruthless prior to every election. In 1871, fifty-three murders were attributed to the Klan in one county in Florida. In Vicksburg, Mississippi, and its environs, two hundred Negroes were killed in the week before the city election of 1874. In the next year, President Grant informed the Senate that "a butchery of citizens was committed [on April thirteenth] at Colfax [Louisiana] which in blood-thirstiness and barbarity is hardly surpassed by any acts of savage warfare. . . . Insuperable obstructions were thrown in the way of punishing these murderers, and the so-called conservative papers of the state not only justified the massacre but denounced as Federal tyranny and despotism the attempts of the United States officers to bring them to justice."

The Senate was powerless to do anything. Indeed, the Democrats, having gained a congressional majority partly by the very means they were now called on to abjure, had no wish to do anything. Were there not Negro militia companies in the South? Let them do something.

But at Hamburg, South Carolina, when a small company of Negro militia tried to do something, they were set upon by a band of better-armed and better-trained whites and many were killed. Negro militia in Mississippi were tricked into disarming. Negroes of the South began to tear up their roots and flee to Kansas, Illinois and Missouri. Between 1877 and 1895 there was no end to this flight. In three years, thirty-five thousand thousand went from Georgia, Alabama and South Carolina. One man, Henry Adams, claimed to have the names of ninety thousand Negroes who wished to leave. Another, Pop Singleton, is said to have taken five thousand with him to Kansas, where a settlement bore his name. By 1880, the end of Radical Reconstruction was simply a matter of forgetting the dead. Terror had put a stop to Negro voting. Not a Southern state but had gone to the Democrats, and the South, unified by a common hate, was the Solid White South at last.

10

THE BLACK

●●

U<small>NTIL THE END</small> of Reconstruction, there was marvelous unity in the ranks of Negroes and among their leaders. They seemed to want only such things as they considered their right and due as freemen— public schools, public health measures and the equal protection of the law. They seemed bound by the conviction that government was for all the people.

The united front of the Negroes held through the factional struggles of the Republican Party in the beginning of Grant's first administration, but toward the close of it, the President's disagreement with Sumner over the plan to annex San Domingo threatened to divide Negroes. Senator Sumner was their proved friend. But was this not also true of Grant? Frederick Douglass showed that he thought so, by working tirelessly for Grant's reelection, though Schurz and Horace Greeley joined Sumner in fighting it. Douglass believed that for the Negro to desert the Republican Party was to go into the camp of the enemy. "The Republican Party is the ship," he said, "all else is the sea." He was able to keep the Negro vote safe and solid for Republicanism in the campaign of 1872, and the Colored National Labor Union, of which he was president, resolved that "By its [the Republican Party's] success, we stand; by its defeat, we fall. To that party we are indebted for the Thirteenth, Fourteenth and Fifteenth Amendment, the homestead law, the eight-hour law and an improved educational system."

A less-easily answered threat to the Negroes' solidarity was the compromise that brought about the election of Rutherford B. Hayes. When the new President almost immediately ordered the withdrawal of federal troops from the South, the Negroes knew that they

183

had been cast out to do their own political fending. And they were bewildered. Despised by one party, abandoned by the other, and with no political organization of their own, they were like babes in a darkening wood. It must have seemed to many of them that a return to the elemental law of human psychology was the only thing possible. Each man for himself. And was not Douglass himself beginning to say that "the true basis of rights is the capacity of the individual"?

What gave this greater point was Douglass' elevation to the office of United States Marshal of the District of Columbia. It seemed to lift him above the grubbing concern of his fellows. It was an appointment which even wealthy and influential white men envied him. It carried with it great political and social responsibilities. But the howls of surprise and outrage which greeted his naming did not come exclusively from white men. Douglass complained later that in the interim between designation and confirmation, when he was the object of much calumny, "no colored man in the city [of Washington] uttered one public word in defense or extenuation" of him. When in 1884 he took for his second wife, Miss Helen Pitts, a white woman, the vast majority of Negroes looked upon him as a traitor to his race. This opinion was not completely modified by Douglass' explanation. His first wife, he said, was the color of his mother, while his second was the color of his father, and he wished to be perfectly fair to both races.

2

Disorganized and heart-sickened by a vague awareness of the forces aligned against them, Negroes in the South—where ninety-five per cent of them were concentrated—fell easy prey to the pressure of progress and the blunt, impersonal enmity of the former Confederates. Whatever of substance there was in the old Southern aristocratic ideal, it began to decay with the coming on of industrialism. If, as is so often claimed, the rural Negro had the plantation owner to turn to as counselor and friend, he began to lose him to the towns and cities, where the opportunities of industrialism were promised fulfillment. For the planters took leave from their acres, became, in fact, absentee owners, and the land was left in the care of those who still dreamed of its possession as the sine qua non of social advancement, to those who had no tradition of noblesse oblige. In short, to overseer types, farm-manager types and horse-trader types—rascals who felt no qualms at using the methods of slavery to control the Negro in freedom.

The Negro had no defense against these, nor against the connivings of the resurgent Southern Democrats. The North was weary of the eternal race question. While the night-rider, the burning cross and the mob were sufficient to reduce the Negro vote by one half within five years and by two-thirds within seven, there were still the permissive laws of the land. Theoretically these allowed the Negro too much freedom and equality. Either the laws had to be held in continued defiance or they had to be changed. Defiance, being an emotional state, could not possibly endure forever. Change, then— or nullification. Everything must be made legal now, even if by illegal means. Political machinations, chicanery, legal subtleties—the Negroes were no match for them.

Actually, there was no more guile in what was done than in the reasons for doing them, and these were frank enough. The white South feared that the Negro's political equality would lead to "social equality." The white South wanted to firmly reestablish and maintain its racial superiority. Using first the instrument of terror, as we have seen, the white South set out to do what it finally completed doing by 1900.

There were all sorts of ways. Registration forms were complicated beyond the intelligence of the average Negro voter. Negroes were required to produce on demand registration certificates issued six months in advance. Polling places were changed overnight and Negroes were not notified. The ballots were not simple. In Virginia, for instance, candidates were listed by office rather than by party, and few Negroes were literate enough to make the proper association. To split the colored vote and assure the election of the white Democratic nominee, a "white-man's-nigger" would be run against the Negroes' own candidate. There was the device of requiring a separate ballot and a separate ballot box for each office voted on. There was the gerrymander.

Nothing was more symptomatic of the dissipation of the aristocratic ideal than the elements that had clawed, crawled and bought their ways into the ranks of the Southern Bourbons. These included hard-eyed industrialists, who had come down from the North to exploit cheap labor; supply merchants, who might have come from anywhere and who furnished everything from gold to guano and men to mules at murderous rates; and ex-carpetbaggers who had seen the error of their ways.

The poor whites were slow to realize that these Bourbons meant them no material good, that on the economic frontier rapidly being established in the social wilderness of the post-war South, these *aristocrats* were the outlaws. Gulled by dreams of attaining planter status, or of rising to foremen, to superintendents, to managers in mills and mines, dirt farmers and poor white laborers listened when they were told that their dreams would come to nothing if the Negro remained politically strong. "If you want to rise," the poor whites were told, "keep the nigger down." And the poor whites were happy to.

But panic in 1871 and again in 1873 and then a depression settling like a blanket, alarmed the poor whites. The credit machinery, where it did not completely disintegrate, ground to a halt. Cotton was in strangling oversupply. In 1878 it was priced at ten cents, and this figure slid constantly lower until in 1890 it plumped to five. The traditionally "rich and aristocratic bankers" refused loans, supply merchants refused to supply. Mortgages were ruthlessly foreclosed. The poor lost not only land, but the means of cultivating it. Taxes on corporations were low; on farmers high. The poor whites began to see the light. "By the middle of the 1890's the acquiescence of the white Southern masses was at an end. The hard times, the deflation policies of the federal government, and the cumulative effects of a too-rapid industrialization of the country goaded them into passionate rebellion." [1]

One of the leaders of this rebellion was an astute but unstable Georgian named Tom Watson. He knew that as a by-product of forming a solid front against the Negro, the lower classes of whites had gained some know-how and had been bribed with a slight measure of political strength by the conservative Democrats. He realized, too, that the conservatives needed all the strength they could muster to maintain the political status quo which he felt duty bound to destroy. "The accident of color can made no difference in the interests of farmers, croppers and laborers," Tom Watson cried. "You are kept apart that you may be separately fleeced of your earnings."

There was already in existence an organization with which the poor whites could make a strengthening juncture. It was the Colored Farmers National Alliance, which had chapters in a dozen Southern states. In some states the strength of the Alliance was considerable, and it was needed by the conservatives. Thus between the Democrats and the poor white rebels, who called themselves Populists, there was competitive bidding for the Negro vote. The bidding was lively and bloody, resulting in riots, resulting in renewed agitation of the question of Negro equality, resulting in the storing up of more racial bitterness for the future. But in the 1890's, the Populists, combining with Negroes and with isolated cells of radical Republicans, took control, and the Negro became a "balance-of-power factor" in Southern politics.[2]

But not for long. And only in North Carolina did the Negroes' use of their power result in anything tangible. There they won political and civil appointments as sheriffs, bailiffs, magistrates, policemen and tax collectors, and in 1896 and 1898 they sent George H. White to Congress, the last Negro elected from the South. Having gained nothing immediately apparent in other states, and reconstruction having accustomed them to measure political strength in terms of patronage and office-holding, Negroes soon sank into that condition of sullen political lethargy in which they remained for a quarter of a century.

Moreover, even at their lowest ebb the conservatives had not ceased to fight the coalition of the black and white masses. Nor had their trusty weapon, racist propaganda, ever been allowed to rust. It was again reasserting itself by the middle 1890's.

Disguised as literature, which most of it laid claim to being, the stories, plays and novels set forth with painstaking detail the golden items of the romantic and legendary South. It was artificial, sentimental and niggling, but it revivified the old concepts and retouched in shining colors the fading portraits in the gallery of Southern chivalry. The handsome cavaliers and lovely ladies had their opposites in the black Uncle Edinburgs and moon-faced mammies who looked back to the good old days of slavery, when " 'for Gawd, dyar warn' no trouble nor nothin'." If there were brave knights ever ready to defend the sweet virtue of white women, there were certainly black men against whom defense was needed—"wild beasts, hyenas, reptiles," brutal and lascivious, waiting with ill-disguised impatience the propitious moment to ravage their former mistresses. Thomas Nelson Page *In Ole Virginia,* Joel Chandler Harris in *Uncle Remus,* Sherwood Bonner in *Sewanee River Tales* and George W. Cable in *The*

Grandissimes eschewed grosser distortion and got at partial truth; but Page's *The Negro: The Southerner's Problem* was literally a bible of reaction, and for bitter hatred of the post-Civil War Negro only one book can beat *Red Rock*. That book was *The Leopard's Spots,* its author a minister named Thomas Dixon, Jr. Through this writer the deadly purpose of the literature of the South found its fullest expression.

The North loved it and largely believed it and generally went into ecstasies over the brave protagonists who came home from the wars to find their lands ruined, their families in rags, and the "niggers riding in the seats of power." The North applauded these heroes as they plunged into the new battles to salvage sacred honor, recoup their plundered wealth and reestablish that broad and gracious way of life in which had been raised up the finest men and the purest women and the most rewarding culture the western world had ever known.

And so, after 1900, the South had nothing to fear from the North— not interference, not even criticism. One Southern state constitutional convention after another contrived means of circumventing the Fourteenth and Fifteenth Amendments. It was the Grandfather Clause in Louisiana, the education test in Tennessee, the property qualification in Mississippi, the character test in Virginia, and everywhere the poll tax and the white primary. At the Virginia constitutional convention of 1901, Carter Glass, the delegate from Lynchburg, gloated: "This suffrage plan will eliminate the darkey as a political factor in this state in less than five years. . . . There stands out the uncontroverted fact that the article of suffrage which the Convention will today adopt does not necessarily deprive a single white man of the ballot, but will inevitably cut from the existing electorate four-fifths of the Negro voters."

By 1910, the Negro in the South was as completely disfranchised as he had been under slavery.

3

Even so, the shape of the Negro's political future was not so discouraging to contemplate as the reality of his economic present. The Northern philanthropists were mistaken in supposing that the schools they built would make easy the Negro's transition to economic sufficiency. It is true that school and factory grew up side by side in the

South and were scions of the same root, but it is equally true that if the Negro wanted the one, the white man was determined to have the other. The old terror of Negro equality haunted the South. Especially did it haunt the common white man, who was unwilling to sink to the level of competing with the blacks.

Certain kinds of work were beneath the dignity of the landless poor whites. The planters found them unsatisfactory as tenant farmers and sharecroppers. In the towns and cities they would not be janitors or personal servants and the like. Unskilled, they were indifferent craftsmen. But there were the mills going up everywhere, and, as Broadus Mitchell says in *The Rise of the Cotton Mills in the South,* these provided an escape from competition with the blacks. So into the mills they went—men and women and children of eight years old, because the whole family must earn mill wages in order to live at all. When a few half-hearted efforts were made to put Negroes into the mills too, the whites struck. Other whites in other places had done it before—in the Arizona copper mines, for instance, against the employment of Mexicans. Southern whites struck thirty-one times between 1882 and 1900. The deed of barring Negroes from the mills was followed by the reasoning word: the blacks were temperamentally unfitted for mechanical work.

It soon developed that there were many kinds of work for which Negroes were unfitted. Chinese coolies were preferred to them on plantations and in railroad building in parts of Louisiana, Arkansas and Tennessee. For Negroes there seemed to be no stable place in the economy. When they moved to the cities to escape sharecropping and peonage, they had to content themselves with the lowliest occupations, no matter what their skills. In the North, competition with European immigrants had been keen since the 1840's, but in the closing decades of the century it grew keener. Italians and Greeks took over bootblack parlors and barbershops, Poles did the unskilled work in industry, the Irish went into the ditches and onto the docks, Germans and other foreigners displaced Negro bellboys and waiters. In 1885, Mrs. Fannie B. Williams outlined the situation in Chicago.

It is quite safe to say that in the last fifteen years, the coloured people have lost about every occupation that was regarded as peculiarly their own. . . . White men wanted these places and were strong enough to displace the unorganized, thoughtless and easy-going occupants of them. When the hordes of Greeks, Italians, Swedes, and other foreign folks began to pour into Chicago, the demand for the Negro's places began. One occupation after another that the coloured people thought was theirs forever, by a sort of divine right, fell into the hands of these foreign invaders. . . . The Swedes have captured the janitor business by organizing and training the men for this work in such a way as to increase the efficiency and reliability of the service. White men have made more of the barber business than did the coloured men, and by organization have driven every Negro barber from the business district. The "shoe polisher" has supplanted the Negro bootblack, and does business in finely appointed parlours, with mahogany finish and electric lights. Thus a menial occupation has become a well organized and genteel business with capital and system behind it.[3]

It is not surprising that under these circumstances the Negroes themselves made cooperative attempts to haggle for places in the economy. Nor is it surprising that these attempts failed. Without nationalization, independent urban workmen's protectives, like the United Laborers and Hod Carriers Association of Philadelphia and the Colored Engineers Association of Baltimore, were practically helpless. It is true that the white National Labor Union had urged Negroes to organize in the 1870's and had granted them the right to representation in its national meetings, but this had no practical result. White craft unions did not grant membership to Negroes. When Negroes formed their own national union, its economic aspect was at once overshadowed by the political in the election of Frederick Douglass to the presidency. For five years organizational activity was feverish and it culminated in the establishment of the National Bureau of Labor, but this was largely a shell, for no Negro labor leader of strength, vision and ability had come along to transform potential into kinetic force. Douglass, who might have been such a one, was immersed in politics, and he succeeded (with the help of John Langston, another Negro politician) in syphoning off a great deal of energy into that channel. "The Republican Party," he said, "is the true workingmen's party of the country." But the Republican Party was in practically uninterrupted control from the end of the Civil War to 1900, and the Negro continued to suffer under economic and industrial disabilities.

This is not to suggest that there were no Negroes who topped the masses. Here and there both North and South we find them, though in small numbers. Probably the most secure of all Negroes were the

120,000 farm owners (as against 1,106,728 farm laborers in 1890). But there were others who had won security. George W. Williams, Benjamin Brawley and Luther Jackson, those unquiet singers of Negro praises, make catalogues of them. There were "captains of industry" (Brawley's phrase) like John R. Hawkins, financial secretary of the African Methodist Episcopal Church, and "capitalists" (Jackson's phrase) like Isaiah T. Montgomery, co-founder of the all-Negro town of Mound Bayou, Mississippi, and Adam Blake, the Albany hotel-keeper whose wealth was estimated at $60,000. In Missouri there was Robert Wilkinson, a barber, with $25,000, and Alfred White, a caterer, with the same amount. There were tailors and stewards and grocers and butchers and other tradesmen in Ohio, Pennsylvania, South Carolina, Georgia and Mississippi who estimated their riches at from $5,000 to $50,000. In 1890, even the smaller amount was great wealth for a Negro. There were banking institutions and insurance companies in the District of Columbia, Virginia, Tennessee, Florida and Alabama. Many of these failed in one crisis or another, and by the turn of the century only the bank established as a subsidiary of the Order of St. Luke could be sure of continued existence.

But if the men who directed these enterprises were neither capitalists nor captains of industry, there were three or four Negroes who contributed to the industrial advance from which the Negro generally was shut out. Many modern lubricating devices are based on patents obtained by Elijah McCoy, who began his work in 1872. Norbert Rillieux, a Louisiana Negro, invented the vacuum pan used in refining sugar. Granville T. Woods, of Ohio, assigned some twenty patents to the General Electric Company and the American Bell Telephone Company and lived long enough—until 1910—to see them in general use. Jan E. Matzelinger, an immigrant Negro shoemaker from Dutch Guiana, was less fortunate. He died in Lynn, Massachusetts, in 1889, without realizing that his shoelasting machine would be the keystone of an American industry that within ten years was doing a business of more than one hundred million dollars a year.

4

To mention these accomplishments is but to underscore the common, and the common for the Negro was an economic situation of oppression and poverty. Indeed, the merciless quality of that position was to be a fundamental factor in contributing to the disruption of that racial unity among Negro leaders spoken of at the beginning of this chapter.

Small differences of opinion there had been. Back in the seventies, the Ohio Negro leader, John Booker, had been heretic enough to suggest that the Negro should end his blind loyalty to the Republican Party, and for this he was excommunicated from the councils of race leaders. In the eighties, Frederick Douglass had disagreed with Richard Greener, first Negro graduate of Harvard and a Howard University professor of law, over the migration of Negroes from the South. Douglass had held that migration was no cure for racial ills, that the Negro had greater opportunities for holding office and getting jobs in the South. Greener contended that the density of the South's Negro population cheapened labor, that a westward dispersion in numbers would benefit those who remained in the South, and, furthermore, that the treatment accorded the Negro in the South was reason enough for him to leave. And Greener dropped back into the quiet of his professorship.

But these had been clashes which evolving circumstances rendered all but meaningless, and the instinct for tribal solidarity soon muted them. By 1895, however, that instinct, especially among a small but growing middle class of Negroes, was noticeably drying up. Differences in opportunity, in attainments, in wealth and in color, fostered social schisms and class differentiation. Out of the middle class an even more snobbish upper class was slowly emerging, and for neither class were tribal solidarity and "race advancement" enough—were not even, in the thinking of some, desirable or important. Many members of these classes were naturally geared to the values of their white relations. They were individualists. They had individual ambitions, and they sought, in the American pattern, personal fulfillment.

Education was a factor here. The philanthropic urge that established Rice Institute in Texas, Vanderbilt in Tennessee, a greater Trinity in North Carolina and Johns Hopkins in Maryland did not stop with these. John F. Slater, George Foster Peabody and, later, John D. Rockefeller, Anna Jeanes and Caroline Phelps-Stokes set up funds from which money poured into the pumps that, to paraphrase Slater, were to uplift the Negro population and confer on them the blessings of Christian learning. The journey from shack and shackles to college halls had been made with the ardent singleness of purpose of a holy crusade. Not that every institution that called itself a college was one in fact—and the universities were certainly not universities: the Yankees who taught in them were not deceiving themselves in this regard. But they and their pupils were deceived nonetheless. Education was no panacea. Some elements in the South hoped it would be a quietus and a salve, but it was not these either. J. L. M. Curry, of Alabama, argued that the Negro should be educated for the simple reason that education was owed him. Henry Grady thought that education, if there was not too much of it, would make the Negro "more useful to whites." The Governor of North Carolina, Charles B. Aycock, saw education as a method of control, as a means of keeping the Negro in his place.

But actually it was none of these and it did none of these. For the interfering, long-nosed, bluestockinged, indomitable Yankees, sent and provisioned and paid by the philanthropists and by the Baptist Home Mission Society, the American Missionary Association and Lutherans and Catholics and Quakers—these Yankees were educating Negroes as they would have educated whites, that is for "manhood." And in Atlanta Baptist College (later Morehouse), in Atlanta University, Fisk, Roger Williams, Talladega and Biddle, they were teaching *First Principles,* the *Anabasis,* Caesar's *Gallic Wars,* philosophy and logic and, with the best of mistaken intentions, were educating Negroes to dissatisfaction.

Or at least dissatisfaction was the somewhat unexpected result. Negroes educated in the liberal programs of the Yankee-taught colleges of the South could feel the cruel impact of discrimination, segregation and prejudice on every phase of their lives. They understood more clearly than their untrained fellows what it meant to be denied the simplest human dignity. They suffered the frustration of having prepared themselves for responsibilities they would never be allowed to exercise. Nor were they so self-centered as not to realize that the only guarantee of professional and economic stability for themselves lay in a measure of financial stability and at least a minimum exercise of citizenship rights for the masses. Without work, or with at best work and wages on the meanest subsistence level, how could the masses keep their children in the schools which the middle classes hoped to teach? Or put money in the banks which the middle classes hoped to found? Or join lodges? Or pay preachers, lawyers and physicians?

It was a Gordian knot of socio-cultural problems that one man undertook to cut through with a program so simple and under a pattern of thought so acceptable to the white South that, but for the outbreak of the World War and the dissolution of certain concepts in that holocaust, he might have succeeded. He might have done this in spite of relentless opposition from members of his own race. Until the emergence of Booker T. Washington, there had been no insuperable differences in purpose and opinion among Negro leaders: after it, Negro thought polarized around two contradictory ideas—cultural integration and the imperium in imperio.

11

A PLACE AND A PATTERN

●●●

Booker Washington was born in slavery a year or two (he himself did not know the date) before the Civil War, just in time to be caught up in the educational tidal wave that swept over the Negro race in the seventies and eighties. The wave landed him at Hampton Institute in 1872. An ambitious youth of ingratiating manner, he soon won the notice and approval of his teachers and of General Samuel Chapman Armstrong, the principal of Hampton. He spent three fruitful years at the Institute, and two years after graduating was called back to be, as he put it, "a sort of house father to a hundred wild Indians." But this was not sufficient outlet for Washington's energies. He took charge of teaching retarded Negroes in night school and within a year he built up his "plucky class" and the night school (again to use his own words) "into one of the most . . . important features of the institution." In 1881, when some white Alabamians were looking for someone to head a Negro school in Tuskegee, General Armstrong had no hesitancy in recommending Booker Washington.

All of Washington's experiences and the mold of his character suited the task that lay ahead. His ambitions were completely organized. He knew an opportunity when he saw one and he could ascribe to himself the most laudable of motives for seizing it. He was certain that a proper education for his race lay remote from the classics, from "culture" and politics. If he had a sense of humor—and he did—it was far overmatched by a sense of personal infallibility that gradually led to the despotism of the God-ordained leader. Above all, though, he had that happy, useful and flexible talent without which all others would have been useless: he could accommodate at no matter what cost to personal dignity—and he could make accommodation pay.

And he did. Tuskegee grew—as a school, in three years from thirty students in a shack to three hundred in half a dozen buildings; as an idea, from a project suspected of ruining the Negro with learning to the sole and complete and unassailable answer to the race problem in America. Washington, the word was, would keep Negroes in the South. Washington would train in them the docility they needed for their prescribed place in society. He would teach them not only to serve but to be servants. The classics, mathematics, the sciences— the study of which had spoiled so many of his race—were impractical for those destined to plow and plane, cook and clean. Washington had said that the individual who "learned to do a common thing in an uncommon manner had solved his problem regardless of the color of his skin, and . . . in proportion as the Negro learned to produce what other people wanted and must have, in the same proportion would he be respected."

This was rather naïve thinking, giving no evidence that Washington knew of the broad currents then running deep through American life—the increasing importance of organized labor, the potentials of planned political participation. Or if he knew of them, he had no sympathy for the Negroes' urge to try them. He opposed labor unions, which only tended to compound the race's habit of laying "too much stress on its grievances and not enough on its opportunities." He disliked politics and deplored the Negroes' participating in them except as they went to "Southern white people . . . for advice concerning the casting of their ballots." He was suspicious of intelligent inquiry, more especially in that it was likely to lead to conclusions differing from his own. His thinking had no future in it—only the present and the past. He saw the white-patron-Negro-suppliant relationship as the salvation of his people. In this Washington was very sincere.

But if he were merely naïve in the beginning, he seemed to some dangerous after the famous Atlanta Exposition speech of 1895. ("In all things that are purely social, we can be as separate as the fingers. . . .") That speech, which Frederick Douglass (dead eight months before its making) would certainly have condemned as weasel, mealy-mouthed and reactionary, lifted Washington to a national status of such power as to make him the virtual dictator of race policy. The New York *World* called him the "Negro Moses"—

and so he proved almost to be.

He was the umpire in all important appointments of Negroes; the channel through which philanthropy flowed, or did not flow, to Negro institutions; the creator and destroyer of careers; the maker and breaker of men. He was all this quite literally, and his latent egomania, scarcely repressed by honorary degrees from Harvard (1896) and Dartmouth (1901) and by being publicly proclaimed by William Baldwin, millionaire president of the Long Island Railroad, an object "almost of worship"—his latent egomania showed itself. Freed of financial harassment for Tuskegee by Andrew Carnegie's gift of $600,000, Washington went ruthlessly about the business of seizing control of every avenue of Negro endeavor. "He was appealed to on any and every subject: how many bathrooms to put in a Y.M.C.A., whether or not to start a day nursery [colored, of course] in some town, and so on." [1] He created what has been called the "Tuskegee Machine," and with petulant pride kept it running in high gear for a dozen years.

2

From white America's point of view, the situation was ideal. White America had raised this man up because he espoused a policy which was intended to keep the Negro docile and dumb in regard to civil, social and political rights and privileges. Having raised him to power, it was in white America's interest to keep him there. All race matters could be referred to him, and all decisions effecting the race would seem to come from him. In this there was much pretense and, plainly, not a little cynicism. There was the pretense, first, that Washington was leader by sanction of the Negro people; and there was the pretense, second, that speaking in the name of his people, he spoke *for* them. Whatever happened to the Negro, whatever long-term policy was set for him, whatever purposes he seemed to lend himself to, white America was not to blame: the decision was the leader's.

Thus Washington was both straw man and dictator, a dual role made classic by Negro slave bosses in slavery, but taking on a dangerous new significance in freedom. Bending every effort to please the whites, the conflicting factors in the circumstances made it inevitable that Washington should injure the deepest aspirations of his people. It may have been tactful to ignore the constantly tighten-ing restrictions on the Negro's legal and social status, but it was playing the white man's game. Ridicule of the Negro's pretensions may have been salutary, but it was the white man's medicine. It may have been all right to frown upon Negro political participation, but how could Washington justify the frown at the same time that he consulted with white politicians, from President to precinct leader, on appointments of Negroes to even the lowliest of political posts? Washington throttled the young Negro press and cajoled and seduced T. Thomas Fortune, editor of the largest Negro paper, to his side. Practically nothing by Negroes touching upon Negroes was brought out in books and magazines without Washington's sanction. Under his direction, "ghost writers black and white" turned out Negro copy. For all practical purposes, and so far as white America knew or cared, Washington's was the only Negro voice in the country.

But there was opposition, and it grew steadily, for Washington could not buy up the scruples of all men. His hatred and fear of opposition argued that there was a basic weakness in his program and a subtle corruption at work in his conscience. He tried to break up opposition; he got others to try. He brought a great deal of per-sonal animus to bear; he aroused it in others. Monroe Trotter, the fiery editor of the Negro Boston *Guardian,* galled by Washington's high-handedness, went to jail for disturbing one of the Tuskegee titan's meetings. W. E. B. Du Bois, more controlled than his fellow graduate of Harvard, felt the full weight of Washington's powerful wrath.

This young New Englander, a teacher at Atlanta University at the time, had once been offered a post at Tuskegee—though what a Harvard Ph.D. in history and sociology would have done in a school devoted to teaching the vocations on a high school level no one knows. Indeed, overtures from Tuskegee continued to reach Du Bois, but as Washington's program became clearer, Du Bois saw more and more in it to disagree with. He did not like the basic com-promise in the acceptance of an inferior race-caste status. He did not believe that vocational education was the complete answer to the race problem. He did not believe that the socio-economic philosophy that had permitted the uncontrolled growth of huge industrial em-pires and that Booker Washington seemed to rely on as the ultimate prop of an independent Negro commercial and cultural structure was valid any longer. As a matter of fact, Du Bois' own studies were proving that it was not.

And it was these very studies, begun at Atlanta University in 1897, that Booker Washington wanted to modify, or drastically curtail, or stop altogether.

So the young scholar was again approached by powerful emissaries from Tuskegee. This time the proposition was that he edit but not have editorial control of a periodical at Hampton. Du Bois refused. But it was Washington's technique to try to overawe where he could not persuade or coerce, and a few months later a group of millionaires, including William Baldwin, a trustee of Tuskegee, Robert Ogden and George F. Peabody, went to Du Bois with another offer—this time to go to Tuskegee at any salary he cared to name. While this matter was still in the discussion stage, Du Bois published *The Souls of Black Folk*. One of the essays in that book was entitled "Of Mr. Booker T. Washington and Others."

It was not really the essay of an enemy, for Du Bois did not become an enemy in any personal sense until Washington forced him. It was rather the work of a member of the "loyal opposition." Though it did point out the very great difference between being forced to accept a leader and commissioning one by "silent suffrage," the essay was entirely impersonal and objective. And logical. Its logic openly joined issues that had long been joined in hidden fact.

Other essays were point-by-point answers to the Washington program. "Of the Training of Black Men" declares boldly for exactly the kind of education that Washington wished Negroes not to have. In "Of the Sons of Master and Man" Du Bois rejoins to Washington's political passivism that "to have the Negro helpless and without a ballot today is to leave him, not to the guidance of the best, but rather to the exploitation and debauchment of the worst . . . to lay any class of weak and despised people, be they white, black, or blue, at the political mercy of their stronger, richer and more resourceful fellows, is a temptation which human nature seldom has withstood and seldom will withstand."

Du Bois saw the Negro problem as a "plexus of social problems, some new, some old, some simple, some complex." He did not believe in the artificial limitations imposed upon man by divisions into race and caste. He believed that the time to fight these restrictions was eternally in the present—to fight them with the weapons of truth

where possible, and with the bludgeons of propaganda where necessary. It was patent to him that Washington soft-pedaled and pooh-
poohed the limitations of class and caste, as if they were merely
nebulous ideas in the foggy minds of malcontents. Du Bois did not
see how any man, so obviously as Washington the tool of power and
privilege, could be the leader of the despised black masses. Finally,
Du Bois believed that for present and not wholly apparent gains,
Washington was mortgaging the future of the Negro.

Washington, with the help of influential friends, tried to destroy
both Du Bois and his position. He caused to be blocked off certain
of the financial resources Du Bois had drawn upon for his Atlanta
University Studies. He succeeded in preventing the publication of
certain of Du Bois' investigative papers, although they had been
authorized and financed by the United States Commissioner of
Labor. Accusations of personal jealousy and of being ashamed of
his race were brought against the outspoken New Englander. While
at the same time the General Education Board, of which and for
which Washington was a kind of ambassador plenipotentiary,
brought pressure on Atlanta University; the Tuskegee coterie made
impossible Du Bois' acceptance of a position as assistant superintendent in charge of Negro schools in the District of Columbia.

The truth of the matter was, however, that to destroy Du Bois
would not have been to destroy his position, for it was no longer
singular—if, indeed, it had ever been. Increasing numbers of Negroes
held it. By 1906, Booker Washington had reason to complain queru-
lously, as Mary White Ovington heard him do, that "those Negroes
up North are hammering at me."

Those Negroes up North had started their concerted hammering
the summer before, when Du Bois called together a representative
twenty-nine of them to launch the Niagara Movement. The group
included such respected leaders as George W. Cook, secretary of
Howard University, Dr. Charles Bentley of Chicago, George W.
Crawford of New Haven, the volatile Monroe Trotter, and the
sharp-minded, sharp-tongued Ida Wells Barnett of Tennessee and
Illinois. In January they set forth a platform of which not a single
plank but opposed Washington's policy with a directness almost
personal. They declared for "freedom of speech and criticism," an
"unfettered and unsubsidized press," "manhood suffrage," the "abolition of all caste distinctions based simply on race and color," the

acquisition of the highest and best training as the privilege of all, and a "united effort to realize these ideals under wise and courageous leadership." Six months later Du Bois summarized these aims in the following words: "We will not be satisfied to take one jot or tittle less than our full manhood rights. We claim for ourselves every single right that belongs to a freeborn American, political, civil, and social; and until we get these rights we will never cease to protest and assail the ears of America."

This was a manifesto born of despondency. Its rigid and uncompromising tone spoke loudly the despair of its framers.

3

Washington had done some good and necessary work. His conciliatory attitude was probably helpful, although it did not prevent the mob violence that spattered the South (and North) with blood even in the climactic years of his career. His insistence on thrift was wholly salutary. His idea of building up a Negro economy and culture within the framework of white society was at least quixotic enough to be stimulating, and it led naturally to the formation of various annual conference groups and to such bodies as the National Negro Business League and the National Lawyers Guild. As a teacher, he pushed a practical approach to the problem of training. He was the first to use farm and home demonstration methods, the first to send the school to the student.

But in all this there was the mistake of overextension, and it was not in the beginning so much his mistake as that of the general society. It was an age of expansive faith in one- and two-shot panaceas, in absolute cures for complex ills. It was an age of large hopes. It was the period of "manifest destiny" and of "dollar diplomacy," in race relations no less than in America's international relations. Nothing must be allowed to divert the energy and distract the interest in establishing capital investments in Europe and South America, of underwriting pineapple and sugar plantations in Hawaii (and the eventual annexation of those islands), of building coaling stations in Samoa, and of backing the Pan-American Congress of 1889, which gave sanction to all this, and a big navy to protect it.

Least of all must the potentially explosive Negro question be allowed to get out of hand. And Booker Washington seemed to have the answer here. President Cleveland, who was against the ascendant imperialism, was definitely for Washington's imperium in imperio. "If our colored citizens," he wrote to Washington, "do not from your utterances gather new hope and form new determination . . . it will be strange indeed."

Washington spread himself like a blanket. It may have meant warmth and comfort to some Negroes, but the more intelligent of them felt it as a smothering weight.

Its psychological effects upon whites in the South and upon Negroes everywhere were perfectly apparent by 1910. The mass of Negroes were beaten creatures, convinced by the unassailable testimony of their position of their inherent inferiority, and more than half convinced that they got from the white man no worse than they deserved. A quarter of a century later, a white Southerner, William Alexander Percy, who lived through those times, summed up the effect upon whites. "To live habitually as a superior among inferiors, be the inferiority intellectual or economic, is a temptation and a hubris, inevitably deteriorating."

Voteless and voiceless, alien to and barred from the sources of liberalism, shackled by proscriptions in economic life, ridiculed with relish, lynched with impunity, more and more it seemed to Negroes that their black skins were a badge of shame, a curse of God. A paralyzing psychosis of defeatism gripped them. "It is better to die than it is to grow up and find out you're colored," the Negro poet Fenton Johnson lamented. "Oh, to be a Negro in a time like this!" To be a Negro meant . . .

But even Booker Washington, though with cautious euphemism, made a fairly accurate catalogue of what it meant. It meant "poor dwelling houses, loss of earnings each year because of unscrupulous employers, high-priced provisions, poor school houses, short school terms, poor school teachers, bad treatment generally, lynchings and whitecapping, fear of the practice of peonage, a general lack of police protection, and want of encouragement." [2]

And the Negroes took it. Perhaps this was a show of their resilience, for which they had been praised by those who did not know the merciless statistics, or, knowing them, praised with cynical flattery.

Though five and a half million Negroes lived in rural areas of the South, only one hundred and twenty thousand owned farms. By 1910, when the number of Negroes in the rural South had increased to six and a quarter million, and when Booker Washington's program should have been showing results in prosperity, independence and thrift, the number of Negro farm owners had increased by only eighty thousand and the average worth of property per owner was less than $300.

Meantime the number of Negro farm wage hands had increased by 237,397 to 1,500,000, and more than a million Negroes were share-croppers. At the beginning of the last decade of the nineteenth century, 2,883,216 Southern Negroes were illiterate, and ten years later 2,717,606 were still illiterate. In the same period the death rate for Negroes showed no appreciable decline, and 34.2 per thousand (34.4 in 1890) was still nearly double the figure for whites. Of every ten thousand Negroes in the South in 1890, twenty-nine were con-victed of crime, as against six in ten thousand for whites. The crime figures were more disproportionate in the North: sixty-nine to ten thousand for Negroes, twelve to ten thousand for whites. In the 1890's North Carolina had a Negro representative in Congress. By 1910, "with the withdrawal of the Republicans from the political arena in the South and the consequent development of the one-party system, the exclusion of Negroes from the Democratic primary pro-vided the coup de grace by which Negro suffrage was nullified from Virginia to Texas." [3] In 1890 the American Federation of Labor encouraged Negro memberships: in 1910, it was actively opposed to it. In 1890, ninety Negroes were lynched: in 1900, one hundred and seven.

The Negro's plight was the source of much of the bitterness directed against Booker Washington. Monroe Trotter, whose news-paper, The *Boston Guardian,* was more and more the rather strident oracle of Northern Negroes, wrote:

As another mark of the treacherous character of Booker Washington in matters concerning the race, comes his discordant notes in support of Secretary Taft. . . . Booker Washington, ever concerned with his own selfish ambitions, indifferent to the cries of the race so long as he wins the approval of white men who do not believe in the Negro . . . leader of the self-seekers, he has persistently, but thank heaven unsuccessfully, sought to entangle the whole race in the meshes of subordination. Knowing the race could only be saved by fighting cowardice, we have just as persistently re-sisted every attempt he has made to plant his white flag on the domains of equal manhood rights and our efforts have been rewarded by the universal denunciation of his doctrines of submission and his utter elimination as a possible leader of his race.[4]

That Washington had been utterly eliminated as a race leader was not true, of course, and it never became quite true. There was little use in fighting him with contumely. Du Bois' plan of opposition was infinitely more sound, but Du Bois and the then-unspoiled John Hope, a teacher at Morehouse College, had small resources of organization. It is true that a militant, free Negro press was rising, and that it was almost unanimously opposed to Washington's compromise and accommodation, but the press had to fight the passivity of the black masses who had been conditioned to associate social force and social control with individual leaders rather than with themselves. Moreover, the Negro press generally did not have the support of the masses. Time and again, Negro editors, politicians and just plain "race men" complained of this. Negro newspapers were "shamefully neglected," declared Frank Trigg, ". . . due to the lack of a proper conception the majority of the race have of the importance of its unity, and of its concert of action in all matters pertaining to the race's weal and woe."

So John Mercer Langston, one of the last of the Negro Congressmen, might declare the Negro "editor is to march boldly forward" and that "nothing must be allowed to weigh even an atom against the Negro's first demand for immediate emancipation from every sort of evil—social, political, or official thraldom," and the Memphis *Free Speech,* of which Ida Wells Barnett was founder and editor, echoing the defunct *Living War,* might inveigh against "notorious and incorrigible Jim Crowists," yet it was pretty much like shouting at the weather, like thunder without God.

4

The intellectuals were more discouraged than filled with Miss Barnett's bitterness. They deplored the intellectual and social climate, but they felt helpless in the face of it. Having graduated, many of them, from colleges and universities in the North, they were utterly unprepared for the racial proscriptions on the one hand and for the excuses they saw for them in the low cultural level of the Negro masses on the other. For leaderless black masses were beginning to crowd up from the South into the cities of the North. Ignorant and sometimes overaggressive, they posed a situation for the Negro upper class that was fraught with dangers—not the least of which was in the almost psychotic care with which the upper classes sought to avoid contact with the lower. In *Lillian Simmons, or The Conflict of Sections,* by Pauline Hopkins, an upper class Negro is made to complain, "You Southern niggers come up here and spoil our privileges . . . with your ignorance and roughness. . . ."

Du Bois was accused in those days of being ashamed of his Negroness, and it is no libel of him now to say that perhaps he was. All the conditions and situations in which the educated Negro was likely to find himself contributed to his feeling of race-shame, and at the same time that he told himself that the hated caste status was imposed from without, the very strength of the tradition of race-caste fostered in him doubts of his worthiness of any other. His mind was curiously warped and dangerously divided. His ambitions were perverted. The broad aptitudes that, except for the matter of color, would have assured him a place of some consequence in the general society, were pressed into the business of defense, or, as we shall see, finding means of escape. James Weldon Johnson summed it all up in his anonymously published novel, *The Autobiography of an Ex-Coloured Man* (1912). "And this is the dwarfing, warping, distorting influence which operates on each and every intelligent coloured man in the United States. He is forced to take his outlook on all things, not from the view-point of a citizen, or a man, or even a human being, but from the view-point of a *coloured* man."

But there was not only this necessity; there was also the fact, equally compulsive, of the white man's point of view about the colored man. This viewpoint was a rationalization from misinterpreted fact, and it was emotional and dogmatic. The white man was certain that, measured by every index—biological, intellectual, moral —the Negro was inferior. He had a different odor, a different speech, a peculiar disposition. There was in some metaphysical corner of the white man's mind an involuted concept of Negro inferiority that resisted all scientific contradictions as stubbornly as it resisted holy writ. The concept was sometimes held in perfect innocence, but that cut no chip of ice. Within the frame of that concept the Negro was forced to function as being and as citizen. A certain way of acting, of thinking, of doing was expected of him, and any deviation from the expected was likely to be ridiculed as sportive, cursed as presumptive, discouraged as imitative, or altogether ignored.

Writing of the verse of Paul Laurence Dunbar who, by 1900, was one of the most popular poets in America, William Dean Howells, one of the most influential critics, said: "It appears to me now, that there is a precious difference of temperament between the two races which it would be a great pity ever to lose, and that this is best preserved and most charmingly suggested by Mr. Dunbar in those pieces of his where he studies the moods and traits of his own race in its own accents of our English. . . . He reveals in these a finely ironic perception of the Negro's limitations. . . ." This was double-barreled praise, and so Dunbar, who was not expected to write them anyway, could find no hearing for his charming lyrics in pure English. Only his "jingles in a broken tongue" were acceptable. Magazines would take only those short stories of his which depicted Negroes as whimsical, simple, folksy, not-too-bright souls, all of whose social problems were little ones and all of whose emotional cares could be solved by the intellectual or spiritual equivalent of a stick of red peppermint candy.

So too, in a different way, it was with Charles W. Chesnutt, another distinguished Negro writer. For a decade and a half after his stories began appearing in the *Atlantic Monthly* in 1887, the fact of his race was kept a closely guarded secret. His novels, however (*The House Behind the Cedars, The Marrow of Tradition, The Colonel's Dream*), all published after 1900, were obviously the work of a Negro, and they were ignored. The Negro characters portrayed in them did not fit into the frame of the expected.

Negro characters on the stage were shaped to the concept. White actors had made popular the comic and/or whimsical Negro who could be laughed at, tolerated, and genially despaired of as hopeless in the modern, dynamic society. Edwin Booth himself had "more than once appeared in the character of what was then termed a 'Dandy Nigger,'" and sometime before the Civil War Thomas D. Rice had created for the commercial stage the "Ethiopian [Negro, blackface] minstrel." Rice was quickly imitated by Daniel Emmett, Charles White, the Christys and Primrose. "For almost fifty years [beginning about 1843] minstrels were the most popular form of American entertainment." When Negroes themselves entered the professional theatre, the minstrel show was fixed in form and spirit, and Mr. Bones and Tambo, the ribald jokes, the coon songs, the breakdown and the buck-and-wing had passed eternally into the folkstuff of America, and, eternally too, it seemed, into the racial concept. Billy Kersands and Sam Lucas were great Negro minstrels in the 1880's, and James Bland's sentimental ballads (for sentimentality also was of the tradition), "Carry Me Back to Ole Virginny" and "In the Evening by the Moonlight" were on their way to immortality. In the 1890's, James Weldon Johnson and his brother J. Rosamond, Paul Laurence Dunbar and Harry T. Burleigh were contributing to the racial concept in the theatre. In that same decade, "the first Negro show to make a complete break from the minstrel pattern" was nevertheless entitled "A Trip to Coontown" and the most popular theatrical sketches were "Cloridy—the Origin of the Cakewalk" and "Jes Lak White Folks," both written by Will Marion Cook.

There developed thus a psychic cleft between the talented Negro and his racial existence. When he did not bow to the tradition, which Washington's program pointed up as his salvation, he sought to escape it altogether. Untold thousands of Negroes passed over into the white race. Most, of course, could not pass. In order to escape, while at the same time remaining within the race, they had somehow to ignore their racial kinship and leave unsounded the profoundest depths of the experiences that were theirs by reason of their race. Some of them won high critical praise for their work in non-racial themes, and were proud of it. For it meant two things to them: they had defied the tradition; and their talents had earned them the right to be judged by the same standards used for whites.

The leader of this group was William Stanley Braithwaite. Save only a few essays written at the behest of his friend, W. E. B. Du Bois, nothing that came from his pen had anything in it to mark it "Negro." His essays in the Boston *Transcript,* his yearly anthologies of magazine verse, and his own poetry might just as well have been written by someone with no background in the provocative experience of being colored in America. Though the other writers of this genre (which was not entirely a genre) developed a kind of dilettantish virtuosity, none carried it to Braithwaite's amazing lengths of self-conscious contrivance. They were simpler and more conventional in their apostasy. Alice Dunbar, the widow of Paul, wrote sonnets of uncommon skill and beauty. Georgia Johnson and Anne Spenser were at home in the formal lyric, and James Weldon

Johnson, not yet grown to his full stature, but having foresworn the old tradition, set in "The White Witch" and "My City" a very high standard for his fellow contributors to Henry Gilder Watson's *Century Magazine.*

5

But given the whole web of circumstances—empirical, historic, psychological—it was impossible to go on forever denying racehood. Functioning simply as human beings, Negroes were of necessity borne back upon themselves for a satisfactory social and cultural life. There were a few who led lives integrated with whites, but their numbers were so small and they themselves of so little consequence that they can be discounted. Segregation and discrimination were everywhere the rule—in residential areas, in labor and industry, in hospitals, hotels, restaurants and practically all places of public accommodation; in government service, in the Army and Navy. The *separate but equal* theory had not been tested in the courts and was nowhere applied. Twenty-two states had laws against intermarriage and thirteen had laws against racially mixed schools. So Negroes went to Negro churches, joined Negro lodges and clubs, sent their children to Negro schools, and patronized—sometimes of necessity— Negro business.

Nor was there any lack of these institutions. The Negro church was defiantly independent. Not only were the great denominations flourishing, but the Negro Baptists had broken away from white control and formed their own national organization. By 1900, Negro churches had property worth $56,000,000 and a total membership of three and a half million, and they were maintaining schools and colleges like Wilberforce in Ohio, Morris Brown and Clark in Georgia, and Philander Smith in Arkansas. The Negro church distributed food and clothing to the poor, bought medical service for the sick and legal service for the troubled. It established hospitals, orphanages and asylums for the aged. The first really important Negro business institutions started under the guidance of ministers. As early as 1881, the Reverend W. W. Brown, a Methodist preacher, organized the Grand United Order of True Reformers, a secret society with insurance features. When Frederick L. Hoffman's *Race Traits and Tendencies of the American Negro* (1896) showed the high incidence of disease and the suddenness of death among the colored population, many white insurance companies refused to handle Negro policies. Negro secret orders began emphasizing their protective features. On the strength of these, and with the added attraction of elaborate ceremonials and gaudy uniforms, the Order of Tents, the Order of St. Lukes, the Knights of Tabor and the Good Samaritans, all mutual aid societies, grew amazingly.

And so did burial associations and penny savings banks, shops and stores, restaurants and bakeries—"the slowly growing seed of cooperative business efforts," Du Bois called them—and social organizations like the National Association of Colored Women, discussion and conference groups, Y.M. and Y.W.C.A.'s, the Negro Alliance, newspapers and magazines (there were more than two hundred Negro weeklies by 1900)—"the slowly evolving organs by which the group [sought] to minimize the anti-social deeds and accidents of its members."

Thus there developed not only a Negro community, but a Negro life; not only a place, but a pattern. Within this isolation Negroes were forced to live. Indeed, they were forced to increase their isolation and to build out of the very proscriptions they endured the walls of race pride. Race isolation and race pride became the outside frames of the pattern and the pattern itself became increasingly protective.

This is not to say that Negroes swallowed the bait of Booker Washington. Rather the opposite. Under the apparent conformity was protest against caste, against the pusillanimous pragmatism that, hoping to win the favors of the strong, made caste the agent of the white man's aggrandizement; protest against the self-interest of whites in supporting accommodating Negro leaders to help them control the Negro group, to help them keep the group within the limits of what Washington called "practical efficiency" and its ambitions within the bounds of allowable progress. The very core of the Negro community was the pathologically intense desire that the Negro prove himself equal to the white man. This expressed itself in a childish exaggeration of the accomplishments of Negroes, in the exaltation of the Negro character, and in an amount of literary whining that called into question the very things the Negro would have the world believe.

On the other hand, as the Negro novelist, Sutton Griggs said,

"Thomas Dixon was writing the Negro down. . . . Thomas Nelson Page was disguising the harshness of slavery under the mask of sentiment . . . [and these] misguided souls ignored all the good in the aspiring Negro, made every vicious offshoot that [they] pictured typical of the entire race; presented all mistakes independent of their environments and provocations; ignored or minimized all the evil in the more vicious elements of whites; said and did all things which [they] deemed necessary to leave behind . . . the greatest heritage of hatred the world has ever known."

The histories, stories, novels and poems that were beginning to get written by Negroes tried to right the balance. Pauline Hopkins spoke not only for Negro fiction but for all Negro writing when she said that it "is of great value to any people as a preserver of manners and custom—religious, political and social. It is a record of growth and development from generation to generation. No one will do this for us; we must ourselves develop the men and women who will faithfully portray the inmost thoughts and feelings of the Negro with all the fire and romance which lie dormant in our history, and as yet, unrecognized by writers of the Anglo-Saxon race."

That was the spirit. Such glorifiers of the race as Joseph Wilson (*The Black Phalanx,* 1888) and E. A. Johnson (*A School History of the Negro,* 1891), made the Negro the bravest in war and the most industrious in peace. Novelists and poets showed the Negro the victim of mass hatred—which he was, of course—but proclaimed the strength and beauty of character that would eventually prevail. The very titles of the works betray them: *Hearts of Gold,* by J. McHenry Jones; *Iola Leroy, or Shadows Uplifted,* by Frances W. Harper; *Contending Forces: A Romance Illustrative of Negro Life North and South,* by Pauline Hopkins; *The Hindered Hand,* by Sutton E. Griggs. "Most of these writers," says Hugh Gloster, "proved themselves as guilty of tedium and literary distortion as were Dixon and Page. Their works are usually poor novels, because they are more polemic than fiction, and often poor polemic because they melodramatically plead the case."

But there were some solid accomplishments in literature, history and the graphic arts. Charles W. Chesnutt had begun the writing of his masterly short stories in 1887, and the very year of the century's close found him preparing his first race-conscious novel, *The House Behind the Cedars.* White scholars spoke highly of George W. Williams' *History of the Negro Race* and *History of Negro Troops in the Rebellion.* Du Bois' *Suppression of the African Slave Trade* had been chosen as the first work in the Harvard Historical Studies series.

In sculpture, Meta Warrick Fuller attracted a great deal of attention. Her masterpiece, "The Wretched," was exhibited in 1893 and drew such comments as, "Under her strong and supple hands the clay has leaped into form: a whole turbulent world seems to have forced itself into the cold and dead material." More striking still was what was being done with the long-neglected spirituals. Using arrangements by R. Nathaniel Dett, Harry T. Burleigh and Will Marion Cook, the Fisk Jubilee Singers and the Hampton Quartet carried these songs all over America and Europe, and literally kept Fisk University and Hampton Institute in existence by music.

But most striking of all was the work of Henry O. Tanner, the man whom Europeans still consider "one of the best America has produced in painting." In 1897, the French government bought Tanner's "The Resurrection of Lazarus" and made it a part of the permanent exhibition in the Luxembourg. Tanner's paintings now hang in many European galleries, in the Pennsylvania Academy of Fine Arts, in Memorial Hall in Philadelphia, and in the gallery of the Chicago Art Institute.

If these were considerable accomplishments, they were not enough. Nothing and no one, it seemed, was quite enough to whiten the stigma of being black. The general level of race fear and hate was at what seemed an insurmountable height, extending to the very rim of the world where, in the reaches of the Caribbean and the Pacific—Hawaii, Samoa, Puerto Rico and the Philippines—and in faraway Africa, black and brown and yellow men were again falling victims to the white man's exploitation and willful ignorance.

But California was not far away, and there had been devised, as early as 1882, the Chinese Exclusion Act; and there and in the state of Washington the thrifty Japanese Americans were being forced to think of themselves as a people apart, a species something less than human, who could not buy land, who could lease it for only three-year periods, and who were the targets of Hearst's "Yellow Peril" campaign. And Michigan was in process of becoming the industrial heartland of America, but from there was soon to pump into "all the towns and out-of-the-way hamlets," says Samuel Tenenbaum, "aided by the magic name of Ford," the corrosive poison of anti-

Semiticism. In this, too, Hearst had a hand, for his papers were making known to uncritical thousands the burlesque "Potash and Perlmutter," and some hotels and restaurants and places of public amusement were beginning to display signs: "Gentiles Only." America was far from the dream of America.

12

DREAM AND REALITY

●●

IN THE FIRST month of the new century, James Weldon Johnson, recently returned to his home in Florida from New York, exhorted his people to sing of the faith taught by the dark past and to face the dawn of their new day.

A new day did seem to be dawning. The gales of race hate seemed to have blown themselves out in the boisterous weather of the Spanish-American War. The dramatic mummery of that sought-for conflict, with its accompanying rash of imperialistic ambitions, had temporarily distracted even the South from the business of validating in law that complex of ideas that stood for the incontrovertible superiority of the white man over the Negro. It had distracted the South from this business so thoroughly that she cheered with the rest of the nation at the news of the heroism of black troops at San Juan, and Southern officers were moved to vie with one another in praising the swarthy warriors.

"It would seem that the colored man was destined to be in the van of Americans who fight and fall in the cause of liberty and humanity. Instead of bringing up the rear, in battle and self-sacrifice, history shows him to be with the foremost and sometimes in the lead. . . . The Spanish-American War gives another proof of this." [1]

If these words were extravagant, they simply reflected the brimming enthusiasm of the times. For in simple truth, black soldiers had not done much in the Spanish-American War. It was not their fault. They had wanted to. Forty-five per cent of the Cuban population was Negro, and Spanish rule had made their plight particularly wretched. Fired by the exploit of the insurgent mulatto leader, Antonio Maceo, American Negroes rushed to answer the first call for volunteers. They were repulsed by the President and the War Department. When Congress finally permitted Negro recruitment, four regiments—the Seventh, Eighth, Ninth and Tenth United States Volunteers—were formed. These, and the outfits which eight states authorized, saw little service. But the 24th and 25th Infantries and the 9th and 10th Cavalries—Negro regulars—went into action at El Caney, Las Guasimas and San Juan. There is no doubt that in the battle of San Juan the Negro cavalry turned a defeat into victory and saved the honor and the hides of Teddy Roosevelt's Rough Riders. When the shooting was over, several of the Negro volunteer contingents, like the 8th Illinois and the 23rd Kansas, did occupation duty.

There were examples of individual heroism and sacrifice by colored soldiers. Quite a few died in battle. Many more succumbed to disease, including thirty-five who volunteered as subjects in experiments to conquer yellow fever. The story of Sergeant Berry, of the 10th Cavalry, became a popular hero legend among Negroes and was made into a moving picture many years later. For "particularly meritorious service in the face of the enemy" at Santiago, four men of the 9th Cavalry and two of the 25th Infantry were commissioned second lieutenants. Medals of Honor were awarded Fitz Lee, Dennis Bell and William Thompson, all of the Tenth Cavalry, for distinguished gallantry at Tayabacoa.

Not much—for the war itself was not much—but enough for the encomiums that followed. A correspondent of the Atlanta *Evening Journal* wrote: "The Negroes make fine soldiers. Physically the colored troops are the best in the army. . . . These colored regiments fought as well, according to General Sumner in whose command they were, as the white regiments. What I saw of them in battle confirmed what General Sumner said. The Negroes seemed to be absolutely without fear, and certainly no troops advanced more promptly when the order was given than they."

Nor did the "enthusiasm aroused throughout the whole country" end in nothing. President McKinley reacted to it. Between 1898 and 1900, he made enough appointments of Negroes to important federal posts to constitute what was later called, partly in derision and partly in respect, the "Kitchen Cabinet." A Negro was appointed as Register of the Treasury, another as Recorder of Deeds, another as Collector of Customs, and yet another as a judge in Washington's municipal court.

McKinley, however, did not have the dramatic flair that his successor possessed. Theodore Roosevelt loved the limelight and very soon after taking office, he monopolized it by inviting Booker Washington to lunch at the White House. The talk of this had no sooner died down than the Crum incident set tongues a-clatter again in blast and counterblast. It was a small enough incident, really, and one which incurred no hazard to the President's political strength. Roosevelt simply refused to withdraw the nomination of William Crum, a Negro, as Collector of the Port of Charleston. He stood up for a Negro against the opposition of the entire white South. The act made him secure friends among Negroes. His toothy smile blossomed from lithographs in nearly every Negro parlor in the land.

A better day coming?

Seemingly there were other signs of it, isolated but heartening. A few individual Negroes were surmounting the barriers of prejudice or facing them boldly on grounds where the ancient inhibitions did not hold. The stories of their triumphs, always overdone in the Negro press, smacked tangily of opportunity, expansion and recognition.

This was especially the case in the entertainment world. A new Negro music was beating in from the Southwest, whether from New Orleans or St. Louis no one can say. But suddenly in the first decade of the century, ragtime was here. Such compositions as "Maple Leaf Rag," "Mandy" and "Ballin' the Jack," and such composers as Scott Joplin, the Johnson brothers and Shelton Brooks were giving America the basis for her only indigenous popular music. Negro dancers, singers and comedians, like Bob Cole, Bert Williams and George Walker, were regularly making the Orpheum Vaudeville circuit and starring in musical plays on Broadway. In James Weldon Johnson's opinion, *In Dahomey* made "Negro theatrical history by opening at the very center of theatredom, at the New York Theatre in Times Square." Isaac Murphy was still the greatest jockey, but other Negroes like Soup Perkins, Bob Isom and Jimmie Lee were riding to racetrack glory in the early 1900's. The most famous and formidable prize-fighters of the day were Sam Langford and Joe Jeannette; and out West, Jack Johnson, who unfortunately was to bring no lasting honor to himself, or the ring or the race, was winning his first fights. The great singer, Sissieretta Jones, called the "Black Patti," had an international reputation.

2

But none of these successes could disguise the fact that for thirty years the status of the Negro as a citizen had been slowly sinking. It was at its lowest ebb since slavery, in the first decade of the century. If the documenting studies which Du Bois was making at Atlanta and if the gloom of the annual race conferences at Hampton had no significance for the unlearned masses of Negroes and were vigorously ignored by others of more intelligence, the meaning of certain electric events in the public realm could be lost on no one. Of course there were attempts to play these events down, or, in the tricky bookkeeping of appeasement, to count them pure gain, as Booker Washington did, and did constantly. A few months after the bloody Wilmington, North Carolina, riot of 1898, for instance, he was telling a white audience in Huntsville, Alabama, that the Negroes were "surrounded, protected, encouraged . . . given the full protection of the law, the highest justice meted out through the courts and legislative enactments. . . ." and that in exchange, Negroes were "loving and trusting" the white people. In 1903, by which time the great bulwark of white supremacy had been thoroughly restored and only the most stupid did not understand that economic and social considerations were subordinate to those of race, Washington told a colored audience: "The Negro in this country constitutes the most compact, reliable, and peaceful element of labor . . . and I believe that, if for no other reason than the economic one, the white people will see that it is worth while to keep so large an element of labor happy, contented and prosperous, by surrounding and guarding it with every protection and encouragement of the laws."

No matter how Booker Washington professed to see it, the outlook was dark, North and South. Communities in the North felt unfairly challenged by the multiplying presence of the Negro. "There are too many Negroes up here; they hurt the city," a white man of Indianapolis told Ray Stannard Baker.[2] This was probably the feeling in Chicago, where in seven years from 1893 the Negro population doubled to 30,000. In Philadelphia between 1890 and 1900, the Negro population increased by 59 per cent to 60,613 and added

25,000 more in the next ten years. New York had 90,000 Negroes by 1910, and they were beginning to spread northward and eastward from West Fifty-third Street and the San Juan Hill district.

The urban centers of the North were no places of refuge. For the most part, Negroes lived in sections already abandoned, in alleys, cellars and garrets. They paid for such quarters, as Robert Weaver shows, from a fourth to a half more than the former white occupants. Employment was precarious. The national total Negro membership in national and international unions and in locals affiliated with the American Federation of Labor was only 32,619 in 1900. There were no Negroes in unions of common labor, the category in which they were mostly employed. Negro wives and mothers frequently carried the burden of their families. Forty and seven-tenths per cent of all Negro women, but only 16 per cent of white women were employed in 1900. Negro children worked too—49.3 per cent of all those between the ages of ten and fifteen. The figure for whites was 22.5 per cent.

Telling figures? But only telling half, for they make another kind of statistics—in unstable family relations, in community disorganization, in crime, delinquency and disease. There were warnings from many quarters, from Negro leaders and white friends of the Negro. Du Bois sounded them constantly. Dr. J. L. M. Curry sounded them in his annual reports to the Slater Fund, of which he was secretary. In a speech delivered in Memphis in 1904, Dr. W. S. Montgomery, assistant superintendent of schools in Washington, D.C., pointed out that:

The poverty and prejudice everywhere encountered, and the fierce competition, constrain these [Negro] people to settle in unsanitary localities, in the alleys, closes, and courts where thousands are rotting and festering in the slums and tenements. . . . Diseases to which they have heretofore been immune claim them as victims, and they become a menace to the general health of the community. The brutal battle for existence develops a violent spirit, cheapens human life, creates a cunning which seeks to win by fair or foul means, producing the thief and sharper who live by their wits. Lack of steady employment does not call out the sterner qualities of patience, honesty, honor, duty and self-control. Competition pushes to the wall, and the man, despised and rejected, turns an Ishmaelite—a law breaker, and swells the criminal list. Politically he is lost as an individual or unit of society, swallowed up in the mass. . . .

"Swallowed up in the mass," but only politically, and this only in the South, where, by all other indexes, his ingurgitation was completely impossible. In 1900, Atlanta, New Orleans and Memphis had Negro populations ranging upward from fifty thousand. Savannah, Montgomery and Baton Rouge had Negro populations larger than the white.

Neither in the North nor South, however, was there lacking a class structure among Negroes. If anything, it was somewhat less flexible than the tripartite organization of white society. The expression "All niggers look alike to me" was a cavalier stupidity which galled Negroes of the upper class. And particularly that their upper-class distinction was based on the same indexes in kind, though not in degree, as those of whites. Family was first. In the cities and towns of the South, the family was counted of worth in direct proportion to the amount of white blood in its veins. The more white blood, the better the family. Though this had bearing in the North, the length of a family's residence in a Northern community was perhaps of equal bearing. Philadelphia, New York and Boston had their Negro "old families" with a tradition of freedom running back five or six generations. If in such families the marks of white ancestry were distinct (and they usually were, for mating below the color line was frowned upon), so much the better.

After family came occupation, education, behavior and income. If not white-collar or professional, the occupation must at least be above the laboring, lunch-box carrying and day's work domestic categories. Physicians, teachers, post office employees, preachers and business men met the qualifications. A college or university education was fine; a high school education would do. Behavior was strict, coldly formal in public, warmer but subdued in the circle of one's friends. Conspicuous consumption, especially in the dress of the women and the furnishings of the home, was desirable. James Weldon Johnson thought the homes of the upper class, with their "heavy furniture, heavy pictures, heavy curtains, and heavy carpets . . . very sumptuous." Incomes had to be high enough and stable enough to support sumptuous tastes. Upper-class Negroes were generally Congregationalists, Presbyterians or Episcopalians. In 1900 the richest Negro church in the world was St. Philip's Episcopal of New York.

It was not exactly easy to rise into this class. As a matter of fact, one of its chief characteristics was a jealously guarded exclusiveness. Certain of its own respectability, the upper strata of Negroes wanted nothing so much as to make unassailably clear their difference from "other" Negroes.

Those "other" Negroes resented this. Especially resentful was the middle class, striving for respectability and thinking to find it in church and lodge and sewing circle. In the upper reaches of this group, largely of the Baptist and Methodist persuasions, family stability was highly prized, but family age and blood ties to whites were less important. A light skin, though, particularly in the female, had advantages both social and economic. "Wanted a light colored girl to do maid service." Northern papers carried many such notices, for the notion was universal that a light-skinned Negro was somehow better than a black-skinned one. A "fair" girl of the middle class, even of the lower middle class, could go places, not barring the sacred precincts of the upper class. A story which seems to have originated in the early 1900's, but which still has some point today, concerns a Negro physician of Washington, D.C., who, after a short vacation, returned with a wife. Introductions to her husband's upper-class friends invariably brought the reply, "I be's please' to meet you," and a nervous giggle. But the white of her skin, the blue of her eyes, and the gold of her hair more than made up for her low middle class and probably illegitimate origin.

It was infinitely easier for members of the middle class to sink to the stratum below than to rise to the one above. In the North the vast majority of the men of the lower class were common laborers. In the South, they were often skilled as carpenters, brick masons and the like. With the help of their working wives, they provided for their families and let the children remain in school a reasonable time, girls usually for a longer time than boys. The youth from this group who somehow managed to go to college took a long step upward. But relatively few of them managed. They were always more likely candidates for the poolrooms, where gambling went on, the saloons, where petty crimes were hatched, and the street corners, where derby-hatted pimps whistled up trade for their whores.

Or if not candidates for these, then highly susceptive to the chronic disease of the lowest class, unemployment. For the gurgling gutters of industrialism did not drain off the surplus of black labor. Though Booker Washington averred that the Negro "does not like an organization which seems to be founded on a sort of personal enmity to the men by whom he is employed," he could not gloss the important fact that this revealed—the great psychological distance between the white working masses and the black. And if unions were founded on personal enmity to employers (which of course they were not), they fed on monopoly, and monopoly turned back upon a desperately harassed society an element that it could neither absorb nor reject—the Negroes of the depths, a class which, as Du Bois says, "in modern industrial civilization is worse than helpless. It is a menace not simply to itself but to every other group in the community. It will be diseased, it will be criminal, it will be ignorant, it will be the plaything of mobs. . . ."

And it was. And so were other groups the playthings of mobs.

3

On the night of August 15, 1900, the cry of the mob to "get Ernest Hogan and Williams and Walker and Cole and Johnson" was for the blood of the best known and most respected Negro entertainers in New York City. The mob did not get any of those for whom it called, but George Walker only narrowly escaped and Ernest Hogan, who was playing at the Winter Garden in Times Square, had to spend the night locked in the theatre.

Others had no such refuge. "A mob of several thousand raged up and down Eighth Avenue and through the side streets from Twenty-seventh to Forty-second." The mob was no respecter of class or sex. Negro men and women were dragged from hacks and street cars and brutally beaten. Running to the police for protection was like escaping the tiger only to confront the lion. The police were out to avenge Robert Thorpe, one of their number, who had been fatally stabbed by a Negro. The beatings they inflicted on Negroes were as cruel as those inflicted by the mob.

When demands for an investigation were made, the authorities hemmed and hawed and passed the buck. Tension did not ease. Led by the Reverend William Brooks and T. Thomas Fortune, editor of the New York *Age,* Negroes formed the Citizens Protective League, engaged legal counsel, and raised money to prosecute the identified guilty policemen. Thus compelled to do something, the Police Department conducted a hearing of its own, but the "coloured citizens who testified to having been beaten by the police were themselves treated as persons accused of crimes. . . ." Police protection as a common right of the Negro was a long way off.

In the South, it was even farther off, for the ordinary restraints on mob violence against Negroes had never held. The demagogues saw to that. The men whom a social conscience, less hardened by the fear of change, would have damned, manipulated the strings of hate with expert precision. "Pitchfork Ben" Tillman, W. K. Vardaman, Hoke Smith and Cole Blease. There were also a host of lesser magnitude, including some who by family, wealth and tradition were gentlemen to other manners born.

Seeing their leaders perverted by the extremes of what appeared to be the good old romantic tradition, it is not to be wondered at that the hoi polloi followed suit. The common masses, for instance, watched the change that came over Georgia's Tom Watson with flatulent satisfaction, for the ex-Populist, who had once advocated the Negro's right to vote and an end to lynching, was become one of them. And this was what the common Southerner demanded—that his leaders be like him. The aristocratic ideals of cooperate responsibility, of yielding to authority, and of noblesse oblige were completely broken down. The demagogue was sure of cheers when, like Vardaman, he bellowed, "The way to control the nigger is to whip him when he does not obey without it, and another is never to pay him more wages than is actually necessary to buy food and clothing."

Because it is true that otherwise and anywise (whether with more wages, or less wages, or no wages at all) the lower-class Negro sometimes got out of hand. Restricted and repressed in all the normal activities of citizenship, he tended to be aggressive in socially unacceptable ways. He loafed when he might and should have been working. He drank more than was good for him. He was ornery, sullen, mean. That these were symptoms of the almost intolerable state of his existence, few stopped to consider. The legal denial of the right to vote? He did not want to vote. Forced to live in teeming hovels on unlighted, unpaved streets and up noisome alleys, it developed that that was what he wanted. Unlearned, what use had he for schools? Unemployed? He could live on next to nothing.

These were the conceptual ingredients in the social pot that simmered in the Southern summer heat of 1906. In Atlanta, Georgia, the pot came to sudden boil. But not without warning. With the organic simplicity of the working out of some natural law, the elements had been combining for months. In a bitter gubernatorial campaign, with Hoke Smith and Tom Watson on one side and Clark Howell and the regular Democrats on the other, nigger-baiting had got full play. Hoke Smith claimed that the Democrats wanted political equality for the Negro. The report was exaggerated, but the Atlanta *Journal* gave it ready confirmation and added something more.

Political equality [the *Journal* said], being thus preached to the negro, in the ring papers and on the stump, what wonder that he makes no distinction between political and social equality? He grows more bumptious on the street, more impudent in his dealings with white men, and then, when he cannot achieve social equality as he wishes, with the instinct of the barbarian to destroy what he cannot attain, he lies in wait, as that dastardly brute did yesterday near this city, and assaults the fair young girlhood of the south.[3]

Other editorials and news items were less devilishly subtle. All through the summer there were rumors, stories and circumstantial accounts of alleged Negro rape of white women. Three such stories were carried by the papers in May, and in July another, and in August two more. "That every one of these stories was afterwards found to be wholly without foundation was of no importance." Fear and hatred slowly tightened its grip on both elements of the population. Rumor begat rumor, and an irresponsible press scattered this progeny with abandon. On the afternoon of September twenty-second, which was a Saturday, the papers outdid themselves.

It was a good day for it. The half holiday was hot. The city market, a sort of boundary between a white neighborhood and the densest Negro area, was full. So were the saloons, in some of which Negroes drank with only a partition separating them from white drinkers. The streets, too, were crowded. Yet there was an unnatural quiet.

Shortly after noon, the papers hit the street. The first editions were extras. The second and third editions were extras. The Atlanta *Evening News,* a new paper, published four extras in six hours. "TWO ASSAULTS!" the second extra screamed in headlines eight inches high. "THIRD ASSAULT!" In its second extra of the afternoon, the Atlanta *Journal* declared: "ANGRY CITIZENS IN PURSUIT OF BLACK BRUTE WHO ATTEMPTED ASSAULT ON

MRS. CHAPIN RESCUED FROM FIEND BY PASSING NEIGHBOR."

That evening the volcano erupted hot terror. Mobs stormed through the streets attacking black men, women and children wherever found. A lame Negro bootblack was found in a barbershop and stomped to death. The barbershop, in Atlanta's Peachtree Street and owned by a Negro but catering only to whites, was wrecked and the barbers beaten. The mobs armed themselves from looted hardware stores and pawnshops. Negroes were made to jump from viaducts to the railroad yards forty feet below. They were hauled off street cars and thrown through car windows to mobs that literally tore them limb from limb. One Negro was disemboweled, another castrated. Thousands of Negroes fled to their "white folks" and were given protection, for there were deeds of kindness and courage done that night too. Making the rounds of mailboxes with his mail-collector father, Walter White, now Secretary of the N.A.A.C.P., saw one such deed.

No sooner had we turned into Marietta Street, however, than we saw careening toward us an undertaker's barouche. Crouched in the rear of the vehicle were three Negroes clinging to the sides of the carriage as it lunged and swerved. On the driver's seat crouched a white man, the reins held taut in his left hand. A huge whip was gripped in his right. Alternately he lashed the horses and, without looking backward, swung the whip in savage swoops in the faces of members of the mob as they lunged at the carriage determined to seize the three Negroes.[4]

Sunday was quiet, but on Monday a new mob surged out into a Negro section called Brownsville. In the center of the city, the hats and caps of Saturday night's victims still hung from telegraph poles. The mob was a mixed horde of private persons and county and city police. In the decent neighborhood of the Negro Clark College and the Negro Gammon Theological Seminary, a neighborhood in which Negroes themselves with their own money had built the only public school, where there were three churches and not a single saloon, where 97 per cent of the residents owned the homes they occupied— here the mob opened fire. The fire was returned, and a police officer was killed. The riot flared anew. Homes were looted and put to the torch. Business places were robbed and wrecked. Four more Negroes were killed. The president of the theological seminary, Dr.

J. W. E. Bowen, was beaten by the police, presumably for daring to ask for police protection.

No one knows the total number of injuries, permanent cripplings and deaths that resulted from the Atlanta riot. Reports vary, but an all-white investigating committee had this to say: "Among the victims of the mob there was not a single vagrant. They were earning wages in useful work up to the time of the riot. They were supporting themselves and their families or dependent relatives. . . . About seventy persons were wounded, and among these there was an immense amount of suffering. . . . Many . . . are disfigured, and several are permanently disabled. . . ." [5]

But the Atlanta *Evening News,* which had promoted the riot more assiduously than ever it had promoted civic welfare, was still unsatisfied. Three months later, on December 12, it said editorially: "No law of God or man can hold back the vengeance of our white men upon such a criminal. If necessary, we will double and treble and quadruple the law of Moses, and hang off-hand the criminal, or failing to find that a remedy, we will hang two, three, or four of the Negroes nearest to the crime, until the crime is no longer done or feared in all this Southland that we inhabit and love."

It appeared that rape had become peculiarly a Negro crime. Where and when such crimes did occur—and they did, though with nothing like the frequency which mass hysteria suggested—the press made the most of them. Every Negro was at heart a ravager of white women. The fear-reaction that this image called up was potent beyond present-day comprehension. As late as 1930, the image was used successfully as the only defense of two white murderers who killed in cold blood and for no ostensible reason a wholly innocent Negro. The cry of rape, or even of attempted rape, raised against a Negro was enough to ignite a holocaust in almost every community in the land.

It did just this in Springfield, Illinois, in August, 1908.

Mrs. Mabel Hallam, having been beaten by her secret lover and desperate for an explanation of her bruises and contusions, claimed to have been assaulted and raped by a Negro. She identified George Richardson, a native of the town, as the alleged criminal. The mob gathered in a twinkling. Failing to find the accused, who had been spirited away, the mob turned its fury on the first Negro it could find, a barber named Burton. His shop was wrecked, and he was cruelly mutilated and burned. This, however, was only an excitant. A white woman already indicted as a criminal and free on bond, led a looting, beating, burning mob raging through the Negro community. All that night and the next day, the city's police were helpless, or pretended to be. On the second night, the state militia quelled the riot, but by then another Negro, eighty-four-year-old William Donegan, had been lynched.

In this riot there was a circumstance so unusual that not a single paper in the state failed to emphasize it. Four white men were killed. This was the first time in an action of this kind that the death toll of whites was greater than that of Negroes. But if the latter drew consolation from the fact, it was short-lived. The city discharged more than fifty Negro employees, although "it was acknowledged that their efficiency and fidelity were not questioned." The state, its capital being Springfield, dismissed others. A thousand Negroes, many of them substantial and respected citizens, left the city for parts unknown. The Illinois *State Journal* commented that "it was not the fact of the whites' hatred toward the Negroes but of the Negroes' own misconduct, general inferiority, or unfitness for free institutions that were at fault."

Negroes everywhere lost heart. In the first decade of the century, nearly a thousand of them were lynched in public spectacles that outmatched the Roman circus for savagery and obscenity. No appeal to conscience was effective. Civil, legal and moral rights meant nothing. The "soft-speaking conformity and sheer opportunism" of Booker Washington did no good, unless to hasten the destruction of the Negro's courage and idealism was good. It looked to James Weldon Johnson "as though the Negro would let his rights and his claim to rights go by default. In that quarter, whence came the champions of justice to the Negro from the whites, there had been a shifting of front, and there was a more or less general admission that the noble crusade had been undertaken in vain. Most of what had been gained as a result of the [Civil] war had been yielded in the struggle on the field where public sentiment is won or lost." [6]

13

THE PRAGMATIC APPROACH

●●●

A WELL-KNOWN WRITER and journalist named William English Walling was in Chicago when the Springfield riot broke. He went at once to investigate and was appalled at what he found. He knew the atmosphere of error and the anatomy of hate. He had seen nothing worse than Springfield in Czarist Russia, whence he had but recently returned, and where his wife, Anna Strunsky, had suffered in the Jewish persecutions.

Yet what moved Walling was not so much what he saw resulting from the "morbid violence of the mob" as it was the initiation of a "state of affairs far worse," and slowly spreading. What he feared was that every hope of political democracy would be eventually destroyed "in the North as in the South" and that "American civilization would have either a rapid degeneration or another profounder and more revolutionary civil war. . . . Yet," he wrote in the *Independent,* "who realizes the seriousness of the situation, and what large and powerful body of citizens is ready to . . . aid?"

The answer was that there was no powerful body of citizens. Du Bois' Niagara Movement, just out of its fourth annual meeting when Walling's article appeared, had already been "done to death by a shameful conspiracy engineered by black men who were paid to make their fellows stop protesting." The Afro-American Council, formed toward the close of the preceding century, was torn by policy and ideological differences. The various city and state Negro conventions were little more than local organizations with weak leaders controlled by conservative whites and manipulated, as often as not, by petty politicians.

But in New York, a wealthy white social worker read Walling's piece. Mary White Ovington's interest in the Negro problem had grown since the day in 1903 when a group of her charges from the Greenpoint Settlement House hurled a childish "Nigger! Nigger! Nigger!" at a group of unoffending colored women. After that Miss Ovington could not let the race problem alone to work itself out. She left Greenpoint Settlement and became a fellow in Greenwich House. Here she launched into a study of the Negro in New York City. Too deeply moved by what she learned to let her study gather dust on an out-of-the-way shelf, she began writing for magazines. Her *New Masses* story, "The White Brute," was a distinct shock to many readers. Her book, *Half a Man,* was in the tradition of the muckrakers, of whom Upton Sinclair said that they wished to "do otherwise than repeat indefinitely the blunders which have proved fatal in the past."

Miss Ovington at once wrote to Walling, requesting a meeting to which Henry Moskovitz was also invited. These three drew up a statement and issued a call "to believers in democracy to join a national conference for the discussion of present evils, the voicing of protests and the renewal of the struggle for civil and political liberty." The response was gratifying. Joined by Du Bois, Moorfield Storey, John Dewey, Jane Addams and Oswald G. Villard, the prime movers formed the National Negro Committee in May, 1909. Only one hitch developed. There were a few who felt that the movement would need Booker Washington's endorsement. There were others, the majority, who were opposed to seeking the cooperation of Washington, because the man's whole drift was contrary to what they sought to do. In the end the majority won, and the group was incorporated in 1910 as the National Association for the Advancement of Colored People. It was committed to an uncompromising program of racial equality.

But the word "equality," which the N.A.A.C.P. refused to define in restricted terms, was a powerful conjure. In the minds of most whites it called up visions of Negroes swarming into the lives of whites, worshipping at their churches, studying in their schools, overrunning their hotels, eating at their dinner tables, and, horror of horrors, marrying their women. For—inexplicable as it was in rational terms, since, contradiction supreme, it implied the easy and willing perversion of the very thing (the inviolable purity of white womanhood) which was claimed as the South's last bulwark against

Negro equality—the center of this nightmare of racial commingling was the Negro male, a conceptual figure born of sick conscience and suckled on fear, brutal beyond exaggeration and of ineffable sexual potency.

The N.A.A.C.P., according to Miss Ovington, was "denounced by nearly every white man who gave to Negro institutions." It was "radical," for how otherwise explain the prominence of Du Bois in it as director of publications and research. It was certainly depraved, for was not this Mary White Ovington the same "high priestess . . . who affiliates five days every week with Negro men and dines with them at her home in Brooklyn, Sundays?" It was subversive, surely, for Walling's wife was probably a Bolshevik, Oswald G. Villard was the grandson of William Lloyd Garrison, and John Lovejoy Elliott was a descendant of the martyred abolitionist Elijah Lovejoy. And then there were the Jews, Walter Sachs, Rabbi Stephen Wise and Dr. Henry Moskovitz.

That the organization was radical in the commonly accepted meaning of the term there can be no doubt. Its organ, *The Crisis,* of which Du Bois was founder and editor, soon proclaimed it so. Within a few months, Du Bois attacked the proposition that had been "the keynote of Mr. Washington's propaganda for the last fifteen years," the assumption that "the truth—the real facts concerning a social situation at any particular time—is of less importance than the people's feeling concerning those facts. There could be no more dangerous social pragmatism. . . . It is a self-contradictory and deceptive position and it has historically led to social damnation in thousands of awful cases." [1] Following the savage lynching of a Negro in Coatesville, Pennsylvania, in 1911, Du Bois wrote: "Let every black American gird up his loins. The great day is coming. We have crawled and pleaded for justice and we have been cheerfully spit upon and murdered and burned. We will not endure it forever. If we are to die, in God's name let us perish like men and not like bales of hay."

Asseverations such as these struck responsive chords in many Negroes. Within a year *The Crisis* had a circulation of twelve thousand, and within two more it was being mailed into every state of the Union and its circulation had increased to fifty thousand. Indubitably Du Bois was the leader of a growing biracial radical group whose special vehicle was the N.A.A.C.P.

Nor was the fiery polemic all that the group went in for. Almost immediately it formed a legal committee of Negro and white lawyers, including Arthur Spingarn, Louis Marshall, Moorfield Storey and Felix Frankfurter, who, working often without fee or even the promise of one, took the fight against discrimination and injustice into the courts. In the United States Supreme Court, they won cases reaffirming the Fifteenth Amendment, invalidating the Grandfather Clause and barring residential segregation. When it sent a young and courageous white woman to investigate the burning alive of a Negro in Waco, Texas, the N.A.A.C.P. began a struggle against lynching that was to identify the organization as ineradicably as Uncle Sam identifies the United States.

2

If the N.A.A.C.P. was considered too radical to merit the support of the philanthropists who gave to Negro causes, the National Urban League was not. The agency was the result of a merger. The New York Committee for Improving Industrial Conditions of Negroes and the National League for the Protection of Colored Women had puttered along in their separate and ineffective ways for five years. They were the favorite charities of women who had Baldwin locomotive and Schieffelin whiskey money to spend. They had got domestic service jobs for Negro women newly come North. They had investigated the pigsty conditions in which urban Negroes lived. They had framed resolutions about the Negro's employment status. Though the two committees had interlocking directorates, it was apparent that they had not seen the similarity of their purposes. George Haynes, a young Negro graduate student in Columbia University, pointed this out to them, and in 1911 the National Urban League on Conditions Among Negroes was formed. On that occasion, Mrs. William H. Baldwin, the League's chairman, said: "Let us work together not as colored people nor as white people for the narrow benefit of any group alone, but together as American citizens for the common good of our common city, our common country." [2]

Eugene Kinckle Jones became the league's first field secretary and the work of the organization underwent a considerable expansion. The board of directors was enlarged in 1913 to include prominent Negroes and whites like Booker Washington, James Dillard, Charles D. Hilles and Kelly Miller—men who could not subscribe to the program of the N.A.A.C.P. Before long, the League was truly national in scope, with branches in various cities where salaried officers sought to broaden employment opportunities for Negroes, to better housing and recreational facilities, and to act as advisors to civic and industrial management. When the league undertook to train promising young Negroes in social work, it attracted the interest of many who have since become outstanding. Ira DeA. Reid, now a professor at Haverford College, became secretary of the New York League. Forrester B. Washington, now head of the Atlanta University School of Social Work, was a member of the national staff. The league's official organ, the *Journal of Opportunity* was first edited by Charles S. Johnson, now the president of Fisk University.

But neither the league nor the N.A.A.C.P. could do much to stem the counterflow of emotionalism running beneath the surface of events as the national elections of 1912 approached. There was a growing reluctance on the part of some white people in public life to be too closely linked to Negro endeavor, a growing weariness or shame at being called "nigger lover." And perhaps it was this that affected Theodore Roosevelt as early as 1906, when, in a decision patently unjustified by the facts, he dismissed without honor a battalion of Negro soldiers charged with rioting in Brownsville, Texas. Though the action was subsequently modified by a congressional Court of Inquiry, Negroes remembered it and brought it up to haunt Roosevelt when he opened his campaign for reelection in 1912.

We are glad [wrote Du Bois], that at least there can be no doubt in any colored man's mind concerning the attitude of Theodore Roosevelt. . . . There were many of us who were disposed, after time had dimmed the bitter memory, to attribute the unjust dismissal of hundreds of colored soldiers who were not even charged with wrong-doing, because of the suspected but far from proven guilt of a few—there were some of us who wished to attribute this official Brownsville "lynching" to the mistaken but sincere impulse of a strong personality rather than to a meaner motive.[3]

If there was any doubt in the minds of some Negroes that Roosevelt was not to be depended on, that his immediate interests played strange tricks with his professed loyalties, that doubt was cleared away at the Chicago convention of the Bull Moose Party. The unpredictable Rough Rider rejected a platform plank that demanded "for the American of Negro descent the repeal of unfair discriminatory laws and the right to vote on the same terms on which other citizens vote." When the party organization proceeded to bar "practically every representative of 8,000,000 Southern Negroes and to recognize delegates chosen by Southern conventions open to" whites only, Roosevelt did not raise a question or a finger.

The campaign that year put Negroes in a quandary. The regular Republican Party had let them down. It was true that President Taft had made some excellent appointments, but he had not really abandoned the position of doing nothing for Negroes that might distress the whites. He had refused to speak out for civil rights. He had incurred the impatience of Negroes by keeping silent in the face of some of the most brutal lynchings and acts of mob violence ever committed in the country. He had made no bones of wishing to keep, and, in fact, to increase the limitations on Negro political activity in the South.

"Deserted by the Republican Party, undesirable, and not wanted in the national Democratic Party, which way shall the Negro turn his face, and whither direct his steps?"

It was no idle question. Inexhaustible debates in the Negro press and on the platform rang loud and fierce—and pathetically indecisive. The Negro's loyalty to the Republican Party was almost paranoic in its intensity. It was the party of Lincoln, and the tyrannical love of the martyred President emanated even from the grave. To split the party, as unaccountably it was split, and so divide the mind and the heart of the Negro, was a monstrous, humorless joke. Nor was this quite all; for now there were Negro leaders who were beginning to hold it no mortal sin to listen to the siren song of the Democrats. And to do more: to mock at those still naïve enough to want to keep their faith in the Republican Party whole.

Wrote Du Bois: "We sympathize with those faithful old black voters who will always vote the Republican ticket. We respect their fidelity, but not their brains. We can understand those who, despite the unspeakable Roosevelt, accept his platform which is broad on all subjects except the greatest—human rights. This we can understand, but we cannot follow."

There were the Democrats then. And who were the Democrats? They were the South, and the South was Negro disfranchisement, peonage and death.

Nevertheless, Wilson and his party were beginning to sound good. Wilson was declared to be "the highest type of a Christian gentleman and scholar." He sounded like one when he said, "I desire to see justice done to the colored people in every matter," and "Should I become President of the United States they [colored people] may count upon me for absolute fair dealing, for everything by which I can assist in advancing the interests of their race in the United States."

It was a prospect good to contemplate; a possibility that, in any case, could not be ignored. Du Bois, by now the most listened-to and the most trusted man of his people, once more took up his pen. "We sincerely believe that even in the face of promises disconcertingly vague, and in the face of the solid caste-ridden South, it is better to elect Woodrow Wilson President of the United States and prove once and for all if the Democratic Party dares to be democratic when it comes to black men. It has proven that it can be in many Northern states and cities. Can it be in the nation? We hope so and we are willing to risk a trial." [4]

Thousands of other Negroes were also willing, and proved it. The importance of this was not that their vote was decisive. But it gave them a sense of political strength to discover that they were the balance of power in New York, Pennsylvania, Ohio and Missouri, and it made it impossible for them ever again to mistake promise for performance.

3

Scholar and gentleman Wilson undoubtedly was, but he was also, and first, a Southerner. With his election (the first of a Southern-born man since 1848) the country turned itself over "to the Democratic Party in general and to the South in particular." Though not a majority in Congress, Southerners had a political power-potential four times greater than Northerners. Half of Wilson's Cabinet was Southern-born. No sooner had Congress convened than it began to consider legislation designed to make it impossible for Negroes to hold commissions in the armed forces, to prohibit the immigration of foreign-born Negroes, and to segregate Negroes in the civil service. This latter thing was accomplished, even without the legislation, and with a niceness of coordination that marked it as policy. A white man, secretly making an investigation for the N.A.A.C.P., noted signs marking off Negro areas in the Treasury and the Post Office

Departments and in the Bureau of Printing and Engraving, and he was told by an official that it was the government's wish "to inaugurate segregation everywhere, but that it was difficult to determine the best way to go about it."

There were protests, of course. Heading a delegation from the National Equal Rights League, Monroe Trotter had a conference at the White House which was abruptly terminated when President Wilson decided that Trotter was impudent—as he probably was. A few liberal white papers in the North published strong editorials, but the nation was generally apathetic. Later that same year considerably fewer papers protested when the United States Supreme Court declared unconstitutional the Civil Rights Law of 1875. Two years later, in 1915, the punitive killing of several hundred black Haitians by United States Marines caused even less comment in the white press. The demagogic political overlords, whom Wilson never abandoned, made capital of this public indifference to the Negro's fate. The determination to nullify Negro citizenship expressed itself in a flagrant abridgement of his simplest rights. In some communities in the South, postmasters cut Jim Crow windows so that Negroes would have no excuse to go inside post offices. Cities in Georgia, Alabama and Florida revived ancient curfew laws, applicable only to Negroes. The South's system of peonage was openly boasted. Denial of justice in the courts, police brutality, mob violence and lynching were too common to be remarked, even by the Northern press.

The white press did rouse itself when Booker Washington died in November, 1915, but only in the South were the eulogies absolute. After all, Washington was the white South's man. The white South had made him, raised him up as the savior of its conscience, and when he died the white South wept. Excepting only the plutocrats, for whom he was in sort also a savior of the conscience and for whom Tuskegee was a kind of sacrificial altar to the god of gold, the North was less stricken in its grief and clearer in its judgment. The New York *Times* averred that Washington "was far from being [the Negroes'] acknowledged leader. . . . There was a multitude who thought him timid and even treacherous." The New York *Evening Post* had seen resentment of him grow "until men openly accused him of selling their birthright for a mess of pottage."

It is no wonder then that there was no wail of anguished lamentation among the Negro people. There was regret for what the man might have done, but did not do. There were recriminations for what he did or helped to do that better had been left undone. "In stern justice," wrote Du Bois, with general Negro approbation, "we must lay on the soul of this man a heavy responsibility for the consummation of Negro disfranchisement, the decline of the Negro college and public school and the firmer establishment of color caste in this land."

And even the South did not mourn for long. It had other fish and some men to fry. Of the latter, sixty-seven in the year of Washington's death. The lynching rate fell from this in 1916 and 1917, as we shall see, but spurted up again in 1918. The next desperate year it went to eighty-three, of whom only fourteen were charged with rape. What happened had happened before, during Reconstruction and in the summer storm of Populism: the white South's dominance over the Negro slipped—and for a variety of reasons.

In the first place, the boll weevil got at the cotton. What the weevil left, floods destroyed in 1915 and 1916. For want of collateral in crops, planters' credit dwindled. For want of cotton, mills closed down. The Negro was caught in an economic pincers. He began to leave the land, to go North. At first there were those in the South who professed to see a blessing in the exodus. The Nashville *Banner* thought that it would "relieve the South of the entire burden and all the brunt of the race problem, and make room for and create greater inducements for white immigration." But what inducements? As the dimensions of the European war expanded, the South had nothing to offer the potential white migrant comparable to the North's war wages, which were luring Negroes too. Those Negroes who remained in the South were not unaware that they had a value to the white man greater than ever before. They grew less tractable, more independent and "sassy." Quite a few of them were lynched for it.

But there were enlightened Southerners who realized that the economic interests of no one were served by visiting violence upon the Negro. The Atlanta *Constitution* was moved to say that:

> The appeal to humanity, to fairness and justice and right, has been, apparently, without effect. It is unfortunate . . . that an appeal to the pocketbook should be necessary to bring back the enthronement of law; but if moral suasion is powerless, the question of personal interest has entered, and in no uncertain degree. . . . There is no secret about what must be done if Georgia would save herself from threatened disaster. . . . In the

first place, there must be no more mobs. Mobs and mob spirit must be eliminated completely, so completely that there will be no danger of recurrence. . . . But more than that, we must be fair to the Negro. There is no use beating about the bush; we have not shown that fairness in the past, nor are we showing it today, either in justice before the law, in facilities accorded for education, or in other directions.[5]

Many Southern papers echoed this point of view.

So the South began a process of mollifying the Negro. Even the Governor of Mississippi, Theodore Bilbo, already infamous for his "nigger-baiting," called a special meeting of the Mississippi State Council for Defense to launch a movement to check the Negro exodus by applying the remedies of "fair dealing, an end to abuses, and higher wages." R. R. Moton, who had succeeded Booker Washington at Tuskegee, was engaged to go through the South and urge Negroes to remain, as he put it in a speech in Montgomery, "with the white men of the South." Moton pictured a sort of rheumy hell for Negroes who went North. "They will take colds and develop pneumonia and consumption, as well as other diseases," he told his audiences. The Beaumont, Texas, *Enterprise* was sure that "the Negroes can do more for themselves and for humanity by working in the fields of the South. . . . The Negro who will work and who will keep his place can find more real happiness in the South than he will ever find in the cities of the North. . . . The climate here is suited to him. The people understand him. They know his weaknesses and his nature and due allowances are made for both." [6]

For all this campaigning, two million Negroes left the South in five years. The South's old, inviolate, absolute surplus of labor was not only absorbed, it was depleted with astonishing celerity. And crops to make. And mills to run. And wages for the white mill hands (who, in order to get wages at all, now needed the black man as much as the planters ever did) up to a fabulous thirty dollars a week! But the hitch was that in the factories and steelyards of the North, a field hand Negro just up from the South could make twice and thrice as much. And labor agents and Negro newspapers were telling him so.

Thus the new enemies to the South's well-being were the labor agent and the Negro press. Municipalities, counties and states tried to liquidate them. Labor agents were exorbitantly taxed (as much as a thousand dollars in Birmingham), endlessly bedeviled. Where their activities remained legal, they were often arrested on trumped-up charges. Montgomery, Savannah and Jackson made it a crime to "entice" Negroes to go North. In Brookhaven, Mississippi, a labor agent was thrown into jail and the two hundred Negroes he had rounded up were hauled off a northbound train, beaten and dispersed.

Negro newspapers were anathema. It became a crime (*inciting to riot*) in Georgia for a Negro to read the Chicago *Defender*. Every week this paper offered Negroes fresh inducements to go North. It set May 15, 1917, as the day for a concerted "Great Northern Drive."

But every day was a day for that. Plantation after plantation was left without a single laboring hand. While the rest of the nation enjoyed a war-inspired prosperity, the South found itself in imminent danger of economic strangulation.

And once again, after the lull of 1916 and 1917, the South took recourse to its ancient weapons, repression and terror. Ticket agents refused to sell northbound tickets to Negroes. The whip came back into general use. Peonage grew widespread. "Extra-legal patrols and sheriff's posses engaged in a campaign of terrorization and forceful restraint." The lynching rate rose. But all this had an effect exactly opposite to what was intended. An unjust jailing, a beating or a lynching was often the final cause of whole Negro communities, with their preachers, teachers, doctors and business men, stealing away in the night.

14

WHITE MAN'S WAR

●●

By November, 1916, when it was evident that America could not stay out of the war, the rumor was already rife among Negroes that President Wilson had said that the war was to be a "white man's war." No one knows where or how it started, but the record of Wilson's first administration made the rumor credible. When, on March 25, 1917, still two weeks before the formal declaration, Newton D. Baker called the First Separate Battalion (Negro) of the District of Columbia National Guard to protect the national capital, the bitter and cynical said that it was still "the white man's war, but the black man's fight." The meaning of the phrase was in dramatic contrast to the slogans that soon blazed from every billboard in the country. "A War for Humanity." "Make the World Safe for Democracy."

The morale of most Negroes was grievously low, but the fact could not be ascertained from the records of early recruiting. Deeply stirred by the promises in the official catchwords, Negroes swarmed to volunteer. But doubts beset them speedily. Five days after America's entrance into the conflict, the War Department ordered a stop to the acceptance of Negroes: the quotas of colored outfits were full.

These outfits consisted of ten thousand men in the 24th and 25th Infantries and the 9th and 10th Cavalries, and another ten thousand in the National Guard, including companies in Massachusetts, Connecticut, New York, Ohio and Illinois. These National Guard outfits had their own Negro officers, but Colonel Charles Young, the highest ranking Negro in the regular Army, being declared physically unfit, was immediately retired. Negroes protested this action as one of pure prejudice. To give the lie to the official finding of ill health,

Young rode horseback from his home in Ohio to Washington, D.C. The army retracted only so far as to send Colonel Young to Haiti as military attaché. Negroes saw this as another dodge to avoid promoting him to the rank of general.

By late spring of 1917, Negroes were thoroughly discouraged. German propaganda was eating at them, reminding them of the ancient Belgian atrocities in the Congo, of the compounded mistakes of Britain's imperial policy in Africa. They did not have to be reminded of the American record of injustice and race violence. In East St. Louis, Illinois, where in three years ten thousand Negroes had been imported from the South, some as strikebreakers, a savage race riot flared in July, 1917. Nearly six thousand Negroes were driven from the city. An uncounted number lost their lives. A young Russian Jewish observer commented that the pogrom-makers of Russia could take lessons from the whites of East St. Louis. "The Russians, at least, gave the Jews a chance to run while they were trying to murder them. The whites of East St. Louis fired the homes of black folk and either did not allow them to leave the burning houses or shot them the moment they dared attempt to escape the flames." [1]

Meantime Negroes had begun agitating for the government to train Negro officers. At a conference in Washington that summer, they demanded "the right of our best men to lead troops of their own race in battle, and to receive officer's training in preparation for such leadership." They memorialized Congress and made representations to the War Department. They were told that the entrance of Negroes into Plattsburg, where white officers were trained, was unthinkable. Joel Spingarn suggested a compromise—a separate training camp for Negro officers. Many Negroes, among them Monroe Trotter, objected to this, and Du Bois had to call them sharply to task.

Where in heaven's name do we Negroes stand? If we organize separately for anything— "Jim Crow!" scream all the Disconsolate; if we organize with white people— "Traitors! Pressure! They're betraying us!" yell all the Suspicious. If, unable to get the whole loaf we seize half to ward off starvation— "Compromise!" yell all the Scared. If we let the half loaf go and starve— "Why don't you *do* something?" yell those same Critics. . . Just now we demand Negro officers for Negro regiments. We cannot get them by admission to the regular camps because the law of the land, or its official interpretation, wickedly prevents us. Therefore, give us separate training camp for Negro officers.[2]

If enough college-worthy Negroes could be found, General Leonard Wood, director of military training, thought a separate officer's training camp might be provided. With tongue in cheek, he suggested finding two hundred Negroes eligible for such training. Within two weeks more than a thousand Negro college men presented their names, and in June, 1917, a special camp was opened at Fort Des Moines, Iowa. The following October nearly seven hundred Negroes were commissioned captains and lieutenants. It was a hurt to some that their training took one month more than the standard three.

But many things were a hurt to some, and now that Booker Washington was dead, there was no one to advise caution, forbearance and soft resilient patience. Negroes cried out when the operation of the Selective Service became discriminatory. (It came out later that 51.65 per cent of all Negro registrants were placed in Class 1, while only 32.53 per cent of whites were so classified. The actual induction of Negroes was 31 per cent of the registrants, as compared to 26 per cent of the whites.) Negroes cried "Shame!" when Colonel C. C. Ballou, commander at Des Moines, called the Negro officer-candidates together and told them that they "need not expect democratic treatment." Later raised to the rank of major general and placed in command of the Negro 92nd Division, this officer issued the hated Bulletin No. 35, which said in effect that the Negro's legal rights meant nothing at all; that the men of his command, remembering that "white men made the Division and they can break it," must not press for what they were legally entitled to. General Ballou was transferred to another command.

What hurt Negroes most in the late summer of 1917 resulted from the Houston, Texas, riot in which members of the 24th Infantry were involved with whites. Just before the trouble there, the chaplain of the 24th wrote: "The battalion has made good and all doubts as to the conduct of the Negro soldier has been dissipated. We are striving to add another page to the glorious history of our regiment." They added a page, but it was spattered with the blood of whites.

In common with most Southern communities, Houston objected to the presence of Negro soldiers. The citizenry goaded them with insults. "To avoid trouble," said the official record, the Negro provost guard were ordered disarmed. Molestations, insults and beatings of soldiers increased. After some days of this, members of the battalion stole the arms that were forbidden them and killed seventeen whites. Speedily tried, thirteen soldiers were hanged and forty-one were condemned to life imprisonment.

The country was in a state of abnormal excitement, even for wartime. Hysteria blew everything up. Nothing was simple. Alarum followed alarum; incident, incident. Almost no one outside the race seemed to sense the gall-distilling incongruity between our stated war aims and our practices at home. No one seemed to realize that the Negro had a tremendous emotional stake in democracy. Whose democracy? the Negro began to ask in bitter jest. And why? And wherefor? There was a great plexus of fear and suspicion which no one deemed it worth while to dissolve, and there was a timid, sad hope which few thought it necessary to encourage. The Negro was expected to give whatever was demanded and to take whatever came.

So matters stood in the fall of 1917.

2

Back in March, Emmett J. Scott, once Booker Washington's confidential secretary and at the time an official of Tuskegee, had written a letter to Julius Rosenwald, a member of the advisory board of the Council of National Defense. The letter expressed concern "at what the attitude of the Administration will be in respect to the Negro people" when America entered the war. At the suggestion of Mr. Rosenwald, Scott drafted a resolution for the Council, and two months later, when Negro morale was dangerously low, he was appointed special assistant to the Secretary of War and, the letter of transmittal read, "confidential advisor in matters affecting the interest of 10,000,000 Negroes of the United States." The appointment was hailed by white and colored as a great step forward in giving official recognition to the Negroes' interest.

Emmett Scott had his work cut out for him. He was sent almost immediately to Spartanburg, South Carolina, where the 15th New York Regiment, renamed the 369th U.S. Infantry, was in training. The regiment had formerly been under the command of the Negro, Colonel Benjamin O. Davis, but he had been relieved and his place taken by Colonel William Hayward, a white officer. Whether this was a factor in what the white citizens of Spartanburg called "nigger obstreperousness and sullenness" no one knows, but trouble broke when one of the most popular men in the outfit was kicked by a white civilian. Only the timely intervention of Colonel Hayward prevented a riot.

The special assistant to the Secretary of War was swamped as the complaints of Negroes piled in. "There was considerable misunderstanding and false impressions at the beginning as to the real function of the office . . . as to the real scope and limitations of the appointment." In his prolix official volume, *The American Negro in the World War,* Scott continues: "Judging from thousands of letters he received, covering every subject imaginable, and from various public comments and utterances . . . it would seem that he had been appointed a 'Special Committee of One' to adjust and settle at once any and all matters and difficulties of whatsoever kind and nature which had any bearing upon the race problem in America."

Scott did what he could, but that was precious little. He must have realized how hopeless his task was when reports on conditions began to come in from two special investigators appointed by the Federal Council of Churches and the Phelps-Stokes Fund. Charles H. Williams and G. Lake Imes visited practically all the camps and cantonments where colored troops were stationed and talked with officers, enlisted men and plain citizens. From the winter of 1917 to the end of the war, both in this country and abroad, they carried on their investigations. They found discriminatory conditions ranging from a lack of sufficient chaplains, morale officers and recreation facilities to "inexcusable brutality" on the part of white Military Police and "lack of proper medical attention and treatment." The books that Scott and Williams wrote, in spite of the glossing in them, are grim anatomies of American color prejudice.

3

The great majority of Negroes in the armed forces functioned as service troops. In the Navy they were messmen and orderlies, the only classifications into which they were accepted. There were no Negroes in the Coast Guard or the Marines. The only Negro who might have served in aviation was Lieutenant Charles A. Tribbett, but on his way to Fort Sill, Oklahoma, for training—in uniform, under orders, traveling on government business on a government-controlled railroad—he was arrested by civil authorities at Chickasha,

Oklahoma. His crime: riding in a coach with white people. The War Department intervened, the Justice Department threatened an investigation, and somehow in all the excitement, Tribbett's orders were changed and his career in aviation cut off before it had begun.

Roughly four hundred thousand Negroes were called into service and two hundred thousand were shipped to France, but only fifty thousand saw combat duty. Most of these latter were men of the 92nd and 93rd Infantry Divisions. The important fighting units of the 93rd were brigaded with French troops, and this made a difference in morale. Unit for unit, the 93rd did more and better fighting than the 92nd. Perhaps of some bearing on the record is the fact that the 92nd was whipped into a fighting organization only after it landed in France. Its various units had been trained separately in camps scattered from Iowa to Maryland.

As combat soldiers, Negroes fought as hard and as bravely as whites. Their record in the war disproved all the stereotypes upon which army policy was posited. The stereotypes, which Horace Mann Bond has catalogued, were: That Negroes do not make good soldiers. They are not susceptible to discipline. They are not brave. Negroes and whites cannot be employed in mixed units. Negroes make good soldiers if commanded by white officers. Negro officers are unable to command the respect of their own race. Negroes have never proved successfully that they could stand up under direct fire, although they make good parade soldiers.

There were white officers who did not believe in the stereotypes. One of these was Colonel William Hayward. Of his 369th Infantry he said: "There is no better soldier material in the world. Given the proper training, these will be the equal of any soldiers in the world." Arriving in France on December 27, 1917, men of the 369th were the first American troops to move up to the fighting front—not, however, without having done service as a labor battalion at St. Nazaire. They went into action in the Bois d'Hauza in April, 1918. For two months they withstood deadly German fire along a whole sector, and then they were relieved for special training in open warfare.

The training was never completed. In September the Germans began their last great offensive in Champagne, and the Allies determined to counter. Supported by Moroccans on the left and poilus on the right, the 369th opened an attack at Maison-en-Champagne that did not lose its drive until it had carried them to the Rhine.

They were in the trenches for 191 days. They never lost a man through capture—nor a trench, nor a foot of ground. Their casualties were 1,100 dead and wounded. The first American soldiers, black or white, to receive the highest decoration of the French government, the Croix de Guerre, were Privates Henry Johnson and Needham Roberts of the 369th. The regiment was eleven times cited for bravery. For the offensive that carried them to the Rhine, the entire regiment was decorated with the Croix de Guerre.

It was this outfit, too, that could boast the famous regimental band led by Lieutenant James Reese Europe and drum-majored by Sergeant Noble Sissle. The band gave morale-building concerts all over France. In a humorous but laudatory article for the *World Magazine,* Charles Welton observed that "on all fronts at this time soldiers who had been dodging Minenwerfers were buoyed up by the promise that Jim Europe had enough jazz in stock to last until the war was over."

But the 369th was not the only battalion to distinguish itself. After only twenty-six days of instruction in French arms and tactics, the 371st went into the trenches as a part of the 157th French Division under General Goybet. It fought in the Champagne in the summer, taking the strategically important Montfauxelles, which was the apex of a triangle formed by four French towns and which the Germans had held to stubbornly for eleven desperate months. In September the outfit was integrated with the main Champagne offensive. In some of the bitterest fighting of the war, between September 28 and October 6, it lost 1,065 of its 2,384 men.

Units of the 92nd Division, like the 367th which saw action in the Metz offensive, and the 368th which fought in the Argonne-Meuse drive, won numerous individual and unit citations, including the Croix de Guerre. It was of Negro American troops that General Goybet spoke when, after calling them "crack regiments," he went on to say that they "overcame every obstacle with a most complete contempt for danger."

And there were more than military obstacles to overcome. First of all, there was the German propaganda, which had been pounding steadily at American Negroes since before the United States entered the war. According to Captain George B. Lester, a military intelligence officer, the directing hand of this effort to demoralize was the German ambassador to Mexico. The publishing source was the Fuehr

Publicity Bureau in New York. This bureau kept "records of every lynching, every attack by a white person upon a Negro, and every item of alleged oppression of the Negro race by the white. . . . The Negroes were told by the propagandists that in Europe there was no color line, that there the blacks were equal to the whites; that if Germany won the war the rights of Negroes throughout the world would equal those of whites."

When the 92nd Division reached the battle lines, the Germans dropped leaflets:

Hello, boys, what are you doing over there? Fighting the Germans? Why? . . . Some white folks and lying English-American papers told you that the Germans ought to be wiped out for the sake of humanity and democracy. What is democracy? Personal freedom, all citizens enjoying the same rights socially and before the law. Do you enjoy the same rights as the white people do in America, the land of freedom and democracy? . . . Can you go to a restaurant where white people dine . . . or can you ride in the South in the same street car with white people? And how about the law? Is lynching and the most horrible cruelties connected therewith a lawful proceeding in a democratic country? . . . You have been made the tool of the egotistic and rapacious rich in England and America, and there is nothing in the whole game for you but broken bones, horrible wounds, broken health—or death. . . . Let those do the fighting who make profit out of the war. . . . To carry the gun in their defense is not an honor but a shame. Throw it away and come over to the German lines.

This was old stuff to Negroes by the winter of 1918.

Older and more vicious and—at first—more instinctive than calculated was the race prejudice which Americans tried to spread in Europe. Currency was given numerous stories, some of them so absurd in their disregard both of scientific probability and empirical knowledge that they could not have come but from the most brazenly ignorant minds. Beneath their tunics, Negroes had tails like monkeys. The peculiar slouch with which they walked was due to the fact that they had no toes to their feet. The kiss of a blue-gummed Negro was deadly poison, and eight of ten Negroes had blue gums which they disguised with pink wax. Negroes in America were locked up every night, for they were incorrigible rapists. Negroes could not learn to read. Among themselves they spoke a phatic language of grunts and growls and shrieks and moans. Negroes could not cultivate the higher senses and desires. For these and other equally pertinent reasons, the French, and especially the French women, should have no contact with black Americans.

Nor did the stories and the warning stay on this level. It may have been in the name of patriotism, cooperation and peace that a section of the American High Command persuaded the French Military Mission to issue the following document to French troops in the summer of 1918:

> American opinion is unanimous on this [the Negro Question] and permits no discussion of the matter. The kindly spirit which exists in France for the Negro profoundly wounds Americans who consider it an infringement of their national dogmas. . . . We should not sit at the table with them and should avoid shaking hands with them. . . . The merits of Negro soldiers should not be too warmly praised, especially in the presence of Americans. . . . The vices of the Negro are a constant menace to the American who has to repress them sternly. The black American troops in France have by themselves given rise to as many complaints for attempted rape as all the rest of the Army. The black is constantly being censored for his lack of intelligence and discretion. . . .[3]

Be it said to the credit of the French that when the French Ministry of War heard of the existence of this black paper, it ordered all copies confiscated and burned.

But by this time the Negro's morale had plummeted to a new low. This is not to say that his effort in the war slackened. He was too much of a realist for that; too much, too, of an American. It is only to say that he was finding no spiritual compensation for fighting and dying. Those morale-building agencies, which were working so effectively among white soldiers and civilians, were at least half blind and three-quarters careless of the Negro's needs. The Y.M.C.A., for instance. A regional director of that institution estimated that "about 25 per cent of the white secretaries served the colored soldiers gladly, about 25 per cent served them half-heartedly, and about 50 per cent either refused to serve them or made them feel that they were not wanted." [4] Nor does this need to be documented further than to cite the case at Camp Greene in North Carolina, where five Y.M.C.A. buildings located in the Negro area of the camp were for the exclusive use of whites. And the case of the canteen worker in France who, rather than serve Negro troops, closed the canteen down.

When the Y.M.C.A. began assigning Negro secretaries to Negro troops, one secretary had often to serve an area containing as many as fifty thousand men. There were only 106 Negro Y workers, including nineteen women, for all Negro troops. Under the direction of John Hope, peacetime president of Morehouse College, the colored Y secretaries did gruelling work. They preached, they entertained, they taught the illiterate. Many of them had to build their own huts out of funds they themselves had to solicit. Some of them went into the trenches with their men, and one of them, T. C. Cook, attached to the 371st Regiment, was cited for bravery. Mrs. Helen Curtis, Mrs. Addie Hunton and Miss Kathryn Johnson, the three Negro women who were sent as Y workers to France, were such rare and welcome sights that the men wept when they saw them. Speaking to the Negro secretaries at a banquet in Paris, E. C. Carter, head of the Y's overseas service, praised: "No group of secretaries has been more successful, nor has any work been on a higher level. I have been impressed most by your spirit. Sometimes you have met with difficulties and have been insulted by workers with the red triangle on their arms, but through it all you have shown the spirit of true greatness as did the Master."

The Knights of Columbus and the Salvation Army had shorter but better records than the Y among Negro soldiers in Europe. Neither organization saddled itself with segregation, and so long as they ran their facilities without interference, there was no trouble. But they were not always allowed to do this. At Tours, France, for instance, the military commander of the cantonment decided that the policy of segregation must apply to the Knights of Columbus facility too. A riot ensued.

In spite of the heavily censored dispatches of Ralph Tyler, the only Negro newspaperman officially accredited to the A.E.F., stories of gross prejudice and discrimination got back to the colored people in America. There was the story of the order, issued by the commander of Zone Five, to the effect that colored officers in the zone were to have their breakfast an hour earlier and their midday and evening meals an hour later than white officers. There were stories of memos from unit officers to division commanders requesting the replacement of colored officers by whites of the same or even lower grades. There were stories of irregular court-martials, of unjust punishment, of Negro soldiers attacked by mobs of white soldiers.

All of these meant to the Negro back home that there was no moratorium on American prejudice abroad. They meant to the whites that Negro soldiers were getting out of hand, that they were learning things from the French that would render them social hazards when they returned to America. Some Negro soldiers had forgot themselves so far as to marry French and Belgian women. They were being spoiled. The thought caused consternation on the highest levels. Now quite comfortable in the shoes of Booker Washington, R. R. Moton was sent posthaste to France as a counteragent. He was given a military escort of the brightest brass. He went among colored troops everywhere, and he made the kind of speeches that Booker Washington might have made. "You will go back to America heroes [and] I hope no one will do anything in peace to spoil the magnificent record you have made in war." He made it clear that the "anything" they might do to spoil their war record was press for the fulfillment of the democracy thousands died to save.

4

For though the Negroes back home were party to a tacit bargain with society, there was tension in the atmosphere—stemming perhaps in part from the whites' realization that there was something calculated in the Negroes' patient forbearance now, something perhaps wily and waiting in his patriotism. Under the taunting title "We Should Worry," Du Bois had written:

The American Negro more unanimously than any other American group has offered his services in this war as officers and soldiers. He has done this earnestly and unselfishly, overlooking his just resentment and grievous wrongs. Up to the present his offer has been received with sullen and ungracious silence, or at best in awkward complaisance. . . . But, "We should worry."

If they do not want us to fight, we will work. We will walk into the industrial shoes of a few million whites who go to the front. We will get higher wages and we cannot be stopped from migrating by all the deviltry of the slave South; particularly with the white lynchers and mob leaders away at war. . . . We'll fight or work. We'll fight and work. If we fight we'll learn the fighting game and cease to be so "*aisly* lynched." If we don't fight we'll learn the more lucrative trades and cease to be so easily robbed and exploited. . . . "We should worry."

But they did worry, and they fussed. Their newspapers and magazines were evidence of it. They gloated too. With that calculation mentioned above—and which is to become a factor of increasing importance in the post-war years—they went into jobs that they had never had before and at wages and under conditions better than they had ever known. Three hundred thousand went into manufacturing. Another hundred thousand went into transportation and communications. Close to seventy-five thousand more were in the mines. They were not blind to the fact that their jobs were mainly the muck-work of unskilled labor, that there was a prevailing assumption of their unfitness for anything else, and that the assumption itself was the rationalization of organized labor's prejudice against them. And there was one thing more to which they were not blind—their importance to the war economy and geared-up industry. The Secretary of Labor made that importance plain in 1918 when he created the Division of Negro Economics and called George Haynes, the sociologist of the Urban League and Fisk University, to head it.

The trouble with the new division was that it had no real power. Its principal function was to build the morale of Negro workers. It tried to do this by forming a State Negro Workers Advisory Committee in fifteen states. It hoped by this means to assure "white employers . . . of a continuing supply of black labor which would serve diligently" and, the division's critics added caustically, "without hope of advancement."

Because even the activity of organized labor among Negroes offered no promise of job advancement. Besides, Negroes were suspicious of labor unions, believing that the unions' interest in them was the result of the depletion of their own white ranks and a consequent diminution of white organized labor's power. Attempts to bar black workers from employment would be futile in the national crisis, so why join unions? (Some Negroes held a view as shortsighted as that.) And especially why join the segregated, rigidly controlled locals that the American Federation of Labor invited them into, in 1919? Many Negroes did join, but there was always the question. Add to this the fact that the government made no practical approach to the basic problems of job security, job advancement and the integration of Negro and white labor, and you have the whole story. A Negro laborer remained—a Negro laborer.

But he and his missus, who likely as not was also a laborer, perhaps walking track or tending crossing on the railroad, or heating rivets in a shipyard, or driving a truck, or operating a machine in a factory, or testing ammunition, or running an elevator—always, of course, at lower wages than those of white girls—the Negro and his missus contributed to the five Liberty Loan drives, the six Red Cross campaigns, the never-ceasing Thrift Stamp drive and the staggering United War Camp effort. If the $250,000,000 estimate of the Negroes' total contribution sounds high, then let it be remembered that no less a person than Mrs. Mary B. Talbert, president of the National Association of Colored Women, is the authority who said that in the third Liberty Loan drive Negro women alone contributed $5,000,000. And let the record be searched for proof—for it is there —that the Negro workers in a single tobacco factory in Norfolk subscribed $91,000 for one drive, and that in another the Negroes of Savannah raised a quarter of a million.

Negro women of the upper classes earned no wages, but they contributed time and an inexhaustible energy not only to their own Negro organizations, but to all the war-created volunteer organizations that did not bar them. They helped with the multifarious problems that came to the Urban League in the wake of continuing migration and employment. They backed Mrs. Emily Bigelow Hapgood in the creation of the Circle for Negro War Relief, and soon sixty units of the organization were spread from New York to Utah. They entertained Negro soldiers and visited their families and bathed and weighed their babies in "baby centers." They found homes for the migrant Negro women so sorely needed in industry. Such women as Mrs. Alice Dunbar Nelson, widow of the poet Dunbar, Mrs. Mary McLeod Bethune, Mrs. John Hope, Miss Ida Cummings and Miss Maria Baldwin were active in the women's division of the Council of National Defense, in the Loan Drives, the Red Cross, the Y.W.C.A., and the War Work Council. They knitted sweaters, made up comfort kits, rolled bandages, fed departing troops and in general, as a phrase of the time went, kept the home fires burning. The emotional conditions under which they worked were sometimes a strain, but they shared with their working and fighting men the hope that the end of the war would bring a new day for the Negro.

And there were those who professed to believe that the new day's dawn was waxing, that there were some faint streaks of light in the sky. The Negro was now ensconced in industry about a million strong, and that was a streak of light. Negroes had been called into the government in advisory capacities, and that was a streak of light. On the battlefield the Negro had "proved his right . . . to a fuller measure of justice, respect, opportunity and fair play in time of peace. . . ." Even white men in the South were saying so. The estimable Reverend George Luther Cady, of the First Congregational Church of Jackson, Mississippi, for instance—had he not preached a sermon on racial tolerance that was published to the world? And had not a Mr. Bolton Smith, "representative white gentleman of Memphis, Tennessee," written to Governor Tome C. Rye as follows?

The Government of the United States is controlled by Southern men. It has called the Negro to the defense of the colors, and the American people will demand that a race thus honored shall be granted the justice of a fair trial when accused of crime. . . . As Secretary of the Tennessee Law and Order League, organized to stop lynching, I urge you to issue a proclamation pointing out the treasonable effects of . . . lynchings.

The Governor issued the proclamation. Another herald of the dawn.

But the light in the sky was not so much false as feeble, for banked on the horizon were the clouds that would obscure it, and drumming across the roofs of the land were the winds of an approaching storm that threatened to uproot the foundations of democracy.

Part Three

15

THE CHANGING PATTERN

•••

THE DRUMMING OF the wind sounded at first like cheers as the boys, black and white, came marching home again. The old 15th New York (the 369th) had not had the thrill of marching away to war, but they were the first returning troops to parade under New York City's Victory Arch. Recalling it later, a white major, Arthur W. Little, wrote: "The multitudes of fellow citizens who greeted us that day—the tens of thousands who cheered, the women who wept—the men who cried 'God bless you, boys!'—all were united to drown the music of Jim Europe's band. They did not give us their welcome because ours was a regiment of colored soldiers—they did not give us their welcome in spite of ours being a regiment of colored soldiers. They greeted us that day from hearts filled with gratitude and with pride and with love, *because ours was a regiment of men, who had done the work of men.*" [1]

That was on February 17, 1919. The next day a Negro was horribly lynched in Georgia. Within that year seventy-six Negroes, some of them still in uniform and one of them not yet recovered from his war wounds, were in like manner done to death. Brought to a maximum by those very things that should have minimized them—that is, by Negro migration, a substantial upturn in the common white man's economic condition, the war and the promise of a period of post-war prosperity—the South's ancestral fears and hates fixed themselves in the old pattern of violence and were bodied forth in the resurrected Ku Klux Klan. Indeed, it was the threatened loss of their better economic position and of the promises of continued prosperity that sparked the revival of the Klan spirit. If the Klan was anti-Catholic, anti-Jew and anti-Negro, it was because, as the South saw

it, Catholic, Jew and Negro were a danger to the Americanism that
the common white man in the South saw physically represented in
his new "standard" wages, a "standard" living level and "standard"
schools. The South had contradictory feelings of inferiority. Though
she wished to remain defiantly herself and *Southern,* she took pride
in approaching the level of progress presumed to obtain North and
West.

And the chief danger to the maintenance of this new level was
the returning Negroes. Whether they were returning from the war
or merely from a sojourn in the North, they were different people
from those who had gone away. They had had new and prideful experiences. They had broken with gloating impunity the old taboos
that undergirded their historic role in Dixie. In the army they had
seen Negro officers take the salute of white enlisted men. Some of
them, for that matter, had been officers themselves. And in the North
they had come in contact with—Bolshevism? Undoubtedly. The
United States government itself investigated, and on November 4,
1919, the Justice Department came out with the statement that "there
can no longer be any question of a well-concerted movement among
a certain class of Negro leaders of thought and action to constitute
themselves a determined and persistent source of radical opposition to the Government and to the established rule of law and order."
Among the salient points noted in the Negro's new attitude were,
"First, an ill-governed reaction toward race-rioting. Second, the
threat of retaliatory measures in connection with lynching. Third,
the more openly expressed demand for social equality, in which
demand the sex problem is not infrequently included. Fourth, the
identification of the Negro with such radical organizations as the
I.W.W. and an outspoken advocacy of the Bolsheviki doctrine."

Southern papers, of course, gave full coverage to this, and Southern white leaders went on from there with calamity howling, warnings, threats. Even so ordinarily sane a Southern white man as W. W.
Alexander was moved to demand the suppression of the Negro press
"in its bolshevistic tendencies and its attempt to inflame the colored
population of America." The South's common whites, always quick
to exaggerate and to personalize, began to have nightmares, in which
every black they had ever known walked with a bolder step, looked
with an insolent eye; and all the blacks, known and unknown, were
planning onslaughts on white government, white jobs and white

women. In short, what their minds misbegot were awful dreams of a revolution of blacks against whites.

It was a simple problem with a simple answer: "Get the nigger before he gets you." Thus, violence, lynching, and the Ku Klux Klan, which the New York *World* charged with "four killings, one mutilation, one branding with acid, forty-one floggings, twenty-seven tar and feather parties, and five kidnappings" in the twelve-month period ending in October, 1921.

The dreams were real bogies in the South, where, for instance, there could be no fear of Negro job competition since "white" jobs and "black" jobs were firmly fixed by a historical precedent which even the disorganization of the war could not destroy. The same was true of the competition for housing, in spite of the N.A.A.C.P.'s victory over residential segregation in the Buchanan-Warley case back in 1917. It is true that the Supreme Court had ruled the Grandfather Clause a perversion of the Fourteenth Amendment, but the Southern answer to this was the lily-white Democratic primary. So there was no political rivalry between black and white in the South, and no such thing there would be for twenty-five years—and then only token.

But more subtly knit into the social fabric, the same complex of fears was apparent in the North as well. Racial competition in all the usual areas was real enough and active enough, and had been even before the close of the war. The second Wilson campaign was the cause of desperate political skirmishing between Negroes and whites. It was basically job competition that led to the East St. Louis riot of 1917. The unslackening Negro migration forced a situation in housing that was certainly not calculated to soothe the interracial temper. What happened in Chicago is a case in point.

In 1916, a pennon strung across Grand Boulevard at Forty-third Street bore the legend: "They Shall Not Pass." The whites put the pennon there, and those who should not pass were Negroes. A year later, Richard B. Harrison, then entertaining at Liberty Bond rallies, dared to defy this warning and moved south of Forty-third. His House was bombed. In the next four years there were fifty-eight bombings of newly acquired Negro residences in Chicago.

But these bombings attracted little attention outside the Negro race. What attracted more was rioting. A riot was sensational, sweeping, far more evocative of mass hysteria. Compared to it, lynching is a private party. The explosive beginnings of riots are not planned; they happen. To be a lyncher, you must first be a member of a mob. Riots sweep into their current even those who have no wish to riot. A lynch mob loiters. It is armed with guns and ropes and knows where the best tree is. Riots are spontaneous. They may organize themselves later, but they do not start with organization. Lynchings are the expression of the conscious anti-social will of the community. Riots may begin, and often do begin, as the expression of an individual in response to pressures that are hardly realized.

Riots shattered the uneasy peace of thirty cities and towns between 1917 and 1925. In the "red summer" of 1919 there were no less than eight major interracial clashes. Only a lucky accident prevented a horrible toll in Chester, Pennsylvania. A gang of white rioters surging into the Negro neighborhood did not meet a mob of Negroes surging toward the white neighborhood. Even so, five whites and seven Negroes were reported to have died. Longview, Texas, writhed in riot for several days after some whites undertook to discipline a Negro for reporting a lynching. Two Negroes and one white man were killed, several Negroes run out of town and sixty thousand dollars' worth of property was destroyed. There were riots in Elaine, Arkansas, and Knoxville, Tennessee. In the nation's capital, heavily armed Negroes prowled the streets in high-powered cars and killed four white men in revenge for a series of beatings.

But by far the most costly riot of that summer occurred in Chicago. On the lake front an imaginary line divided not only the beach but the water itself into white area and black area. When a young Negro swimmer drifted past this line, he was stoned by whites and drowned. Negroes who happened to be present demanded that a white policeman arrest George Stauber, one of the stoners. This was refused. The Negroes attacked the officer. The riot began. It roared on through the night and the next day and for eleven days thereafter —and this in spite of the National Guard who were called out on the fourth day. Rumors spread virulent poison. "Negro women of the stockyard district had had their breasts hacked off after being subjected to sexual violence." "Negroes were being soaked in gasoline, set afire, and made to run like living torches until the flames overcame them." "Gangs of Negroes were raping white women." "Negroes were firing the houses of white people." A city alderman, Joseph McDonough, warned that the Negroes possessed "enough ammunition for years of guerrilla warfare."

When the official casualty list was made, it contained the names of twenty-two Negroes and sixteen whites killed and more than five hundred of both races wounded.

2

In what was called the Negroes' "ill-governed reaction toward race-rioting," the whites saw, or claimed to see, to their unspeakable horror, an element of calculation of great danger. This Bolshevik-promoted calculation, so Congressman James F. Byrnes of South Carolina declared in the House on August 24, 1919, was inspired by the "incendiary utterances of would-be Negro leaders, circulated through Negro newspapers in New York, Boston and Chicago. . . . [These] are responsible for racial antagonism in the United States."

Byrnes went on at some length. On the evidence already mentioned, he asserted "that Negro leaders deliberately planned a campaign of violence before the Washington and Chicago riots." He cited articles in the *Messenger,* a magazine edited by A. Philip Randolph and Chandler Owen, and proclaimed it palpable that the magazine was supported by a source "antagonistic to the United States. . . . It appeals for the establishment in this country of a Soviet Government. . . . It pays tribute to [Eugene] Debs and every other convicted enemy of the Government." Finally, calling on Attorney General Mitchell Palmer to start espionage proceedings against W. E. B. Du Bois, Byrnes quoted from a *Crisis* editorial of May, 1919.

We sing: this country of ours, despite all its bitter souls have done and dreamed, is yet a shameful land. It lynches. It disfranchises its own citizens. It encourages ignorance. It steals from us. It insults us. . . . This is the country to which we soldiers of democracy return. This is the fatherland for which we fought. But it is our fatherland. It was right for us to fight. The faults of the country are our faults. Under similar circumstances, we would fight again.

But, by the God of Heaven, we are cowards and jackasses if now that the war is over we do not marshal every ounce of our brain and brawn to fight a sterner, longer, more unbending battle against the forces of hell in our own land.

We return. We return from fighting. We return fighting. We make way for democracy. We saved it in France, and by the Great Jehovah, we will save it in America or know the reason why.

But Byrnes was wrong, for Du Bois' was not a text taken from a foreign ideology. Bolshevism had about as much weight in determining the Negro's post-war attitude as the cry "Come, seven" has in determining the fall of dice. Communism simply did not fit the average Negro's concept of himself. And this, but for hysteria, the white man—and especially the Southern white man, who claimed a God-like knowledge of the Negro—should have seen. Communism was revolutionary far beyond the limits of what the Negro saw as necessary. Communism was godless, and that was against it. Communism was supported by a dogma and explained by an esoteric jargon that the Negro was by nature impatient of and emotionally unresponsive to. Communism made the fatuous assumption of class alliances which necessitated the breakdown of all race lines, and this, the Negro knew, was not then or in his foreseeable future possible. Communism proposed, among other things, the establishment of a forty-ninth Negro state, and the idea was anathema to the Negro. Mostly, though, communism was un-American, and the average Negro was American through and through.

Not that there were no Negro Communist-sympathizers. A. Philip Randolph and Chandler Owen were at least deeply moved by the possibilities of Bolshevism. A delegation of American Negroes attended the Third Congress of the Third Internationale. Though not an official delegate, a West-Indian-born New York Negro poet addressed the Fourth Congress (November, 1922) of the Internationale in France. His speech aroused the American press to alarmed comment, for this was the same poet, Claude McKay, who had written:

> If we must die, let it not be like hogs
> Hunted and penned in an inglorious spot,
> While round us bark the mad and hungry dogs,
> Making their mock at our accursed lot.
> If we must die, O let us nobly die
>
> Oh, Kinsmen! We must meet the common foe;
> Though far outnumbered, let us still be brave,
> And for their thousand blows deal one death blow!
> What though before us lies the open grave?
> Like men we'll face the murderous cowardly pack,
> Pressed to the wall, dying, but fighting back.[2]

But this was not Bolshevism, really, although it first appeared in the "radical" *Liberator*. It was something much more familiar and much better understood than its new mask of bitterness let be apparent. It was Americanism, though frustrated. It was the American impulse, the American spirit, reelectrified in the Negro people by the war and the war aims and by a thousand charges of current coming directly from the war, and it galvanized the Negro people into an assertiveness that led to the coining of the phrase "New Negro."

3

Of course there was nothing new about the N.A.A.C.P. and the National Equal Rights League. The Commission on International Cooperation was new, but this Southern white liberal's idea of a militant organization was curiously weak. It was weak even where it was supposed to be strongest—in making personal appeals to white Southern leaders who might, and often did, have influence over the Southern mind. W. W. Alexander, Robert Eleazer and Mrs. Jessie Daniel Ames were potent personalities, but their Commission enslaved itself from the very beginning. It enslaved itself by accepting segregation as the sine qua non of race relations, and even the combined force of the personalities it enlisted, including Howard Odum, John Hope, Plato Durham and R. R. Moton, was not enough to break through to anything approaching democracy. Besides, these campaigners in parlor sociology were sometimes quickly dismayed.

But the N.A.A.C.P. had in it not only Mary White Ovington, Oswald G. Villard, Moorfield Storey and Du Bois, battle-scarred fighters who were never dismayed, it could now call on the fresh energies of Walter White and the firm diplomacy and rocklike patience of James Weldon Johnson. This latter at forty-five had had a successful career as teacher, composer of musical comedies, poet and diplomat (consul in Venezuela and Nicaragua). He joined the N.A.A.C.P. staff as field secretary in 1916. Next to Du Bois, Johnson understood the temper of his people and the prevailing attitude of whites better than any Negro of the day.

By the early 1920's, the N.A.A.C.P. was in the midst of its campaign for the passage of H.R.13, an anti-lynching bill presented by Congressman Dyer of Missouri. The organization had built up to this through a series of first-hand investigations carried on by Elizabeth Freeman and Roy Nash, both white, and Walter White. It had published a grisly diagnostic record, *Thirty Years of Lynching in the United States*. It had got the Negro press fully behind the campaign. Negro school children sent letters to their congressmen. James Weldon Johnson was certain that the campaign for the Dyer bill brought out the greatest concerted action colored people had ever taken. After several delays, debate on the bill opened before packed galleries. When it passed the House by a vote of 230 to 119, the Negroes rose and cheered.

But their jubilation had plenty of time to cool in the six months it took H.R.13 to reach the Senate sub-committee of which Borah of Idaho was chairman. Claiming that its constitutionality was doubtful, Borah was reluctant to report the bill out of committee. Only the pressure of a petition to the Senate Republican leader brought the bill out. The petition bore the signatures of twenty-four governors, thirty-seven mayors, eighty-eight bishops and churchman and half a hundred other dignitaries, but it did not divert the Republicans from their game of run-around, nor Southern Democrats from their filibuster. In the end, the bill did not come up for a vote in the Senate. Threatened by Alabama's Senator Underwood, the Republicans withdrew it. Other anti-lynching bills have been submitted subsequently, and all have failed.

The N.A.A.C.P. carried on the fight along other fronts too. Its lawyers, Scipio Jones and Moorfield Storey, won a notable victory in the case of the Negro farmers of Elaine, Arkansas, six of whom had been sentenced to death as a result of the riot of 1919. Twice the date of their execution was set and twice it was postponed, the last time on an appeal to the United States Supreme Court. On February 23, 1923, the court ruled in effect that the willful exclusion of Negroes from a jury trying Negroes in criminal cases was a departure from due process of law. The decision set a precedent which led to the addition of Negroes' names to jury rolls in districts where Negroes had not served as talismen since Reconstruction days.

When the N.A.A.C.P. extended its activities outside the United States, the talk of foreign influences on the American Negro did not quiet any. But there was even less basis for it now, for the matter was just the other way round. Not just lately aroused to the plight of Negroes in other parts of the world, the Association was trying primarily to create a wider forum and to enlarge the bounds of its influence. Four times between 1919 and 1927, Du Bois called together in a Pan-African congress Negroes from the United States, the West Indies, Europe and Africa. They met in London, Brussels and Paris in 1919, in Paris again in 1921, in Lisbon in 1923, and in New York in 1927.

Not too much was accomplished by these meetings, but intelligent Negroes were made aware that the color bar was "a cardinal principle of modern civilization" and that, as Du Bois phrased it, "the problem of the twentieth century is the problem of the color line." It took another kind of man than Du Bois (and another kind of program than the N.A.A.C.P.'s) to bring this truth home to American Negroes everywhere.

4

The man was Marcus Garvey, and he came screaming out of the British West Indies onto the American stage in 1916. His screaming was to little purpose at first, but when the Lusk Legislative Committee named his paper, the *Negro World,* as dangerous to the *comfort and security* of whites, Garvey's voice deepened into a thunderous roar. His movement was called the Universal Negro Improvement Association, and, though Garvey was a monumental liar, there is no reason to dispute his claim of forty-one world-wide chapters in 1919. Indeed, there may have been even more a year later. On August 4, 1920, the New York *Tribune* estimated that twenty-five thousand Negroes "from all parts of the world" were assembled in the city for a thirty-day convention of U.N.I.A.

But even this number was an infinitesimal fraction of Garvey's dream. As President-General of U.N.I.A., he declared to the world that he would organize four hundred million Negroes "to draw up the banner of democracy on the continent of Africa." He went about it with prodigious energy, an unfailing sense of drama, and a flair for phrase-making and phrase-taking. "Africans for Africans," he shouted more than once, and, blinking the occasion on which Senator John Sharpe Williams had used it, "Race is greater than law." [3] He appealed to race pride and race courage. "We have died for five hundred years for an alien race. The time has come for the Negro to die for himself." He dressed his key followers in brilliant uniforms and organized auxiliaries that appealed to the parade-sense of the naïve masses. There were the Black Eagle Flying Corps, the Universal Black Cross Nurses, the Universal African Motor Corps and the Universal African Legion. Proclaiming himself Provisional President of the Empire of Africa, he created orders of nobility like the Knights of the Distinguished Order of Ethiopia and the Duke of Uganda. By these palpable means, Garvey attracted thousands of the simple and ignorant. (His own figure was two million American Negroes by 1922.) He also attracted a squad of the "wise boys" who cut themselves in on the take. And, if his wife can be believed, there was a tremendous take—ten million dollars in the three years from 1919 to 1921.

The less spectacular Negro organization leaders ignored Garvey for as long as they could. Du Bois was moved to warn Negroes that charlatans and scoundrels of both races were offering impossible returns "in cash and race adjustment" on a very small investment. "Do not invest in the conquest of Africa," Du Bois cautioned. "Do not take desperate chances in flighty dreams."

Though this reference to Garvey was plain, the attacks on the man and his program did not remain oblique and hidden. Negro leaders grew fierce and scornful. Garvey was not their kind. His aims were not theirs. The dream of organizing a great black host and leading it back to Africa was fanciful and foolish, the deceptive cover for a mountebank preying upon the hopes, ambitions and fears of the ignorant masses.

Garvey was not the kind to ignore attacks, no matter from what quarter. Du Bois, James Weldon Johnson, Eugene Kinckle Jones were "weak-kneed and cringing . . . sycophant to the white man. . . . The 'Uncle Tom' Negroes must give way to the 'New Negro,' who is seeking his place in the sun."

Garvey threatened law suits and tried to promote dissension in other groups, but these were merely diverting tactics. His great energies were spent in another more profitable direction. With part of the tribute, collected from thousands of followers, Garvey bought three ships and organized the Black Star Steamship Line. The idea was to use the ships not only as transportation for the black emigrés, but for commerce between United States ports and those of Africa and South America. The scheme fell through. Charges of using the mail to defraud were brought against Garvey, and in 1923 a federal court sentenced him to prison for five years. He tried to sustain and direct the movement from his cell in Atlanta, but this effort failed too. His followers—seventy-five per cent of whom were ignorant and hard-working West Indians—scattered, and the U.N.I.A. evaporated like steam. Pardoned by President Coolidge in 1927, Garvey was deported to Jamaica, B.W.I., from whence he went to London where, in 1940, he died.

The Garvey movement cannot be dismissed merely as the aberration of an organized pressure group. The least that can be said of it is that it was an authentic folk movement. Its spirit of race chauvinism had the sympathy of the overwhelming majority of the Negro people, including those who opposed its objectives. For this was the potent spirit of race consciousness and race pride that informed the "New Negro."

5

In the beginning this new Negro was led in the direction of aberrancy as much by a misprized notion of his relation to the body politic as by the social content of the early post-war period. Before his transformation he had always been an object of charity and of *special* treatment. Things had been done to him, with him and for him. But the great metastatic tide of race consciousness that swept through him purged the Negro of many of the old fallacies, and particularly of the fallacy of excusing himself because of the way he was treated. But even more particularly of the false notion that he could survive in an inimical civilization by means of social and cultural mimicry. Purged, he grew overnight into a manhood's fullness of initiative and self-reliance. This was the entire sum of the "radicalism" so much deplored and so misunderstood to be merely a temporary aftermath of the war.

But it was not so transient. The new initiative and self-reliance, which Alain Locke saw as marking a "spiritual emancipation," demanded fulfillment of itself in the most diverse and dynamic ways. The Garvey movement was but a single instance. Negro-founded and Negro-controlled organizations sprang up everywhere. In 1920, the Friends of Negro Freedom was founded to promote race solidarity in all areas. The American Negro Labor Congress came into being in 1925. The Colored Merchants Association came a little later. In an effort to channel the Negro consumer dollar into a kind of race pool, the Colored Housewives League was formed. All kinds of Negro enterprise flourished. The Chicago *Defender* and the *Afro-American,*

Negro weeklies, had capital assets, including advertising revenue, of close to a million dollars. By 1927, Madame C. J. Walker, Indianapolis scrubwoman, had earned two million dollars from her cosmetics and hairdressing business. By then, too, the Atlanta Life Insurance Company, the North Carolina Mutual Insurance Company and the Liberty Life Insurance Company—all completely Negro owned and controlled—were multi-million dollar corporations. When it came, the depression, such as had wiped out earlier Negro business efforts, could not shake them.

Nor were these businesses all, or even the major part of the matter. The Negro had an intellectual side to him too, and this was thoroughly awakened by the war and post-war series of social explosions. The repudiation of dependency and the sentimental appeal was no exclusively emotional matter. It sprang as well from a conscious and careful examination of the formula that had composed the "old" Negro. The new Negro did not like what he found. He did not like it in intellectual terms. He did not like the obedience to white folk's expectations, the submission to white folk's thought and the aping of white folk's way. And so he began that reappraisal of himself that was at once revelation and vindication.

It started naturally with the scholars—with Du Bois and Alain Locke and Carter Woodson and Charles S. Johnson and James Weldon Johnson. Of course Negro social historians had preceded Du Bois: he had begun his own work in historics in the 1880's, but, like his scholarly predecessors, he had not aroused even a decently supporting interest in his early contemporaries. By 1916, however, he must have thought that such an interest was ready to spring to life, for it was then that he established the first Negro book publishing concern. In that same year Carter Woodson founded the Association for the Study of Negro Life and History and brought out the first issue of the *Journal of Negro History*. Charles S. Johnson at about the same time was editing *Opportunity* on an informed and creative level. And as for Alain Locke, Phi Beta Kappa, Rhodes Scholar and professor of philosophy at Howard University, no man did more to stimulate, direct and stabilize this new intellectualism than he.

But if the Negro voluntarily began a reexamination of himself, the whites were literally forced to reexamine him. What was this strange, new creature? What were these stirrings, organizations, books? The whites began to take a closer look and to recompose their notions, not excluding the one that to know the Negro was but to question the family cook or to pass the time of day with the yardman. Chicago set up a Commission on Race Relations. Social agencies put in departments of Negro work. Books by whites about Negroes streamed from the press: Robert Kerlin's *The Voice of the Negro*, Herbert J. Seligman's *The Negro Faces America*, F. J. Woofter's *Negro Problems in Cities*, Frank Tannenbaum's *Darker Phases of the South*, F. G. Detweiler's *The Negro Press in the United States*. America went to school to the Negro, and America learned much.

6

It learned: from the bitterness and defiance and race passion of Claude McKay, from the historical revelations of Woodson and Logan, from the tom-tom beats of Langston Hughes, from the jazz of nameless musicians and the blues of nameless singers, from the polished lyrics of Countee Cullen, and, in review, again from the bitterness, defiance and race passion of a hundred thousand tones and lights and weathers of the Negro soul. Which is to say that Claude McKay's "If We Must Die" pretty well established the emotional tone of this period in the Negro's development.

Yet the scholars, writers and artists mentioned above differed widely, except for one thing. They were alike in the urge to damn the old imperative to use their art and their intellectual gifts for prettifying and excusing the Negro. Their position was exactly opposite to that of most of their predecessors. The new Negro writer and artist expected to satisfy no one, either black or white. "If," Langston Hughes remarked, "white people are pleased, we are glad. If they are not, it doesn't matter. And if Negroes are pleased, we are glad, but their displeasure doesn't matter either." The new Negro writer had attained an objectivity that must sometimes have seemed brazen, posturing and withal defensive.

Take McKay as novelist. As poet he had had his powerful say by 1922. But as novelist, from *Home To Harlem,* his first, to *Banana Bottom,* his last, there is a progressive concentration on atavistic reversion, on social degeneration and on moral decadence, reaching its nadir in the character of Herald Newton Day, the young preacher-teacher of *Banana Bottom.* Or take the degenerates, the parasites and the vampires who slink through the slimy demi-world of Wallace Thurman's novels, or the weaklings, misfits and psychotics in the novels of Nella Larsen, Walter White, Zora Hurston and Langston Hughes, and one finds that they are but various projections of atavism, pessimism and futility. Hughes might praise the new Negro writer's sense of liberation and declare that he stood as it were free on the mountaintop, but even there on the mountaintop he seemed to breathe a noxious and despairing air. His self-revelation sickened him.

And what, about himself, did the Negro reveal? What, perhaps, did he reveal without being aware of it? What was he thinking? Truth to tell, he was becoming a first-class cynic—excusable perhaps by virtue of the fact that it was a cynical age. He deserted the church, that bulwark of bourgeois conservatism, in great numbers. Indeed, he began to laugh at religion, and some, like Major J. Divine (afterwards called "god" and "father") and Elder Becton (afterwards murdered), began to use it as the gimmick in inexplicable shenanigans. The Negro lost all sense of ethical progression and, like his white fellows in that boomtime, acquired an exaggerated sense of the equalizing power of the dollar. He went in for rackets, like banking the numbers and bootlegging, and accepted into his best society the denizens of the underworld. Caspar Holstein, a gambling king, was given as much respect as the Reverend A. Clayton Powell, messiah-like pastor of the largest Negro church in the world. The Negro's Republican faith, long undermined by political opportunism, collapsed totally. He laughed at the uniforms, the unmanned and rotting ships of the Black Star Line and the leader of U.N.I.A., but it was a strained laughter. For he was shocked and angered by Marcus Garvey and called him the "monkey man" and a "monkey chaser," and parodied him and his followers in jingles.

> "When I git on t'other side, goin'a live like white folks, yas'r.
> Goin'a marry me a ring-tail gal and be a monkey chaser."

The new Negro was shocked, alarmed, amazed at the gigantic demonstration of the herd instinct. He was confused, confounded and humiliated by the public disclosures of graft and "nigger incompetence" that an examination of the U.N.I.A. revealed. For all his vaunted objectivity, he could not dissociate himself from whatever onus attached to race. His illusions of freedom settled about him like choking dust. The old hounds of inferiority bayed on his trail. He began to believe that but two ways were left open to him: indifference—if it could be managed—a kind of desperate joy; and escape—escape through conformity, or through desertion (a great many Negroes expatriated themselves for a longer or a shorter time), or through submission, or through reversion to the old "type."

For what else can George Schuyler's *Black No More* mean—a humorous book so indifferent to the judgment of the Negro its every line implies that the humor scalds like boiling tar? What else can Jessie Fauset's *There is Confusion* mean except that the way to escape is to conform? What else Paul Robeson's long sojourn in Europe, and Hughes' wandering over the face of the earth and Toomer's pale loitering in France, except escape by desertion? And Walter White's *Fire in the Flint*—what else does it show, besides the cruelty of Southern whites, save that the Negro can escape by submission?

Much of the new Negro's brooding pessimism was encouraged by the work of certain white writers whose books were beginning to find a wide public in the 1920's. Julia Peterkin's *Black April* and *Scarlet Sister Mary* were undoubtedly written with great sympathy and sincerity, but the fact of their return to old concepts and stereotypes was a shattering blow to the Negro's new image of himself. Dowd's sociological *The American Negro* lent authority to the race prejudices of the South. The primitivism of DuBose Heyward's Porgy, Crown and Bess and of O'Neill's Brutus Jones seemed to indicate that the Negro was still a raw savage. Van Vechten's *Nigger Heaven* pictured him as absorbing all the vices and none of the virtues of white civilization. These books and others like them, either in a humorous or carping vein, were enough to offset the Rosenfeld-Frank-Calverton-Mencken belief that the new Negro, both as man and artist, had a rich and particular gift to make to American culture.

7

And so the new Negro was caught as the old had been. It was in bitterness that Hughes exclaimed:

> We cry among the skyscrapers
> As our ancestors
> Cried among the palms in Africa

> Because we are alone,
> It is night,
> And we're afraid.[4]

And it was not so much revelation as catharsis that Wallace Thurman was after in *The Blacker the Berry,* that White was after in *Flight,* Nella Larsen in *Quicksand* and McKay in *Banana Bottom.*

But it would be wrong to give the impression that all was un-relieved bitterness, cynicism and pessimism. There was, for instance, a refunding of folk material and a reshaping of folk legend that was much more than mere transcription and that led to some works of enduring value and beauty. Jean Toomer's *Cane* (1923) was a nug-get of gold. The moods of this book were hot, colorful, primitive. Through the book's prose and poetry gushed a tide of ecstasy in a return to a heritage too long ignored. Toomer came "like a son re-turned in bare time to take a living full farewell of a dying parent; and all of him [loved and] wanted to commemorate that perishing naïveté."

> . . . Thy son, I have in time returned to thee. . . .
> In time, for though the sun is setting on
> A song-lit race of slaves, it has not set;
> Though late, O soil, it is not too late yet
> To catch thy plaintive soul, leaving, soon gone. . . .
> O Negro slaves, dark purple ripened plums,
> Squeezed, and bursting in the pine-wood air,
> Passing, before they stripped the old tree bare
> One plum was saved for me, one seed becomes
>
> An everlasting song, a singing tree,
> Caroling softly souls of slavery,
> What they were, and what they are to me,
> Caroling softly souls of slavery.[5]

With surer artistry, James Weldon Johnson made the same return in *God's Trombones,* published in 1927. These seven Negro sermons in verse were immediately hailed by H. L. Mencken, whose *Ameri-can Mercury* had published two of them, as masterpieces of folk ex-pression. Sterling Brown and Langston Hughes among the poets, and Zora Neale Hurston, Willis Richardson and Eulalie Spence, play-wrights, and, again Langston Hughes, among those who wrote prose, made effective use of folk material.

Indeed, only one major writer of the period did not, and that was Countee Cullen. "What is Africa to me?" he questioned, and went on from there in a conscious effort to prove that Africa was nothing to him, "one three centuries removed from the land his fathers loved." Cullen could not beat the tom-tom above a whisper, nor know the primitive delights of black rain and scarlet sun. His gifts were delicate, elegant, and he used them best in the delightfully personal love lyrics for which he was (and is) deservedly admired. Keats was his man, with just a touch of Shelley, and just more than a touch of that master scorner of his heritage, William S. Braithwaite.

But to go back to Hughes, for he is after all the most prolific and representative of the new Negro artists, and he is—or was back in the twenties and thirties—the one most divinely capable of realizing and giving expression to the dark perturbation in the soul of the Negro. Go back to him, and this remains to be said: race and the race experience and the race mold, if you will, with all of its complex of false concept and impacted reality, were for him the most volatile, appealing and compelling forces in the world.

8

And so it was with others who had other ways of expressing it, and some of whom had been expressing it in these other ways before the emergence of the new Negro and the artistic renaissance. Take jazz, for instance, and the men who made it. Jazz was new in the twenties only in the sense that it was first given serious attention then. It had come up from God knows where, but certainly from earthy origins in the peasant soul of the Negro. Come up to St. Louis and Chicago before the World War, before the turn of the century. Such men as Scott Joplin and William Christopher Handy took it, and then they took it to New York. It was there by 1917, for James Reese Europe's Fifteenth New York Infantry band was playing it there then. That was the year Scott Joplin died there too. It was still, in condescending terms, "Negro stuff," not counted as much, but it packed the theatres on the Negro vaudeville circuit, and made a living for Will Marion Cook and Will Vodery, Ford Dabney, Jelly Roll Morton and three youngsters, Fletcher Henderson, Duke Ellington and Louis Armstrong.

The "new music" soon attracted white listeners, who made the trek to Harlem just to hear it, and who, titillated, invited jazz players downtown. Fletcher Henderson was one of the first to go, but others followed him shortly. The National Association of Negro Musicians encouraged it, and soon a toned-down jazz was being heard in Rector's and Delmonico's.

In 1921 an all-Negro musical show opened on Broadway. *Shuffle Along* revived in more brilliant fashion the old days of Williams and Walker, of J. Rosamond and James Weldon Johnson, of *Abyssinia* and *Bandana Land* and *In Dahomey*. It was full of bouncy jazz and muted minors—"I'm Just Wild about Harry," "Love Will Find a Way," "Wang-Wang Blues"—and it was all written and produced by the Negroes, Flourney Miller, Aubrey Lyles, Eubie Blake and Noble Sissle. In pairs or singly, these men went on to write other shows with the same ebullience, the same raciness and raceness— *Runnin' Wild,* with its new Charleston dance, *Chocolate Dandies,* to which, in 1923, audiences flocked to watch the boneless pantomimes of Josephine Baker, and *Dixie to Broadway,* which brought Florence Mills to wide notice. In 1926, she was raised to stardom. When she died the next year, all Broadway and Harlem wept, and neither the rich voice of Ethel Waters in *Africana* nor the dancing of Bill Robinson in the second *Blackbirds* could make the theatrical world forget.

Meantime the Negro was finding his way in serious music and on the legitimate stage. Roland Hayes, the tenor, made his American debut at Town Hall in 1924. He sang German lieder, French arias and, best of all, Negro spirituals arranged for him by Negro composers. Already a fixture at the white St. George's Episcopal Church, Harry T. Burleigh gave occasional concerts. Paul Robeson had begun in 1920 to give small private concerts to help pay his way through Columbia Law School. He gave his first full-scale concert of spirituals at the Greenwich Village Theatre in 1925. During that same year Marian Anderson gave a recital in Town Hall, but criticism was so harsh that she "vowed never to sing again." She broke that vow the next year, and to the world's applause. Dorothy Maynor was still a student at Hampton in 1925, but her great teacher, R. Nathaniel Dett, was even then predicting a shining future for her.

As for the legitimate theatre, the Negro had had his own in Harlem since 1909. He had supported a talented stock company since 1916. Though the folk plays of Willis Richardson and Eulalie

Spence were worthy, the Lafayette Players preferred *Within the Law* and *Over the Hills*. Some of them got their first experience with Negro plays in 1917, when Mrs. Emily Hapgood produced *Three Plays for the Negro Theatre,* by the white playwright, Ridgely Torrence.

The event marked an epoch, James Weldon Johnson said, for the Negro on the stage. Such drama critics as Robert Benchley and Francis Hackett agreed with him. In 1919, Charles Gilpin, sometime elevator boy and director of the Lafayette Players, was called on to play William Custis in Drinkwater's *Abraham Lincoln.* The epoch waxed, or seemed to. Gilpin was chosen to play O'Neill's *Emperor Jones.* His performance was honored as one of the ten best in 1920, and, though by 1921 he was again running an elevator for a living, he had placed Negro acting on its highest level and had aroused audience interest in serious drama of Negro life.

The interest was still there when Paul Robeson played opposite a white actress in *All God's Chillun Got Wings* in 1924, and when Paul Green's *In Abraham's Bosom* won the Pulitzer Prize in 1926. Paul Green had written many Negro plays for the Carolina Playmakers at Chapel Hill, where he taught. He had a sense of Negro life that not even Marc Connelly had then acquired. The roles in *In Abraham's Bosom* were extremely difficult, but he wanted no white actors black-faced. He chose Rose McClendon as one of the principals, with Richard Huey, Abbie Mitchell and Frank Wilson. In 1927 came the Heywards' *Porgy,* and for her portrayal of Crown's Bess, Rose McClendon, too soon to die, was recognized as the first lady among Negro players.

And if she was the first lady, then Richard B. Harrison was certainly the first gentleman. He opened as De Lawd in Connelly's *The Green Pastures* in 1930, and turned what might easily have been burlesque into folk art of the simplest, purest kind. He brought to his role not only the Negro's ancestral reverence for God, but the human dignity and beauty of character that had endeared him to hundreds of Negro high school and college audiences for a half century. *The Green Pastures* ran for five years.

But even before *The Green Pastures* opened, whites less understanding than Marc Connelly, H. L. Mencken, and the Heywards had begun to capitalize on the genuine interest in the Negro and to turn it into a commercialized fad. Harlem was, in an expression of the time, a "natural" as a center for this. There, were concentrated all the diverse elements of Negro life—or, better perhaps, non-white life—Sudanese and Bengalese and Sengalese, Camaroons and Filipinos and Cubans, black Jews and West Indians and native Negro Americans. And not just a handful, but half a million packed in two square miles. There was one Negro newspaper printed in English, Spanish and French and another printed in Yiddish. Most of the great race movements started in Harlem, where race organizations, radical and otherwise, had their headquarters. Negro artists, writers, composers, students, preachers and peasants found their way there. It has been said of other corners in other cities, but in the twenties and thirties it was literally true that anyone standing at 135th Street and Seventh Avenue was likely to see pass every Negro he had ever known.

Life in Harlem seemed to have a buoyancy and dynamism, a flavor of exoticism and the very odor of primitive virility. That this was largely as synthetic as Harlem's gin anyone who cared to look could have discovered. But no one cared to look, and the Negroes themselves were not averse to being synthetic, so long as there was money in it. "Nigger heaven," a white writer called Harlem, and there, the well-advertised belief was, Dullness was dethroned; Gaiety was King! The pale-faced revolters from Sauk Center and Winesburg, from Main Street and Park Avenue sought carnival in Harlem. "Life," the burden of the dithyrambics ran, "had surge and sweep and blood-pounding savagery."

> Here dat music . . .
> Jungle night.
> Hear dat music . . .
> And the moon was white.
>
> Jungle lover . . .
> Night-black boy . . .
> Two against the moon
> And the moon was joy.[6]

The moon was also papier-mâché.

Such was the vicious commercialization of Harlem that Negroes, who were generally too poor anyway, could not—that is, were not permitted to—enter the best-known Negro night club in the world.

But an end to the blatancy of all this was at hand. For now were developing the circumstances that would strip Negro life, in Harlem and elsewhere, of almost all that was extraneous to mere survival; circumstances, indeed, that would bring to the general American life the kind of revolution that might have spelled—and seemed for a time actually to spell—the demise of all those attitudes embodied in phrases like "the American way" and "rugged individualism." The revolution promoted the implementation of a strange political philosophy. It unleashed amorphous forces to counteract the collapse of the familiar philosophy of abundance. It necessitated the restatement of the relations of man to government and of man to man. The revolution was good for the Negro. It was good for America.

16

AND CHANGING LEADERS

●●

THE REVOLUTION WAS the New Deal, which was more a social than a political program—and so Roosevelt, the very incarnation of hope and confidence, declared it. Roosevelt came at a time when politics, having reached a low of ineffectiveness under Mr. Hoover, could solve nothing. He came believing that government could solve everything. He came believing, not so much that government was of and by the people, certainly, but that it was for the people.

This was not a new concept of government. In fact, the South would have said that its misapplication in Reconstruction had brought ruin to Dixie. But even that section of the country, completely and helplessly caught in the grip of social forces that had no name save Depression and that, with the South's aversion to analysis, had brought first bafflement and then terror and then humility—even the South was quite willing to try it again. Especially willing to try it was the common man in the South, like common men everywhere. And of these, particularly the Negro.

The national government now assumed that it had responsibility for the welfare of all the people. Roosevelt brought back into usage the old Canute phrase from Caribbean folk lore, "the little people." Quite contrary to what his stewardship of the state of New York had seemed to indicate, Roosevelt professed himself a humanitarian and his program one based on humanitarian principles. The Negro had heard such professions before, but he had not been convinced by them. Somehow he believed Roosevelt. Enough, after 1932, to vote for him again and again—and again.

Not that the New Deal fulfilled all of its promises. It could not. It met increasing opposition from exactly that section of the country where it was first most joyously hailed. In four years the South recovered from its early enthusiasm only to discover that the New Deal's basic policies were just contrary to its own. The leveling process, as in wages-and-hours legislation, was a case in point: it was bad. When the A.A.A. program began paying benefits directly to tenants, of whom the majority were Negro, it was suddenly bad. The encouragement of labor organizations was bad. Because the South thought it might some day become less important to the Democratic Party than the Northern Negro, the wooing of the Negro vote was bad. So in Congress and elsewhere, Byrd and Glass of Virginia, George and Cox of Georgia, Smith and Byrnes of South Carolina did all they could to void the benefits that might come to the Negro from the New Deal.

2

The intensive social reshuffling brought to the top of the deck some new organizations headed by new Negro leaders. The old leadership had been outstripped. It had been too weak to encroach upon the basic assumptions that supported the status quo ante. It could not make the transition from the imperatives of one social policy to those of another. The Negro college presidents, the Y.M.C.A. officers and the bishops had lost their power with the loss of the philanthropies that supported them, and though they still had the ear of certain white folk, they could speak only in whispers.

The new Negro leadership was thoroughgoing in its representativeness. A. Philip Randolph was president of a Negro labor organization of eight thousand members. Walter White had helped to increase the membership of the N.A.A.C.P. from fifteen thousand to well over two hundred thousand by 1936. By the time of the second Roosevelt campaign, the National Negro Congress, a composite of many Negro organizations, was ready to burst into being with fifty thousand members. Lester Granger had moved up in the National Urban League and commanded the allegiance of League affiliates in thirty strategic cities. Carl Murphy was in editorial control of the potent *Afro-American*. Robert L. Vann, who owned and published the Pittsburgh *Courier,* was influential enough for Roosevelt to call him to serve in the councils of the Democratic Party. Quietly but effectively, the Youngs—father and two sons—of the Norfolk *Journal and Guide* gave tongue to the new leadership in the

South. And so did the Scott chain of newspapers in Georgia and Alabama, and the string of weeklies owned by Carter Wesley of Texas.

These leaders and spokesmen organized or got behind any movement that promised relief of the Negro's political and economic condition. The Urban League of St. Louis engineered the first Negro boycott of chain stores that solicited the trade of Negroes but refused to hire them. Using the slogan, "Don't Buy Where You Can't Work," the Jobs-for-Negroes campaign spread west and east, and south to Atlanta, where a chain store in a Negro neighborhood was forced to close.

The New York Citizens League for Fair Play took up the boycott in full fashion. Negroes picketed stores and shops on bustling 125th Street. Negro telephone subscribers refrained from using their telephones on special days, hoping thereby to bring the telephone company to a realization of the vast revenue from Harlem. The same method was used against the electric company. Tension grew in Harlem, and finally led directly to the riot of March, 1935, when white-owned stores were wrecked and looted to the extent of $2,500,000. An interracial Committee on Conditions in Harlem reported that Negroes were simply resentful of racial discrimination and poverty.

The boycott was successful beyond hopes. The telephone company employed Negro operators and inspectors. The electric company employed Negro meter readers and clerks. Stores along 125th Street hired Negro salespeople. And, excepting the riot, what happened in New York happened also in Chicago, Cleveland, Detroit, Los Angeles, Philadelphia. Even in some places in the South, white merchants and utility companies employed Negroes in capacities formerly reserved for whites. The Southern Bell Telephone Company hired Negro salesmen in Atlanta, Birmingham and Montgomery. Automobile sales agencies in Durham, Nashville and Louisville employed Negro salesmen.

On the political front, the new leaders helped push the Negro-for-Roosevelt vote up from a few dissidents in 1932 to sixty-five per cent of the total Negro vote cast in 1944. Back in 1928, Negroes had seen the Republican wind blowing South, fecundating lily-white Republicanism and carrying for Hoover the normally Democratic states of Virginia, North Carolina, Tennessee, Florida and Texas. They were reminded of this by their leaders in 1936 and in 1940 and in between. In 1936 the Negroes of the First Illinois Congressional District got together and sent to Congress Arthur W. Mitchell, the first Negro Democrat ever to sit in the national government. Mitchell replaced the ineffective Negro Republican, Oscar DePriest.

On the state and local scene, too, the new Negro leaders in the New Deal effected some notable political changes. Negro representatives—all of them Democrats save only in New York and Kentucky—went to the legislature in Kentucky, Kansas, Illinois, Indiana, New York, New Jersey, Ohio and Pennsylvania. Negro city councilmen, school and health board members and officers and clerks in municipal agencies became a dime a dozen. Even Winston-Salem, North Carolina, sent a Negro to its City Council in 1947, and many Northern cities, led by New York (with a total of seven) put Negro judges in municipal courts.

The momentum gathered by this movement for Negro participation in state and local government had not died in 1948. In that year, Richmond, Virginia, elected its first Negro Councilman, and in that same year, Robert T. Nelson became Deputy Director of Public Safety in Philadelphia.

Wendell Willkie's candidacy in 1940 threatened to put an end to the rapport between Negroes and the New Deal. Willkie sounded as good as Roosevelt, as sincere as Henry Wallace. Moreover, Willkie was a Republican. It is not necessary to emphasize what this meant to Negroes, many of whom felt uncomfortable under the aegis of the Democrats, and none of whom forgot for a moment that Southerners were chairmen of seventeen of the thirty-three standing committees of the Senate and of twenty-five of forty-eight standing committees of the House. They remembered how "Cotton Ed" Smith had huffed out of the Democratic national convention in Philadelphia when Marshall Shepard, a Negro minister, was called upon to pray. They knew that Southern Democrats were actively and openly opposed to Roosevelt's social policies, and that the President had not been able to do anything about it. In fact, he seemed particularly friendly with George of Georgia and Byrnes of South Carolina.

So Negroes gave more than casual ear when Willkie said, "I want your [Negroes'] support. I need it. But irrespective of whether Negroes go down the line with me or not, they can expect every consideration. They will get their fair proportion of appointments, their fair representation on policy-making bodies. They'll get the same consideration as other citizens."

But in its Chicago convention of that year, 1940, the Democrats nailed into the party's platform a plank on which Negroes felt they could stand. It cited past performances—"Our Negro citizens have participated actively in the economic and social advances launched by this Administration, including fair labor standards, social security benefits . . . work relief projects, decent housing. . . . We have aided more than half a million Negro youths in vocational training, education and employment. . . ." It made promises for the future. "We shall continue to strive for . . . safeguards against discrimination. . . ."

Negroes had substantial reasons for believing this. Because they had been hardest hit by the depression, the New Deal agencies seemed a special boon to them. It is true that they had been discriminated against in the operation of the N.I.R.A., the W.P.A. and the A.A.A., but this was clearly the fault of prejudiced local boards; and in housing, the C.C.C., N.Y.A. and the school lunch program, they had received a proportionately larger share than the one-tenth formula called for. Negroes, although only 9.4 per cent of the population in 1933, constituted 18.4 per cent of all people on relief. In New York City, 13.3 per cent were on relief, in Detroit 29.6, and in Birmingham, 69.1. Nor did Negroes fail to associate rent checks and food checks with Roosevelt and the New Deal. Roosevelt was laughingly and lovingly referred to as "the man what am: he brings the ham." Negroes in Southern cities, of course, got what could be spared from relief for whites, but New York, Philadelphia, Chicago and Cleveland distributed relief funds without regard to race.

Moreover, and perhaps finally, Negroes had from the New Deal a patent assurance of consideration, because right there in Washington were people of their own kind to see to it that they got it. These were the race-relations advisors, Negro men and women, "reformers and idealists" chosen by the government on the basis of their knowledge and ability. They came in for a great deal of criticism from some Negroes who claimed that they "performed no useful service to the agencies in which they were employed or to the people whose special interests they are supposed to serve." But these Negro consultants and advisors were also criticized by whites, and the point of this need not be labored. And if proof of their reforming zeal and idealism is needed, let it be remembered that not one of them but left the security of a permanent position to take the low pay, the buffets and the uncertainty of an appointive post. Let it be remembered also that William Hastie, special assistant to the Secretary of War, resigned in outrage when the principle of integrating Negroes into the armed services—a principle sanctioned by the Democratic platform of 1940—was persistently flouted.

Mary McLeod Bethune served with the N.Y.A. and brought in R. O'Hara Lanier, now president of Texas Negro State University, as her assistant. Under the N.Y.A.'s. student work program, some sixty-five thousand youths received benefits that enabled them to stay in school. The racially famed tennis player, Edgar Brown, served as advisor on Negro affairs in the C.C.C., an agency which employed many Negro educational directors and made the toughest years of the depression bearable for two hundred thousand Negro boys. Frank S. Horne of the Federal Public Housing Authority (for which he still works) did not break down all discrimination in federal public housing, but it is largely due to him that there is bi-racial housing tenancy in some Northern cities and that one third of all government housing elsewhere is allotted to Negroes. Robert Weaver as advisor to Harold Ickes, Ira DeA. Reid as consultant to the Social Security Board, Abram Harris, Ralph Bunche, Rayford Logan and George Evans—all of them earned the gratitude of Negroes and the highest respect of the whites with whom they worked.

In the war years, the government called on other Negroes. Truman Gibson, a lawyer, took Hastie's job in the War Department. Ted Poston, a newspaperman, went to O.W.I. A woman, and probably the only out-and-out politician in the group, Crystal Bird Fauset, went to O.C.D. Colonel Campbell Johnson became assistant to the head of National Selective Service. There was now scarcely a department or major government agency that did not have a Negro race-relations officer.

3

By no means all Negroes became "Roosevelt men." In the first place, most of the Negro upper class, like most of the white upper class, remained Republican. In the second place, communism had never counted itself out. Contrary to popular white opinion, communism had missed its main chance, for reasons which we have seen, right after the first World War. Some Negroes of stature had repudiated capitalistic democracy then, but what they embraced was socialism rather than communism. By 1930 the Communist planners of the American revolution had learned the errors of their earlier ways and were awaiting another chance. The chance came in 1931.

It came in the guise of the Scottsboro Case, an affair shaped to the exact order of the Communists. There was no shadow of a doubt in the mind of anyone, including the Southern white man, that the nine Negro boys arrested in Alabama on a charge of raping two hoboing white girls were innocent. But the South was determined to affirm her independence, and the more the pressure brought upon her, the more determined she became to have her own way with the boys. The pressure was great. It started in New Orleans two days after the Scottsboro boys were arrested. The racially mixed Marine Workers Industrial Union, called a meeting "to take the offensive and to expose the rottenness and corruption of Southern justice before all the American people."

After an interval of observing the direction of the wind, the International Labor Defense jumped in with all guns firing. It fought for and won from the N.A.A.C.P. the opportunity to defend the Scottsboro boys. It bombarded the world with propaganda. It called mass meetings in almost every city in America, and the reports of similar meetings in foreign capitals filled the press. In these meetings, the well-posted Communist puppets never failed to make a solemn pledge of party support for the "self-determination of American Negroes." Exactly what this phrase meant no one seemed to know, but when Robert Minor, one of the leaders of Northern communism, uttered it at a meeting of the All-Southern Conference for the Scottsboro Defense, his mixed Chattanooga audience, some weeping, all transformed, rose like one man and cheered.

Actually, though, none of these pyrotechnics saved the Scottsboro boys. In spite of the brilliant and incontestable defense of the great criminal lawyer, Samuel Leibowitz, the boys were found guilty in their first trial. Numerous appeals followed, during the course of which the Communists withdrew and the responsibility for the defense was taken over by an N.A.A.C.P. committee headed by Dr. Allen Knight Chalmers, pastor of New York's Broadway Tabernacle. The Communists, however, continued to make hay in the sunshine of the case. They materially strengthened their position among Negroes, and this position they exploited energetically as the depression deepened and the New Deal delved into labor problems.

For certainly it was on the labor front that the Communists found further opportunities. Represented by the Industrial Workers of the World, they had pointed out earlier in the century the obvious fact that the interests of white workers were no different from those of black. But the simple insistence on this had got them nowhere. In 1935, there were still twenty-four international unions that positively forbade membership to Negroes, and the scarcity of employment at the time tended to make for an extension of this restriction. Only the United Mine Workers freely admitted Negroes. The U.M.W. had one national and several district Negro organizers.

Though in 1927 the conservative faction in U.M.W. had defeated a Communist bloc, communism retained a considerable influence in the organization. This influence made itself felt when the Central Executive Committee of the Communists International condemned dual unionism in 1930 and John L. Lewis, head of U.M.W., began calling for the organization of labor on an industry-wide basis. Action followed in 1935. The Committee for Industrial Organization was formed, and known Communists, including some Negroes, were sent to organize the steel industry, the packing house industry and, for the most part unsuccessfully, the textile industry. Hundreds of Negroes joined the Communist Party and a C.I.O.-affiliated union. The passage of the Wagner Act, which strengthened the authority of the National Labor Relations Board, assured these Negroes of receiving more employment benefits than had seemed possible a decade earlier.

During these same years, the Communists attracted some Negroes of consequence on another level. Langston Hughes, the poet, once seemed to be a sympathizer. Though he is now actively anti-communist, Richard Wright publicly admitted to being a "card-bearing Communist" in the early 1940's. Angelo Herndon is now forgotten, but he was a pet of American Communists for years, and he eventually went to Russia as a guest of the Russian state. Paul Robeson is said to be a Communist sympathizer, and if he is not, then his fulminations against the "capitalist press"—which, incidentally, has treated him very well—are completely inexplicable. James W. Ford, like Herndon, is also forgotten, but three successive times —1932, 1936 and 1940—he was the Communists' Vice-Presidential candidate. Ben Davis, whose father was the Negro Republican boss of Georgia two decades ago, was the lone Communist member of the New York City Council from 1943 to 1949.

In the intensive and sometimes hysterical drive against Communists since the second World War, the boldness has gone out of some Negro Communists, or they have been driven underground. Many C.I.O. unions have purged themselves of the red tint, but the party policy operated sufficiently among them to promote the liberal interracialism that characterizes the United Mine Workers, the United Automobile Workers, the Steelworkers, the Amalgamated Clothing Workers, the Ladies' Garment Workers and the International Longshoremen's and Warehousemen's Union. The C.I.O. fights racial discrimination through a committee headed by George Weaver, a Negro; and Willard Townsend, the forthright Negro president of the United Transport Service Employees, is a member of C.I.O's Executive Board.

Even so, the imminence of war was to prove that there was still much discrimination in employment in the 1940's. By then war plants were running full blast and every white man who wanted a job had one, but only two million of five and a half million Negro workers were employed. There were only twenty thousand in the automobile industry. The aircraft industry had even fewer. Of thirty thousand employees in ten war plants in New York, on Long Island and in northern New Jersey, less than two hundred were Negroes. The excuse for this was that war plants needed skilled workers and Negroes were generally unskilled. The federal government was sponsoring programs of employment-training, but, thanks to the connivance of certain unions and in spite of the dictum handed down by the United States Office of Education that there should be no discrimination in such programs, Negroes were usually barred. When the management of a Wright aeronautical plant employed two Negroes—in unskilled capacities—in 1941, the white workers went on strike. An inquiry conducted by the United States Employment Service revealed that the disposition of industrial management was set against the hiring of Negroes, and neither Persident Roosevelt, the Office of Production Management, nor the National Defense Advisory Committee seemed able to change it.

Senator Wagner tried to wrangle through a Senate resolution calling for an investigation of the exclusion of minorities from employment in war plants, but the Southern bloc killed it. Following this, Walter White held a conference with Senator Harry Truman, urging upon the Missourian the idea that his Committee Investigating the National Defense Program was the proper one to work on the matter. Senator Truman was sympathetic but frank: it would be at least six months before his committee could get to it, and even then they would be able to hear "not more than three or four witnesses." The N.A.A.C.P., the National Urban League and Negro leaders like Channing Tobias and A. Philip Randolph made appeals to the President and to others in high places, but in vain.

Then the calculation, heretofore noted as part of the equipment of the new Negro, again found its uses. A. Philip Randolph began quietly organizing a Negro March-on-Washington. The purpose was to dramatize not only the plight of Negro labor, but the waste of manpower involved in discrimination in employment. As the movement got under way, all the channels of Negro expression, press, pulpit and corner curb, gurgled with the enterprise. At least fifty thousand Negroes were to converge on Washington from all parts of the country. It was not an original plan of protest, but it had the support of the Negro man-in-the-street. A few Negroes, remembering the Bonus March of 1932, were skeptical and frightened, but no Negro leader was. Even the kindly warning that Mrs. Roosevelt sounded in a conference called by Mayor LaGuardia gave them no pause. "You know where I stand," Mrs. Roosevelt told them. "But the attitude of the Washington police, most of them Southerners, and the general feeling of Washington itself are such that I fear that there may be trouble if the march occurs."

The determination of the Negro leaders forced the President's hand. On June 18, 1941, with Robert Patterson, Frank Knox, William Knudson and Sidney Hillman backing him up, he conferred with Randolph and White. What did they want anyway? he wanted to know. They wanted him to issue "an unequivocal executive order to effectuate the speediest possible abolition of discrimination in war industries and the armed services." All right, the President said in effect, draw up the order.

Segregation and discrimination would never have recovered from the document that Randolph, White, Frank Crosswaithe, Aubrey Williams (head of N.Y.A.) and Mayor LaGuardia drew up. But the original was considerably softened, and on June 25, the President issued Executive Order 8802, creating the Committee on Fair Employment Practices. The Committee functioned all through the war, but, in its later days, under the control of a Congress none too friendly to its purposes. Still, there is no doubt that the Committee materially reduced racial discrimination in industry in the North. There is no doubt, either, that it set the pattern for such agencies in individual states. New York, Rhode Island, Massachusetts and Wisconsin now have commissions or boards to encourage (where they have no power to enforce) fair employment practices. In 1948, the Democratic Party pledged to create a permanent F.E.P.C.

Discrimination in industry continued generally unchecked in the South. Governor Dixon of Alabama epitomized the Southern attitude when, refusing a federal contract for his state, he declared that "the provisions against discrimination in employment are a threat to the ways of the South."

4

One thing more needs noting. Neither to the courage, the calculation or the foresight—to the spirit in any of its manifestations—of the new Negro did Negro schools or the people wholly, or even mainly educated in them since, say 1925, contribute anything commensurate with the influence Negro education boasted of having. No talent to the art, no scholarship to the intellectual life, no energy to the striving. To be sure, Howard, Hampton, Morehouse and Lincoln each produced, almost in spite of themselves, a few "radicals" and a modicum of social-minded rather than society-minded brains. But even these schools by no means kept pace with the times. The rest of the private schools were way behind, and the public state-supported schools were way behind these. Of course, the Negro state schools had to think of legislative appropriations, and the private schools had to think of the sensibilities of their historically conservative white donors, but even these considerations hardly excuse the morbid fear of liberalism that ran through private and state schools alike from before the onset of the depression until recently, when, under younger and bolder men, they have given signs of getting up and going somewhere. . . .

Somewhere other than to the venality and social-class security of the 1920's and '30's. For the acquisition of an education in those boom-and-bust times was no longer posited upon the assumption that educated Negroes would go out to serve and lead their people. The college generation of Walter White and Ira DeA. Reid and Franklin Frazier was about the last to imbibe that tradition. And even in their college days, the ghosts of Ware and Cravath, of Howard and Armstrong, and of Andrews and King were being laid by the mighty conjurations of selfish values. So effectively laid, indeed, that the most authoritative study [1] of the Negro college graduate of 1914 to 1936 lists "service to the race" and "service to humanity" only eighth and tenth of twenty reasons for going to college. Far from envisioning a life of service, the Negro college man of the twenties and thirties concentrated upon acquiring "yellow money, a yellow car and a yellow woman." The Negro college woman aspired to be the yellow woman and to share the money and the car.

But even the winning of these goals called for some training; and the student in the average Negro college was handicapped. He was handicapped before ever he got to college. The South notoriously has practiced shocking inequities in the distribution of educational funds to Negroes. In 1949, the United States Office of Education reported that "in states with segregated schools, white children get an education twice as expensive as that for Negroes." In 1945, North Carolina, undoubtedly the most advanced of Southern states, had a differential in per capita expenditures of four to one between white and Negro children, and this in spite of a program of equalization vigorously begun under Governor Broughton. In 1949, the "average expense for each white pupil in daily attendance was $104.66 a year, [and] for each Negro pupil, $57.57."

What such inequalities meant (and mean) need not be left to the imagination. They meant not only poor equipment, or no equipment, but poor teachers, unfitted educationally and socially for the task of training the young. The inequalities meant Negro schools so overcrowded that in cities like Atlanta, Charleston and Jacksonville a nine-hour teaching day was split into three sessions of approximately two and a half hours each, only half an ordinary teaching day. Overcrowded white schools meant new schools. Overcrowded Negro schools meant pupils hardly trained even in the fundamentals.

Realizing the inadequacies in Negro education, such philanthropic agencies as the Rosenwald Fund, the Jeanes Fund and the General Education Board poured money into the breach. The Rosenwald Fund helped finance the building of 5,232 Negro schools between

1913 and 1932. When it ended its scholarship aid in 1948, the Fund had also spent several million dollars to further the training of Southern Negro (and white) teachers. The Jeanes Fund concentrated on putting the industrial and domestic-science training of Negroes on a decent level. The General Education Board financed scholarships; paid entirely, or equalized with whites, the salaries of some special Negro teachers, and paid the salaries of some supervisors of Negro education on the primary and secondary levels.

Such assistance did not always have the effect of shaming the South into carrying the fair share of its admitted duty to black citizens. For years Elizabeth City County of Virginia refused to build a much-needed Negro school because Hampton Institute, a private college, maintained, for teacher-training purposes, a well-equipped elementary and high school to which pupils could go at no cost to themselves or the state. So long as Hampton (or Rosenwald, or the General Education Board) looked after the colored children, why need the public bother? And, of course, so much the addition of funds for the education of the whites.

Moreover, such assistance, generous as it was (and is), was not nearly enough. To say that the dual system of education is expensive is supererogatory. To say, on the other hand, that it encourages a cast of mind completely opposed to the American spirit is understatement. Where dual systems on the lower level developed in certain parts of the North, race prejudice grew and expressed itself, during the war, in strikes and other disturbances that followed upon the admission of Negro children to "white" schools. Thus in Berwyn, Pennsylvania, in 1945, Trenton, New Jersey, in 1946, and Gary, Indiana, in 1947. And it is still the dual system which, more than any other factor, contributes to the superior-inferior ideology that perpetuates the inequalities.

And finally, of course, the inequalities on the lower level are reflected on the higher. They are reflected in the complex of emotion and idea known as character. They are reflected in the teaching and the teacher and the taught in Negro colleges. They are reflected in the calibre of the Negro mind. Negro students with the measured reading ability of fifth and sixth grade pupils still register as freshmen in many—perhaps in most—Negro colleges. And the colleges have to accept them—state colleges because their funds are allotted on the basis of student enrollments; private colleges because every penny of every student counts. The result is a standard of education even lower than that of which educators complain as prevailing in public schools and colleges generally. The result is found in the thousands of Negro college graduates who are not equipped to deal with ideas, or even to express their own. And this has a corollary in a positive fear of ideas, and a consequence in an emphasis upon vocational training that leaves the Negro race destitute of Negro-trained scholars, writers, editors, preachers, teachers and leaders.

Thus it is not surprising that of the 21,526 living Negroes who graduated from college between 1914 and 1936, only 2,459 were registered voters in the latter year. It is not surprising that the Negro college graduates listed in *Who's Who in Colored America* number no more than those only vaguely and indefinitely educated. It is not surprising that of eighty-one known Negroes with college degrees listed in *Who's Who in America* in 1944–1945, only sixteen were educated in Negro colleges.

The new Negro mind and spirit manifested in the 1920's and '30's did not have their growth in the Negro college.

To point out Du Bois, James Weldon Johnson, Channing Tobias and Mary McLeod Bethune (among the first fruits of the new tree), in no way modifies the conclusion. When Du Bois went to Fisk, Johnson and White to Atlanta, Tobias to Payne and Mary McLeod to Scotia, the teachers in these institutions were still Yankee whites, absolutely committed to the quest and the conquest of reason and reasons. Not that the Yankee teachers turned out no Negro Babbitts more zealous to exploit than to improve the race; but for the black Babbitts there was more scorn than jealousy, more condemnation than praise, and they were careful to talk, if not to live, "lives of service."

In the humanities, Alain Locke was a Harvard graduate and a Rhodes Scholar; the historian, Carter G. Woodson, was from Harvard. McKay, poet and novelist, left Tuskegee in disgust and went to Kansas. Jean Toomer studied in Paris. Countee Cullen was Phi Beta Kappa from New York University. Langston Hughes attended Lincoln, but Lincoln then had no Negro teacher of professorial rank. The scientists, George Washington Carver, E. E. Just, Julian Lewis, Percy Julian and William Hinton were exclusively the products of white schools. Wallace Thurman, the novelist, came from the Far West, as did Arna Bontemps. Jessie Fauset was from Cornell University, Rudolph Fisher from Brown and Sterling Brown from Williams College. The radicals George Schuyler, A. Philip Randolph and Chandler Owen were largely self-taught.

Fortunately some of these men of the early Negro renaissance period turned or returned to teaching in the 1930's and '40's. They brought a spiritual and intellectual counterbalance to the material loss most Negro colleges suffered in the depression. A new analysis and criticism entered Negro college teaching. It was no longer likely that a Negro college president would inquire whether a prospective teacher of science could teach "Christian biology." A new crop of students, matured by the sobering influences of the depression, developed astonishingly in the more lucent and freer atmosphere. Charles S. Johnson and James Weldon Johnson went to Fisk, where Arna Bontemps followed them. Du Bois returned and Rayford Logan went to Atlanta University, where they exposed hundreds of students to ideas that formerly had been interdicted. E. E. Just, Alain Locke and Sterling Brown stayed on at Howard, and E. Franklin Frazier went there. George Washington Carver carried on his chemurgical research and taught at Tuskegee. Langston Hughes, A. Philip Randolph and George Schuyler lectured at Negro colleges here and there. Walter White was always available for lectures, discussions and seminars.

And these were soon joined by younger colleagues, some of whom they had exposed to ideas. John Hope Franklin, for instance, now a competent historian, studied with Charles S. Johnson at Fisk, and then went on to St. Augustine College and from there to North Carolina College for Negroes, and from there to Howard. Frank Yerby, the popular novelist, took James Weldon Johnson's creative writing course. Margaret Walker learned about poetry from John Matheus at West Virginia State College. St. Clair Drake, co-author with Horace Cayton of the brilliant *Black Metropolis,* had Allison Davis as a teacher at Hampton. Horace Mann Bond taught at Dillard in New Orleans and at Fort Valley in Georgia before becoming president of Lincoln in Pennsylvania.

The list of brilliant Negro scientists, historians, sociologists, political scientists and artists who have gone into teaching in the past fifteen years is long. Their contribution to the growth of the present-day Negro mind is incalculable. William Hastie, formerly Governor of the Virgin Islands, taught law at Howard, and Ralph Bunche, now a United Nations' official, taught political science. Charles Drew, perhaps *the* authority on blood plasma, Lawrence Reddick, Margaret Walker, the poet, and Hale Woodruff, the artist, Robert Weaver and Abram Harris all went into college teaching. They helped to raise the standard of Negro education on the college level, so that at least fifteen Negro colleges, with enrollments roughly totaling twenty five thousand, were rated "A" by the Southern Association of Colleges and Secondary Schools in 1949. Five of the fifteen are on the approved list of the Association of American Universities.

5

As Negro education developed on the higher level, the pressure for an expansion of opportunities for more and more training grew stronger. This pressure was directed against the dual-system states which, in 1938, were forced to take steps to provide Negroes an education "equal" to that given whites. A Supreme Court decision declared that the individual states must make possible, within state boundaries, the education of Negroes in all the fields open to whites. Consequently some states—Maryland, Oklahoma, Arkansas and Kentucky—opened to Negroes the doors of certain "white" graduate schools. These states, however, seemed to consider this only a temporary expedient, for in 1945 they joined with eight other Southern states in a so-called "regional plan" of higher education. Under the terms of this, the states designate as "regional" universities certain segregated schools and undertake to defray the cost of graduate and professional training of native Negroes and whites. First proposed by the Conference of Southern Governors as early as 1940, the plan began to operate in a tentative fashion in 1949.

Negroes opposed this development and the N.A.A.C.P. pledged to fight it as contrary to both the letter and the spirit of the Supreme Court decision of 1938. The notion prevails among Negroes that segregation without discrimination is impossible. The history of race relations in America seems to support such a conclusion. Negroes have been apathetic about such organizations as the Southern Regional Council, which, in 1944, was set up "to attain . . . the ideals and practices of equal opportunity," but to attain them within the pattern of segregation. As Lillian E. Smith, editor of *South Today* and author of *Strange Fruit,* pointed out at the time, "it is difficult [for Negroes] to believe that any group is 'doing good' when the fundamental ideology of the group is a regressive belief in segregation."

But it cannot be taken as a defense of segregation to point out that without it many notable careers among both white and colored would never have been, and that much that has enriched the culture of the world would have been lost. The whole web of American Negro life would never have been woven. It is quite conceivable that American music would not have been quickened by jazz and the spirituals, nor the dance by the joyful abandon of the Charleston, the Black Bottom and the Lindy Hop, nor literature by the folk method and manner of dialect expression. It is conceivable, too, that there would have been no special glory in the voices of Marian Anderson and Dorothy Maynor. Richard Wright might never have written at all. The rich and heady variety, the deep and fundamental emotions, the startling contrasts and contradictions that make life in America a constant sharp experience would have dribbled away. And there must be no one who does not realize that all this has had civilizing value, and that in a very peculiar—and at last perverted— way, the development of Negro life in America has been permissible only by virtue of the growth of Democracy.

Yet, there is a basic contradiction of evil consequences, not the least of which is the cruel split in the American psyche, the terrible division, the "war of impulses." When the Negro question is raised, white America suffers an anxiety-guilt complex: she is caught in what Gunnar Myrdal calls a peculiar American dilemma. When black America raises the color question, she finds herself in a quandary. Which way to go, toward isolation or integration? While she has constantly sought and fought for opportunities to go in one direction, black America has been forced to go in another. The resulting frustration has been as hard a thing as any people has ever been asked to bear.

17

"IF WE MUST DIE—"

●●

IT IS COMMONLY admitted now that the political and moral deterioration that was a direct cause of the first World War did not end with that conflict. The steps in its rapid progress after 1919 were interspersed with great leaps into social chaos—continuing revolution in Russia; serious dislocations, unemployment, inflation in Germany; the still-born League of Nations; the failure of naval disarmament; the Black Shirt revolution in Italy and the rise of Hitler in Germany; the paralysis of depression creeping slowly over Europe and locking America in its grip even before the stock market crash of October, 1929. Finally, there was the return to international violence when Japan invaded Manchuria in 1931. After that, every day brought news of further degeneration on the international front. Immured in her "splendid isolation" and struggling with the problems of a depression which, incidentally, isolation intensified, many Americans paid little heed to the spread of fascism, except to hope that the "strong men" then rising in Europe would be good for the European world.

Least of all did American Negroes pay heed. In spite of the pioneering of Du Bois, the N.A.A.C.P. and the forgotten Marcus Garvey, American Negroes felt no cultural or racial ties with black peoples outside the American borders. It is true that they cheered mightily when a French colonial Negro, René Maran, won France's Prix Goncourt with the novel *Batouala*. Some of them even read the book, but their reaction to the African life depicted in it only emphasized the absence of ties with foreign Negroes. The average American Negro, so far as that goes, resented even the West Indians who were establishing themselves in solid and competing numbers in the States.

To compete with "foreign West Indians" for jobs, for living space and for social honors . . . Why didn't they stay where they belonged? It was galling, only less so than the impact of Jim Crow.

Besides, American Negroes had more immediate and pressing concerns than the rise of fascism in Europe. In 1935, in the non-farm areas of the country, fifty-three per cent of all Negroes fourteen years of age or over were unemployed. Twelve per cent of these did not have even work relief. Sixty per cent of the Negro population of Detroit was out of work. In New York, 24,292 Negro families were on relief. When it is remembered that the overwhelming majority of Negroes who were employed were agricultural and domestic workers and therefore did not come under the protection of the Social Security Act of 1935, nothing more need be said.

But Negroes were distracted from their immediate problems when Italy pounced upon Ethiopia in 1935. They saw the attack as a further working out of the sickening pattern of white aggression on blacks. When Haile Selassie finally took refuge in England, American Negroes implored him to come to this country, where they were already raising funds for his comfort and for the relief of his unfortunate country. Negroes of Chicago organized the Peace Movement of Ethiopia and talked of recruiting a regiment or two of American Negroes to fight for the Lion of Judah. New York Negroes formed the Council of Friends of Ethiopia and sent Dr. Willis N. Huggins, a New York schoolteacher, to plead Ethiopia's cause with the League of Nations. Negro newspapers made banner headlines of the war and inveighed against "the connivance of England and France" in blocking the sanctions against Italy proposed by Russia. Mussolini and that son of his who spoke of Italian bombs bursting like "beautiful flowers" on Ethiopian villages were the men American Negroes hated most in the world. As the war crashed on to its inevitable result, they were not comforted by the memory of an Alabama black boy's prize-ring defeat of an Italian Carnero.

Hatred of the Fascist ideology was very real among Negro Americans—and very personal. Max Schmeling, no longer the "Black Uhlan" but the "Aryan Knight," knocked out Joe Louis in 1936. That same year there were reports that Hitler, excusing his action on the claim that he was saving the German people from corrupting influences, ordered expelled from Germany American-born Negro entertainers and musicians who had long been resident in Germany.

Substance was given this story by the later one to the effect that Jesse Owens, American Negro Olympic champion, and his Negro team-mates were pointedly snubbed by Hitler at the Olympic Games. The rape of Ethiopia, nazism, fascism, the subservient truckling of the rest of the world to the brass of Mussolini and the hysteria of Hitler—American Negroes felt that they had plenty to be fearful of and to hate.

And yet, when Pearl Harbor happened in December, 1941, Negroes were moved to no patriotic fervor of revenge. Except for the death of Dorie Miller, the Negro messman who manned a machine gun that fateful Sunday, Negroes felt a satisfaction in the damage which non-white men had inflicted on white men. Many Negroes were sorry there was not more of it. The peoples of India, also non-white, were stirring restively against British rule, and this, too, was good. The same thing was happening in Dutch Indonesia, in Africa, in the far reaches of the Pacific—and it was good, all good. If Pearl Harbor had been worse, or if what was to follow could be really, really bad for America, then, the Negro knew, as Horace Cayton, a sociologist, said, that "the graver the outside danger to the safety of this country, the more abundant the gains [for Negroes] will be likely to be." The thought was the theme of many a Negro editorial.

And so, when the danger became palpably great, from the fall of France to the fall of the Philippines, Negroes watched for signs of improvement in their American lot. They thought they saw them in —the amendment of the 1940 Selective Service Act which did away with discrimination in the draft; the promotion of the Negro Colonel Benjamin O. Davis to the rank of brigadier general; the establishment of senior reserve officers' training corps at several Negro colleges; the gradual breakdown of economic discrimination; the issuance of Executive Order 8802.

There was, too, the still warm memory of the New Deal days and the efforts of men like Harold Ickes, Aubrey Williams. W. W. Alexander and Clark Foreman to make federal agencies distribute benefits to Negroes too. There was the gradual easing of the etiquette of race. And, to close it off, there was the Atlantic Charter and the whole moral basis upon which America claimed to be fighting the war. In pledging a war against fascism, America pledged to wipe racialism and the threat of racialism from the earth. The creed of the war was also the creed, though unfulfilled, of the government in peace.

2

In 1940 less than 3,000 Negroes were called under the draft law, augmenting the 4,000 in the two Negro Cavalry (9th and 10th) and two Negro Infantry (24th and 25th) units. In 1940 there were not quite 4,000 Negroes in the Navy. But by 1942 there were 500,000 Negro men and 2,500 Negro women in the armed services, and by D-Day 1,000,000 Negroes were in uniform, including 700,000 in the Army, 170,000 in the Navy and 25,000 in the Marines and Coast Guard.

At first it looked like the same old Army and Navy. Certainly the men who comprised these organizations had pretty much the same suspicions, fears and prejudices that their fathers had harbored during the first World War. There were riots and brawls between Negroes and whites, just as before. The situation at Fort Bragg, Fort Dix and Camp Lee was particularly bad. It was reported that the white Military Police at these encampments were allowed to carry sidearms, but that Negro M.P.'s were not. Scarcely a Saturday night passed but what white soldiers did not come across some Negro soldiers somewhere in town and give them the works. "The white Military Police seldom interfered."

Negroes, of course, protested. Their newspapers never failed to report fully and often luridly every instance of alleged abuse and discrimination. The Negro press reported that in some camps Negro soldiers had to wait behind until PX service and transportation service had been given to all white soldiers who wanted them. The Negro press reported that colored soldiers were no better than servants in the Army. There was serious trouble outside Camp Claibourne, Louisiana, when white soldiers, some of them M.P.'s, allied with civilians in the beating of Negroes.

Actually, there was considerably less mandated discrimination than ever before. There was no branch of the Army in which Negroes were not permitted to serve. In 1940, the Army opened the Air Force to Negroes. The five men who were trained that year formed the nucleus of the all-colored 99th Pursuit Squadron when it was organized in 1941, with Lieutenant Colonel B. O. Davis, Jr., as its commander. Though Negroes protested the segregated status of Negro pilots, the use of Negroes in the air was perhaps the most forward step taken by the military. Before the end of the war, Negroes were

getting training in multi-engine bomber craft, in air corps administration, and as bombardiers and navigators. In 1941, too, the Army integrated colored officer training with that given whites, and by 1944
there were some six thousand Negro officers, about one tenth of
whom were of field grade.

Nor was the Navy quite the same after a while. Negroes began
hammering away at the President as early as 1940. The President
passed the buck. Secretary of the Navy Knox yielded nothing. The
Navy tradition of confining Negroes to messmen and of barring
them from the naval trades was strong. But following the death of
Knox, the Navy's policy loosened to a remarkable degree. The new
Secretary of the Navy, James Forrestal, was willing to listen to such
Negro leaders as Lester Granger and Walter White and Mary Mc-
Leod Bethune. Camp Robert Smalls was set up for the training of
Negroes as yeomen, seamen, gunners and boatswain's mates. In
1944 this training was extended to include training for commissions. One Negro, a Massachusetts Institute of Technology-educated
engineer named Edward Hope, attained the rank of lieutenant, senior
grade, and there were a dozen ensigns and nearly as many lieutenants, junior grade.

Most of the half million Negro soldiers who went overseas served
in labor battalions, but in the second World War such service had
little or none of its former stigma. The engineering and transportation troops were absolutely indispensable. The nature of the terrain
in the Pacific and the kind of war it was in general made them so.
The Engineers, who often landed with the first wave of combat
troops, remained to fight holding actions and to build airstrips and
roads on many a steaming island in the Pacific. Negro engineers
helped build the Ledo Road in India, achieving a record of fifteen
miles of construction in a month. Negro engineers saw service on
New Guinea, Guam, the Treasury Islands, Saipan and Okinawa.

There were Negro combat units, too, in the Pacific theatre. Two
days before the Battle of the Coral Sea, the 24th Infantry met and
defeated the Japanese in the New Georgia Islands. From there this
unit proceeded to Saipan, where its "exceptionally meritorious conduct in routing the enemy" won it a citation. The 93rd Division,
which had been trained for desert warfare, first fought at Bougain-
ville—a far cry from desert fighting—in 1944. They fought their way
to the Treasury Islands and the East Indies and were in on General

MacArthur's return to the Philippines. Six other Negro battalions also fought in the Pacific theatre. Among these was the 234th Anti-Aircraft Artillery, without which "Saipan would have been impossible to hold."

Approximately 200,000 Negro soldiers were in on the war against Japan, and 70,000 more were sent from Europe to the Philippines within a few weeks after V-Day.

But the story of the Negro in the second World War is the story of the European theatre. Here went the most highly publicized Negro outfits—the 92nd Division, the 99th Fighter Squadron, the 332nd Fighter Group, the 761st Tank Battalion. It was to the European theatre that most Negro newspaper correspondents, some eighteen in all, were accredited, and to which Brigadier General B. O. Davis, the highest ranking Negro officer, was assigned. When the Army was at its top strength in 1945, there were a quarter of a million Negro troops in Europe. Negro soldiers waded ashore from LSI's and LST's in the first assault wave on the Normandy coast on D-Day. Negro troops attached to the Third Army swept through the Avranches Corridor and took the brunt of Von Runstedt's counteroffensive in the Ardennes. The 969th Field Artillery Battalion received the Distinguished Unit Citation for its part in the desperate struggle at Bastogne. Its "outstanding courage and resourcefulness and undaunted determination" were "in keeping with the highest traditions of the service."

On March 19, 1945, the *Stars and Stripes* announced that Negro riflemen, newly trained at Noyens, France, were fighting as platoons in infantry and armored divisions of the First and Seventh Armies. "Long contemplated," the Army paper said, "the plan of mixing white and colored doughboys in fighting units was launched not as an experiment in race relations but as an answer both to the needs of the military situation and repeated requests by Negro service troops for an opportunity to get into the war as combat men." They served well, even with distinction. Major General Lanham presented combat medals to eleven Negroes attached to the 104th Infantry and declared to the entire battalion: "I have never seen any soldiers who have performed better in combat than you."

Negro soldiers did all that was asked of them in combat against the Germans in Western Europe, but the fact remains that their greatest service was in the Engineering and Transportation Corps—in Port

Battalions, truck companies, and the like. A total of 124,514 gave such service in the E.T.O. Men of the Service of Supply rehabilitated rail lines, unloaded ships, strung thousands of miles of wire, repaired port facilities and bridges, set up communications and brought up supplies. The "Red Ball Express," for instance, manned almost entirely by Negroes, was the backbone of the Normandy offensive. As the supply lines lengthened, the job became more gruelling. Between August 25 and November 13, Red Ball Express drivers, making a round trip of 546 miles, averaged thirty-six hours on the road without sleep. They hauled 1,500 tons per day more than the scheduled maximum.

Negro airmen gave a good account of themselves. The 99th Pursuit Squadron went overseas in April, 1943, and was attached to the Twelfth Air Force in Tunisia. Under the command of Colonel Davis, this outfit did so well that Negro flyers were taken out of the "experiment" class and Colonel Davis was recalled to the States to organize another Negro air-combat group. This group, the 332nd Fighter Group, was assigned to the Fifteenth Air Force in Italy. They escorted bombers, they strafed, they dogfought. They shot down eighteen planes over the Anzio beachhead. On a single operation over Rumania, they destroyed eighty-three enemy planes on the ground. Altogether they flew 3,500 missions before D-Day, at which time they were a part of the air umbrella over Southern France. Eighty-eight Negro pilots, including Colonel Davis, who himself led many missions, won the Distinguished Flying Cross.

But the records achieved by these and other units got less attention from the white press than what was called the "shameful record" of the 92nd Division. That it deserved no such opprobium is a patent fact now. First committed to action in August, 1944, combat teams of the 92nd Division crossed the Arno River in September and sustained a successful drive until December. In February they were badly beaten in the Valley of the Po, but when their attack was reorganized, they won their objective, Genoa. They lost more than 3,000 killed, wounded and missing. They were awarded sixty-five Silver Stars, one hundred and sixty-two Bronze Star Medals and one thousand three hundred Purple Hearts. General Mark Clark, to whose Fifth Army the division was attached, called the 92nd "glorious."

Back home, however, the division's defeats in the early days of the Po Valley offensive were what the whites seemed determined to remember, to exaggerate and to make representative of the military performance of Negroes on all fronts. Ably seconded by other Southern colleagues, Senator Rankin of Mississippi charged that Negro soldiers had proved themselves "cowards" and that no self-respecting commander wanted Negro troops. The strictures against Negro soldiers in general and the 92nd Division in particular grew so severe that the War Department took official cognizance of them. Truman K. Gibson, successor to William Hastie as Negro civilian aide to Secretary Stimson, was sent abroad to investigate. He had an unfortunate press conference upon his return. He was widely misquoted as saying that Negro soldiers were failures.

3

Of course, all this lowered further an already low Negro morale. The Negro division of the Office of War Information labored under a severe handicap. Negroes were less willing than ever to believe the handouts from O.W.I. Earlier one of these handouts had brought from Lester Granger, Executive Secretary of the National Urban League, an angry comment: "The recent O.W.I. publication called *The Negro and the War* is a monumental mistake and a disservice to the government and the Negro. . . . It is like kicking a man who is down and congratulating him because he is not yet dead."

And down the Negro was, for the truth seemed to be that his morale was no longer susceptible to artificial stimulation. As a case in point, Negroes were happy about the rank of Brigadier General Davis, but they were cynical about it too—more especially when the General was assigned morale work among Negro troops in Europe. If the Inspector General thought that General Davis' rank alone could do the job, he was mistaken. The "front man" pattern of building Negro morale was passé. The Negro was less naïve, less patient, less willing to remember that there was always tomorrow. There was much less of the element of phantasy as a factor in his morale. During the war, it was common for him to say, "If I've got to die, I might as well die right here fighting for myself as to go abroad and die fighting for somebody else." Walter White heard it time and time again. Kenneth B. Clark, a Negro associate professor of psychology at New York City College, put it fairly when he said that Negro morale in the second World War was more "reality-bound," that it tended "to express directly the objective realities of the Negro's status in American life."

And that status was reflected in the Detroit riot of 1943, when white policemen stood by and let white mobs terrorize and beat Negroes. It was reflected in the Los Angeles "zootsuit riots," when Negroes as well as Mexicans were the victims of lawless whites. It was reflected in the impunity with which a Negro soldier could be killed by a white man in North Carolina and another be beaten to permanent blindness by a white policeman in South Carolina. It was reflected in the constant sneering reference to Negro members of the Women's Army Corp as "Wac-coons," in the general disregard of the War Department order of July, 1944, that segregation in recreation and transportation facilities be put to a stop on all army posts. It was reflected in the aggressive anger with which Negroes met these outrages and debasements—an anger which brought accusations of subversiveness against the Negro press and people.

4

It cannot be denied that there were organizations—and individuals —that tried to make an end of the pattern of segregation and discrimination in the areas of their influence. Though it foolishly insisted on segregating Negro blood in blood banks, the Red Cross did employ a Negro administrator and train and employ Negro field officers. The national office of the United Service Organizations, which had Henry W. Pope as Negro advisor, tried to discourage segregation by its member groups. Separate U.S.O. facilities for Negroes were maintained in the South, but the general officers saw to it that they were equal to those for whites. Some U.S.O. clubs in the North had bi-racial staffs, and in all of them Negroes and whites were treated alike. Negro artists and entertainers and figures of popular interest, like Lena Horne, Paul Robeson and Henry Armstrong, the boxer, went abroad to entertain troops under U.S.O. auspices. The policy of the organization affected the Travelers Aid Society, an affiliate, to the extent that the Society engaged Negro workers. The Stage Door Canteen in New York and Los Angeles had no segregation. The Negro press gave much publicity to the photograph of Bette Davis, the motion picture star, dancing with a grinning Negro G.I.

Some government agencies were particularly mindful of the Negro's stake in the war and of his usefulness on the home front. The Office of War Information had a large Negro staff, not all of whom worked with the special Negro division headed by Ted Poston. The same was true of the Office of Civilian Defense. The Office of Price Administration encouraged the voluntary participation of Negroes and engaged qualified Negroes in important positions. The chief of the New York District Legal Enforcement Division of O.P.A. was a Harvard-trained Negro lawyer under whose direction a dozen white lawyers worked. Negro economists, investigators, statisticians and clerks worked for O.P.A.

These manifestations gave many Negroes hope that the ideals for which they fought the war could be realized at home. They gave many Negroes the hope that there were people in high places who realized that America's moral leadership depended upon her active will to enforce and protect not only the four freedoms abroad, but "a fifth freedom—freedom from penalty of race"—at home. These hopefuls knew that in order to do this, the legislative, the judiciary and the executive arms of government must, with honesty and eagerness, join in the attack against repression, inequity, discrimination and segregation. And some Negroes felt that there was an assurance of just this.

18

THE LARGER HOPE

●●●

WHILE AMERICA WAS still just the "arsenal of democracy," Negroes were aware that the requirements of victory over the Fascists would subject the traditional world pattern of race relations to insupportable strain. Negroes knew, some vaguely, some clearly, that if America got into the struggle, such liberalizing tendencies as were apparent in the very nature of the conflict had of necessity to find stronger expression in their own country.

America did get in, and the names with which Americans themselves tagged the war made plain the country's commitment to certain moral ideals. After the speech and phrase-makers got through, America had no choice. "A People's War," and "The war to usher in the Century of the Common Man" were the phrases of Henry Wallace, who also declared that "there can be no privileged people." Wendell Willkie declared it a "war of liberation" and defined his One World in terms of opportunity, freedom and equality. The courageous and outspoken Eleanor Roosevelt was even more explicit. "The nation," she said, "cannot expect colored people to feel that the United States is worth defending if the Negro continues to be treated as he is now."

When the war ended, the Negro was in a stronger moral, political and economic position than he had dared hope. The F.E.P.C. had gained him admission to heretofore closed employment. The War Labor Board had given him equality of wages. The Supreme Court had decided in his favor against white primaries. The Army and Navy had lowered many of their bars to Negro advancement. The Negro was increasingly active in organized labor. Even the South had taken cognizance of the war's reaffirmation of the concept of equality, and certain Southern liberals had assumed the initiative in getting together with Negroes on a program "to give assurance of our sincere good will and desire to cooperate." Virginius Dabney, influential editor of the Richmond *Times Dispatch,* had gone so far as to advocate doing away with segregation in public transportation. He later retreated from this position, but the fact that he had advanced to it at all was significant.

If these attitudes and gains were brought about—as cynicism was quick to suggest—by the compulsive logic of historical events, rather than through changes in the hearts of men, so much the better. Good will is at best an "unstable commodity on the market of race relations," and American Negroes were no longer willing to depend upon it. They knew that the war had tied in their fate with that of minority, dependent and colonial peoples the world over and that the final determinant of this fate was political and economic. Negro scholars like Rayford Logan, Ralph Bunche and W. E. B. Du Bois were making this clearer every day. Walter White, who went to the war as a correspondent, underscored the fact of mutuality of minority peoples' fate in his book *A Wind Is Rising.* If politics and economics, the determinants, were informed by humanitarianism, well and good.

This attitude on the part of Negroes was not rejective of good will. Far from it. They knew that many measures for their good had started in good will. The shock and sadness with which Negroes greeted the untimely death of President Roosevelt was in some measure certainly for the loss of his humanitarian interest in them. But the fact remains that Negroes were looking beyond men to measures, beyond loving to strategy, beyond suppliance to strength, and, finally, beyond a messiah to machinery. Good will might propagandize and promote their cause, as, indeed, it had done throughout the war, but it could never alone win it.

And so Negroes looked hopefully toward the conclave of nations called the United Nations Organization. In that organization they saw a possible blueprint for the furtherance of those political and moral ideals for which, presumably, millions of people had died. They saw it reflected in those representatives of colonial and minority people who, like themselves, must have come to include in their thinking and feeling an intelligent opportunism and an urge to seize advantage from every turn of political, economic and moral circumstance. Surprising numbers of Negroes went to the San Francisco Conference. Ralph Bunche was there in his official capacity as the State Department's Acting Chief of the Division of Dependent Territories. Walter White was there, Du Bois was there; P. B. Young, Jr. and Mary Bethune were also there. Every important Negro newspaper sent a correspondent. The informed element of the Negro population showed an extraordinary interest.

And there was precedent for the Negro's hope of protection and advancement by international agreement. For instance, a protective provision had been made for the Jews of Rumania in the Treaty of Berlin. In 1919–1920, the Allies had got treaties from the Balkan countries and from Austria, Hungary and Turkey which at least defined the rights of minorities. The Council of the League of Nations had been charged with the responsibility for supervising those rights. So there was precedent enough. Negroes did not see how their peculiar American plight could be divorced from world problems. As one Negro writer put it, this was no private affair. Had not the treatment of the Jews in Germany been one of the causes of war? And prior to that, had not Germany made—however falsely—the plight of Sudetenland nationals the excuse for her "peaceful" invasion of Prague?

The Charter of the United Nations Organization sounded good. "We the people of the United Nations determined . . . to reaffirm faith in fundamental human rights, in the dignity and worth of the human person, in the equal rights of men and women and of nations large and small. . . ." Thus the Preamble, while Article I declares it one of the purposes of the United Nations "to achieve international cooperation . . . in promoting and encouraging respect for human rights and for fundamental freedoms for all without distinction as to race, sex, language, or religion."

The machinery looked even better. Part of that machinery was the Economic and Social Council which, in 1946, adopted the following resolution:

The Economic and Social Council, being charged under the Charter with the responsibility of promoting universal respect for, and observance of, human rights and fundamental freedoms for all without distinctions as to race, sex, language or religion, and requiring advice and assistance to enable it to discharge this responsibility, Establishes a Commission of Human Rights . . . [whose work shall be] the protection of minorities [and] the prevention of discrimination on grounds of race, sex, language and religion.

This seemed to Negroes enough to go ahead on. In 1947, the N.A.A.C.P. prepared "An Appeal to the World, A Statement on the Denial of Human Rights to Minorities in the Case of Citizens of Negro Descent in the United States and an Appeal to the United Nations for Redress." The appeal got nowhere. Indeed, its presentation drew a rebuke from Attorney General Thomas Clark, who expressed dismay "that any citizens of this country should feel compelled to go over the heads of their government in seeking redress of grievances."

2

The rejection of the appeal did not discourage Negroes too much. The concept of their problem as a world problem was too new for any but the most enlightened to be distressed by its rebuff. For three hundred years Negroes had been seeking redress within the framework of the nation, for it was the nation that was doing them hurt, and they were, after all, Americans, though black. Within the framework of the nation, then, they would continue to concentrate their energies in the struggle for final and complete emancipation. With the turn of some further circumstance, the coming of some event of compulsive logic, or by the practical exertion of that good will in which they had no absolute faith, Negroes felt that the struggle might be won.

The circumstance, the compulsive logic and the good will combined. The circumstance was Henry Wallace's third party movement which seemed, in late 1946, to entice Negroes to a new political banner. The compulsive logic, we have already seen, was the moral logic of the war. The exerted good will was a considerable segment of the American people.

This segment's chosen representative, Harry S. Truman, had an excellent reputation among Negroes. As a senator, he had twice voted for cloture to put an end to the filibustering of anti-lynching legislation. As Vice President, he had once declared that "every citizen of the United States is entitled to cast his vote." In 1946, as President, he had asked Congress to pass a bill providing for a permanent F.E.P.C., and in the same year, to general applause, he made the precedent-shattering appointment of a Negro, William Hastie, as Governor of the Virgin Islands.

If Negroes were inclined to be suspicious of the motives behind all this, they had only to remember, as Channing Tobias told them, that "politically the President had more to lose than to gain," and that he was, after all and still, the people's representative. Only a pigmy corps of Southerners marched in the shambling phalanx of the Dixiecrats and pledged themselves to defeat President Truman in 1948; only a boisterous handful rebelled when a committee of prominent citizens was named to investigate the status of civil rights in America. This committee recommended, among other things:

The elimination of segregation, based on color, creed, or national origin, from American life.

The enactment of a federal Fair Employment Practice Act prohibiting all forms of discrimination in private employment, based on race, color, creed, or national origin.

A long term program of public education to inform the people of the civil rights to which they are entitled and which they owe one to another.

The committee outlined the permanent machinery by means of which its recommendations could be implemented.

President Truman hailed this report as "a declaration of our renewed faith in the American goal—the integrity of the individual human being, sustained by the moral consensus of the whole Nation, protected by a government based on equal freedom under just laws."

When, later, the report was made the basis of a national civil rights program, Negroes knew that whatever came, the direction of inexorable and unforgiving history was set, as indeed—though in doubt and terror and pain and blood (which may not cease till the millennium)—it had been all along, toward the fulfillment of democracy and the total equality of American men.

NOTES ON SOURCES

● ●

There are many studies of the Negro, general and particular, without the use of which this book could not have been written. It would seem an unnecessary use of academic apparatus to list all of these sources here. By far the best bibliography on the Negro is the one prepared by Professor Roscoe E. Lewis and Mr. Mentor A. Howe and privately issued by the Library at Hampton Institute (1940). Other helpful bibliographical listings are: *The Negro: A Selected Bibliography* (1935), prepared by members of the staff of the New York Public Library, and Dorothy Porter's *A Selected List of Books By and About the Negro* (1936). No one of these is exhaustive, because of course no one of them could go beyond the date of its publication. Miss Florence Murray's *Negro Handbook* (1939, 1942, 1946, 1949) and the Tuskegee *Negro Year Book* keep check on current material by and about Negroes.

Included in no list are many important sources. At Hampton Institute, for instance, there is a set of more than a hundred bound volumes of newspaper clippings, going back to 1890 and encompassing thirty-odd years of Negro life in America. They carry material to be found in an organized form nowhere else. Here are caught with lively immediacy the mass movements, the meetings, the detailed accounts of Negro life. Here one finds abstracts of many of the unpublished and forgotten speeches of Booker T. Washington, Du Bois, Monroe Trotter; editorials that reflect all phases of thought and make revealing comment on all kinds of Negro activity, and news stories that sometimes tell volumes. No source that I know of recreates so fully and in such detail the general character of the Negro life between 1890 and 1925.

Indeed, but one other area of Negro life in America is so well preserved, and that is the period of slavery. The sources for this are very rich, ranging from collected slave narratives, through historical and sociological studies to travel accounts. Outstanding collections of slave narratives are: B. A. Botkin (ed.), *Lay My Burden Down* (1945); *Unwritten History of Slavery*, Social Science Source Documents No. I (1945); Roscoe Lewis' unpublished collection; and a collection made by Charles H. Nichols (1946–1948). While not a true collection of narratives, *The Negro in Virginia*

(1940) does contain first-hand slave accounts and is very useful. Then there are, unforgettably, the slave autobiographies and biographies, such as those by Frederick Douglass, Josiah Henson, Charles Ball, John Thompson, Sarah H. Bradford and Arthur Huff Fauset.

The most thoroughgoing historical and sociological studies of slavery are those which confine themselves to an examination of the institution in individual states. Jeffrey R. Brackett's *The Negro in Maryland: A Study of the Institution of Slavery* (1895), James C. Ballagh's *A History of Slavery in Virginia* (1902), Guion G. Johnson's *Ante-Bellum North Carolina* and Harrison A. Trexler's *Slavery in Missouri* (1914) are but four of many excellent examples. Of an entirely different nature, but valuable are: Helen T. Catterall (ed.), *Judicial Cases Concerning American Slavery and the Negro* (1930–1935); Elizabeth Donnan (ed.), *Documents Illustrative of the History of the Slave Trade to America* (1930–1935); W. E. B. Du Bois, *The Suppression of the African Slave Trade to the United States of America* (1896); and U. B. Phillips, *American Negro Slavery* (1918)—the latter, long taken as standard but which new scholarship now proves must be used with a skeptical eye for ideological ambushes.

But there is no need to draw these notes out. Here, then, is a selected list of books of a general and inclusive nature which I found useful.

Adams, James Truslow, *The March of Democracy: The Rise of the Union*. New York: 1932.
Allen, James S., *Reconstruction: The Battle for Democracy*. New York: 1937.
Aptheker, Herbert, *American Negro Slave Revolts*. New York: 1943.
———, *Essays in the History of the American Negro*. New York: 1945.
———, *Negro Slave Revolts in the United States, 1526–1860*. New York: 1939.
———, *The Negro in the Civil War*. New York: 1938.
———, *To Be Free*. New York: 1948.
Baker, Ray Stannard, *Following the Color Line*. New York: 1908.
Bancroft, Frederic, *Slave-Trading in the Old South*. Baltimore: 1931.
Barnes, Gilbert H., *The Anti-Slavery Impulse: 1830–1844*. New York: 1933.
Beard, James Melville, *K.K.K. Sketches*. Philadelphia: 1877.
Bond, Horace Mann, *The Education of the Negro in the American Social Order*. New York: 1934.
Bontemps, Arna, and Conroy, Jack, *They Seek a City*. New York: 1947.
Botkin, B. A., *Lay My Burden Down*. Chicago: 1945.
Bowers, Claude G., *The Tragic Era*. Boston: 1929.
Bradford, Sarah H., *Harriet—The Moses of Her People*. New York: 1901.
Brawley, Benjamin G., *The Negro Genius*. New York: 1937.
———, *The Negro in Literature and Art*. New York: 1930.
Bridges, Horatio, *Journal of an African Cruiser*. Edited by Nathaniel Hawthorne. New York: 1853.
Buckmaster, Henrietta, *Let My People Go*. New York: 1941.

Cash, Wilbur J., *The Mind of the South.* New York: 1941.

Chambers, William, *American Slavery and Colour.* London: 1857.

Coffin, Joshua, *An Account of Some of the Principal Slave Insurrections.* American Anti-Slavery Society, 1860.

Conrad, Earl, *Harriet Tubman.* Washington: 1943.

Curti, Merle, *The Growth of American Thought.* New York: 1943.

Davis, Allison, and Dollard, John, *Children of Bondage.* Washington: 1940.

Davis, Susan Lawrence, *Authentic History of the Ku Klux Klan, 1865–1877.* New York: 1924.

Dewey, D. M., *The Constitution of the United States With all the Acts of Congress Relating to Slavery.* Rochester: 1854.

Dollard, John, *Caste and Class in a Southern Town.* New York: 1937.

Donnan, Elizabeth, *Documents Illustrative of the History of the Slave Trade to America.* (4 vols.) Washington: 1935.

Douglass, Frederick, *Life and Times of Frederick Douglass.* Hartford: 1881.

——, *My Bondage and My Freedom.* New York: 1855.

Dowd, Jerome, *The Negro in American Life.* New York: 1926.

Drake, St. Clair, and Cayton, Horace, *Black Metropolis. A Study of Negro Life in a Northern City.* New York: 1945.

Du Bois, W. E. B., *Black Folk Then and Now.* New York: 1939.

——, *Black Reconstruction in America.* New York: 1935.

——, *Dusk of Dawn.* New York: 1940.

——, *The Souls of Black Folk.* (17th ed.) Chicago: 1931.

——, *The Suppression of the African Slave Trade.* New York: 1896.

Elliot, E. N., *Cotton Is King and Pro-Slavery Arguments.* Augusta: 1860.

Fitzhugh, George, *Cannibals All! or Slaves Without Masters.* Richmond: 1857.

Franklin, Hohn Hope, *From Slavery to Freedom.* New York: 1947.

——, *The Free Negro in North Carolina.* Chapel Hill: 1943.

Frazier, E. Franklin, *The Negro Family in the United States.* Chicago: 1939.

George, James Z., *Political History of Slavery in the United States.* New York: 1915.

Gloster, Hugh M., *Negro Voices in American Fiction.* Chapel Hill: 1948.

Grenshaw, Ollinger, *The Slave States in the Presidential Election of 1860.* Baltimore: 1945.

Gross, Bella, *Clarion Call.* New York: 1947.

Guthrie, James M., *Camp-Fires of the Afro-Americans.* Philadelphia: 1899.

Herskovits, Melville J., *The Myth of the Negro Past.* New York: 1942.

Higginson, Thomas Wentworth, *Army Life in a Black Regiment.* Boston: 1870.

Holmes, Dwight O. W., *The Evolution of the Negro College.* New York: 1934.

Hutton, Laurence, *Curiosities of the American Stage.* New York: 1891.

Isaacs, Edith J. R., *The Negro in the American Theatre.* New York: 1947.

Johnson, Charles S., *Shadow of the Plantation*. Chicago: 1934.
——, *The Negro College Graduate*. Chapel Hill: 1938.
Johnson, Guion Griffis, *Ante-Bellum North Carolina*. Chapel Hill: 1937.
Johnson, James Weldon, *Along This Way*. New York: 1933.
——, *Black Manhattan*. New York: 1940.
Johnson, Oliver, *William L. Garrison and the Anti-Slavery Movement*. Boston: 1881.
Johnston, Harry, *The Negro in the New World*. London: 1910.
Kemble, Frances A., *Journal of a Residence on a Georgian Plantation in 1838–1839*. New York: 1863.
Little, Arthur W., *From Harlem to the Rhine*. New York: 1936.
Lloyd, Arthur Y., *The Slavery Controversy: 1830–1860*. Chapel Hill: 1939.
Locke, Alain (ed.), *The New Negro*. New York: 1925.
Logan, Rayford W. (ed.), *What the Negro Wants*. Chapel Hill: 1944.
Loggins, Vernon, *The Negro Author: His Development in America*. New York: 1931.
Lynch, John R., *The Facts of Reconstruction*. New York: 1915.
Martin, Asa Earl, *The Anti-Slavery Movement in Kentucky Prior to 1850*. Louisville: 1918.
Mays, Benjamin E., and Nicholson, Joseph W., *The Negro's Church*. New York: 1933.
McDougle, Ivan E., *Slavery in Kentucky 1792–1865*. Lancaster: 1918.
Myrdal, Gunnar, *An American Dilemma*. New York: 1944.
Negro in Virginia, The. Virginia Writer's Program; Preface by Roscoe E. Lewis. New York: 1940.
Odum, Howard W., *Social and Mental Traits of the Negro*. New York: 1910.
——, *The Way of the South*. New York: 1947.
Olmsted, Frederick Law, *A Journey in the Seaboard Slave States*. New York: 1856.
——, *The Cottom Kingdom*. (2 vols.) New York: 1861.
Ovington, Mary White, *The Walls Came Tumbling Down*. New York: 1947.
Phillips, Ulrich B., *American Negro Slavery*. New York: 1936.
——, *Life and Labor in the Old South*. Boston: 1929.
Pierce, Joseph A., *Negro Business and Business Education*. New York: 1947.
Powdermaker, Hortense, *After Freedom*. New York: 1939.
Puckett, Newbell N., *Folk Beliefs of the Southern Negro*. Chapel Hill: 1926.
Quarles, Benjamin, *Frederick Douglass*. Washington: 1948.
Raper, Arthur F., *The Tragedy of Lynching*. Chapel Hill: 1933.
Reuter, Edward B., *The American Race Problem*. New York: 1938.
Scott, Emmett J., *The American Negro in the World War*. Washington: 1919.
Seligmann, Herbert J., *The Negro Faces America*. New York: 1920.
Silvera, John D., *The Negro in World War II*. Military Press: 1946.

Smith, Samuel D., *The Negro in Congress, 1870–1901*. Chapel Hill: 1940.
Smith, William Henry, *A Political History of Slavery*. (2 vols.) New York: 1903.
Soper, Edmund D., *Racism—A World Issue*. New York: 1947.
Spero, Sterling D., and Harris, Abram L., *The Black Worker*. New York: 1931.
Still, William, *The Underground Railroad*. Philadelphia: 1872.
Stone, William, *Studies in the American Race Problem*. New York: 1908.
Stonequist, Everett V., *The Marginal Man*. New York: 1937.
Styron, Arthur, *The Last of the Cocked Hats*. Norman: 1945.
Tenenbaum, Samuel, *Why Men Hate*. New York: 1947.
To Secure These Rights (Report of the President's Committee on Civil Rights). New York: 1947.
Voorhis, Harold Van Buren, *Negro Masonry in the United States*. New York: 1945.
Washington, Booker T., *Up From Slavery*. New York: 1901.
Weatherford, Willis D., *The Negro from Africa to America*. New York: 1924.
Weaver, Robert C., *The Negro Ghetto*. New York: 1948.
Wesley, Charles H., *Negro Labor in the United States*. New York: 1927.
Wiley, Bell Irvin, *Southern Negroes, 1861–1865*. New Haven: 1938.
Williams, Charles H., *Sidelights on Negro Soldiers*. Boston: 1923.
Wilson, Henry, *History of the Rise and Fall of the Slave Power in America*. (3 vols.) New York: 1873.
Woodson, Carter G., *A Century of Negro Migration*. Washington: 1918.
———, *The African Background Outlined*. Washington: 1936.
———, *The Education of the Negro Prior to 1861*. New York: 1915.
———, *The History of the Negro Church*. Washington: 1922.
———, *The Negro in Our History*. Washington: 1928.
Woofter, T. J., Jr., *Black Yeomanry*. New York: 1930.
———, *Negro Problems in Cities*. New York: 1928.

CHAPTER NOTES

Chapter One

1. *Evidence of the Slave Trade*, American Tract Society, New York, 1859.
2. *The Myth of the Negro Past*, by Melville Herskovits, p. 87.

Chapter Two

1. *The Rise and Fall of the Slave Power in America*, by Henry Wilson, Vol. I, p. 3.

Chapter Three

1. *An Account of the Slave Trade on the Coast of Africa*, by Alexander Falconbridge, p. 30.
2. *The American Slave Trade*, by John R. Spears, p. 79.
3. *Sermons Preached on Plantations to Congregations of Negroes*, by Alexander Glennie, p. 21.
4. Quoted in *The Negro in Virginia*, p. 23. All quotations from *The Negro in Virginia* by permission of the publisher Hastings House, Publishers, Inc.
5. *The Anti-Slavery Movement in Kentucky Prior to 1850*, by Earl A. Martin, p. 14.
6. *The Negro in Virginia*, p. 88.
7. Quoted in Henrietta Buckmaster, *Let My People Go*, p. 6.
8. *The Negro, Past, Present and Future*, by J. A. Price, p. 47.

Chapter Four

1. *The March of Democracy: The Rise of the Union*, by James T. Adams, p. 241.
2. *The Cotton Kingdom*, by William E. Dodd, p. 34.
3. *Slavery and the Domestic Slave Trade in the United States*, pp. 25–26.
4. *The Narrative of William Wells Brown*, Massachusetts Antislavery Society, 1847.
5. *Excursion Through the Slave States*, pp. 119–120.
6. "Review of the Debate on the Abolition of Slavery in the Virginia Legislature of 1831 and 1832," *The Political Register*, Vol. 2, No. 25 (October 16, 1833).

7. *Lectures on the Philosophy and Practice of Slavery,* p. 150.
8. *Cannibals All! or Slaves Without Masters,* by George Fitzhugh, p. 153.
9. *An Inquiry into the Character and Tendencies of the American Colonization and the American Anti-Slavery Societies,* p. 12.

Chapter Five

1. *The Negro in Virginia,* p. 60.
2. *Lay My Burden Down,* B. A. Botkin (ed.); by permission of the publishers, The University of Chicago Press.
3. *Judicial Cases Concerning American Slavery,* by Helen Catterall.
4. *Slavery in the United States: The Life and Adventures of Charles Ball,* p. 49.
5. Quoted in *Judicial Cases Concerning American Slavery,* Vol. II, p. 442.
6. *The Last of the Cocked Hats,* by Arthur Styron, p. 421.
7. Quoted in "Maroons Within the Limits of the United States," by Herbert Aptheker, *Journal of Negro History,* Vol. 34 (April, 1939).

Chapter Six

1. *Negro Orators and Their Orations,* by Carter G. Woodson (ed.), p. 95.
2. *Ibid.,* p. 155.
3. May 29, 1854.
4. *Life and Times of Frederick Douglass,* p. 307.
5. *William Lloyd Garrison,* by Archibald Grimké, p. 366.
6. *Works of Charles Sumner,* Vol. IV, p. 279.
7. *Harriet Tubman,* by Earl Conrad, p. 26.

Chapter Seven

1. *White Supremacy and Negro Subordination,* pp. 201–202.
2. *Journal of a Residence on a Georgian Plantation in 1838–1839,* p. 11.
3. *Negro Masonry in the United States,* by Harold Van B. Voorhis, pp. 8–9.
4. *Black Reconstruction,* by W. E. B. Du Bois, pp. 52–53.

Chapter Eight

1. *Southern Negroes, 1861–1865,* by B. I. Wiley.
2. *History of the Negro Race in America,* by George Williams, Vol. II, p. 244.
3. *Grant, Lincoln and the Freedmen,* by John Eaton and Ethel O. Mason, p. 2. Quoted by permission of Longmans, Green & Co., Inc. Copyright, 1907.
4. *The Negro in Virginia,* p. 211.
5. *History of the Black Phalanx,* by Joseph Wilson, p. 456.
6. Quoted in *ibid.,* p. 490.
7. *Slavery and Four Years of War,* by Joseph W. Keifer, Vol. II, p. 214.

Chapter Nine

1. "Proceedings of the National Convention of Colored Men Held in Syracuse, New York, October 4–7, 1864," pp. 48–61.

2. Quoted in *To Be Free*, by Herbert Aptheker, p. 139.
3. *Reconstruction and the Constitution, 1866–1876*, by John W. Burgess, p. 133.
4. Quoted from *Black Reconstruction in America*, by W. E. B. Du Bois, p. 391.
5. *The Southern States Since the Civil War*, p. 30.
6. Quoted in Henrietta Buckmaster, *Let My People Go*, p. 366.
7. From *The Tragic Era* (p. 306), by Claude G. Bowers; by permission of the publishers, Houghton Mifflin Company.
8. From *Lay My Burden Down*, B. A. Botkin (ed.); by permission of the publishers, The University of Chicago Press.
9. *Ibid.*
10. *Ibid.*

Chapter Ten

1. "The Conservative South—A Political Myth," by William G. Carlton, *Virginia Quarterly Review*, Vol. 22, No. 2.
2. *Balance of Power: The Negro Vote*, by Henry Lee Moon, p. 72.
3. New York *Age*, June 15, 1885.

Chapter Eleven

1. *The Walls Came Tumbling Down*, by Mary White Ovington, p. 76.
2. New York *Times*, November 26, 1904.
3. *Balance of Power; The Negro Vote*, p. 79.
4. September 3, 1908.

Chapter Twelve

1. *Camp-Fires of the Afro-Americans*, by James M. Guthrie, p. 682.
2. *Following the Color Line*, by Ray Stannard Baker, p. 118.
3. Quoted in *A Man Called White*, by Walter White, p. 8.
4. *Ibid.*, p. 9.
5. *Ibid.*, p. 15.
6. *Along This Way*, by James Weldon Johnson, p. 311.

Chapter Thirteen

1. *Crisis*, Vol. 2, p. 63.
2. "The Urban League Movement," by L. Hollingsworth Wood, *Journal of Negro History*, Vol. 9, p. 121.
3. *Crisis*, Vol. 4, p. 235.
4. *Ibid.*, p. 29.
5. Atlanta *Constitution*, February 3, 1917.
6. Beaumont *Enterprise*, January 12, 1917.

Chapter Fourteen

1. Quoted in *They Seek a City*, by Bontemps and Conroy, p. 128.
2. *Crisis*, June, 1917.

3. Quoted in Willis D. Weatherford and Charles S. Johnson, *Race Relations*, Boston, Heath, 1934, p. 235.
4. *Sidelights on Negro Soldiers,* by Charles H. Williams, p. 109.

Chapter Fifteen

1. From *Harlem to the Rhine,* by Arthur W. Little, p. 361. Quoted by permission of Mrs. Arthur W. Little.
2. From *Harlem Shadows* by Claude McKay, copyright, 1922, by Harcourt, Brace and Company, Inc.
3. In September, 1919, Williams rose in the Senate to defend some Omaha lynchers. "Race is greater than law now and then," he said, "and protection of [white] women transcends all law, human and divine."
4. Reprinted from *The Weary Blues* by Langston Hughes, by permission of Alfred A. Knopf, Inc. Copyright 1927 by Alfred A. Knopf, Inc.
5. From a "Song of the Son" from Jean Toomer's *Cane* published by Liveright Publishing Corporation, copyright 1923 Boni & Liveright, Inc.
6. Reprinted from *The Weary Blues* by Langston Hughes, by permission of Alfred A. Knopf, Inc. Copyright 1927 by Alfred A. Knopf, Inc.

Chapter Sixteen

1. *The Negro College Graduate,* by Charles S. Johnson.

INDEX